THE MAGICIANS™

NEW CLASS

THE MAGICIANS CREATED BY **LEV GROSSMAN**.

WRITTEN BY
LILAH STURGES

ILLUSTRATED BY
PIUS BAK
CHAPTER 3 INKS BY **MARIANO TAIBO**

COLORED BY
GABRIEL CASSATA

LETTERED BY
MIKE FIORENTINO

Published by
ARCHAIA™
Los Angeles, California

COVER AND CHAPTER BREAK ART BY
QISTINA KHALIDAH

DESIGN BY
**MARIE KRUPINA
& SCOTT NEWMAN**

EDITORS
**MATTHEW LEVINE
& SOPHIE PHILIPS-ROBERTS**

EXECUTIVE EDITOR
SIERRA HAHN

Ross Richie CEO & Founder
Joy Huffman CFO
Matt Gagnon Editor-in-Chief
Filip Sablik President, Publishing & Marketing
Stephen Christy President, Development
Lance Kreiter Vice President, Licensing & Merchandising
Arune Singh Vice President, Marketing
Bryce Carlson Vice President, Editorial & Creative Strategy
Kate Henning Director, Operations
Spencer Simpson Director, Sales
Scott Newman Manager, Production Design
Elyse Strandberg Manager, Finance
Sierra Hahn Executive Editor
Jeanine Schaefer Executive Editor
Dafna Pleban Senior Editor
Shannon Watters Senior Editor
Eric Harburn Senior Editor
Matthew Levine Editor
Sophie Philips-Roberts Associate Editor
Amanda LaFranco Associate Editor
Jonathan Manning Associate Editor
Gavin Gronenthal Assistant Editor

Gwen Waller Assistant Editor
Allyson Gronowitz Assistant Editor
Ramiro Portnoy Assistant Editor
Shelby Netschke Editorial Assistant
Michelle Ankley Design Coordinator
Marie Krupina Production Designer
Grace Park Production Designer
Chelsea Roberts Production Designer
Samantha Knapp Production Design Assistant
José Meza Live Events Lead
Stephanie Hocutt Digital Marketing Lead
Esther Kim Marketing Coordinator
Cat O'Grady Digital Marketing Coordinator
Breanna Sarpy Live Events Coordinator
Amanda Lawson Marketing Assistant
Holly Aitchison Digital Sales Coordinator
Morgan Perry Retail Sales Coordinator
Megan Christopher Operations Coordinator
Rodrigo Hernandez Operations Assistant
Zipporah Smith Operations Assistant
Jason Lee Senior Accountant
Sabrina Lesin Accounting Assistant

BOOM! Studios, 5670 Wilshire Boulevard, Suite 400, Los Angeles, CA 90036-5679. Printed in China. First Printing.

ISBN: 978-1-68415-565-1, eISBN: 978-1-64144-731-7

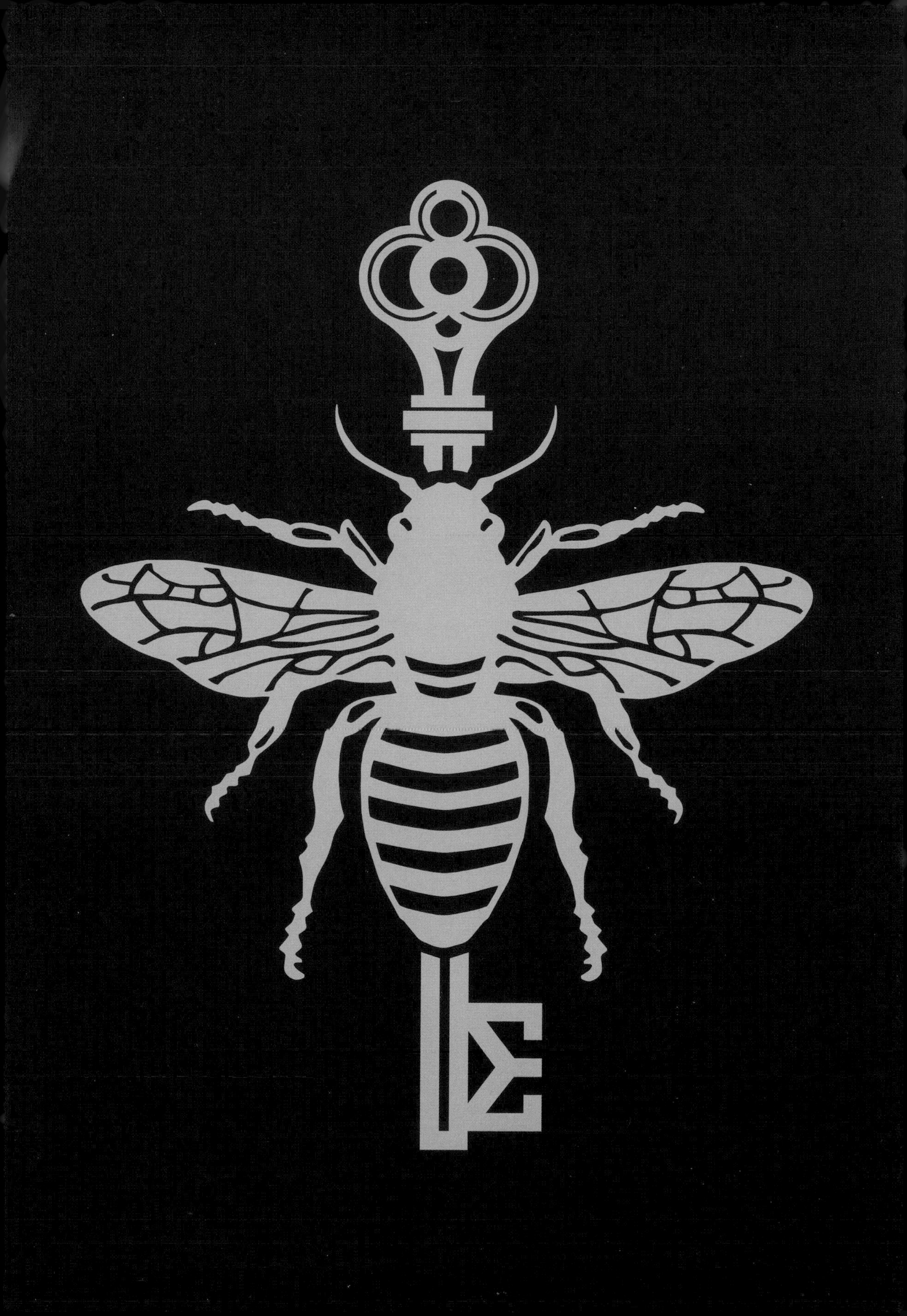

CHAPTER
ONE

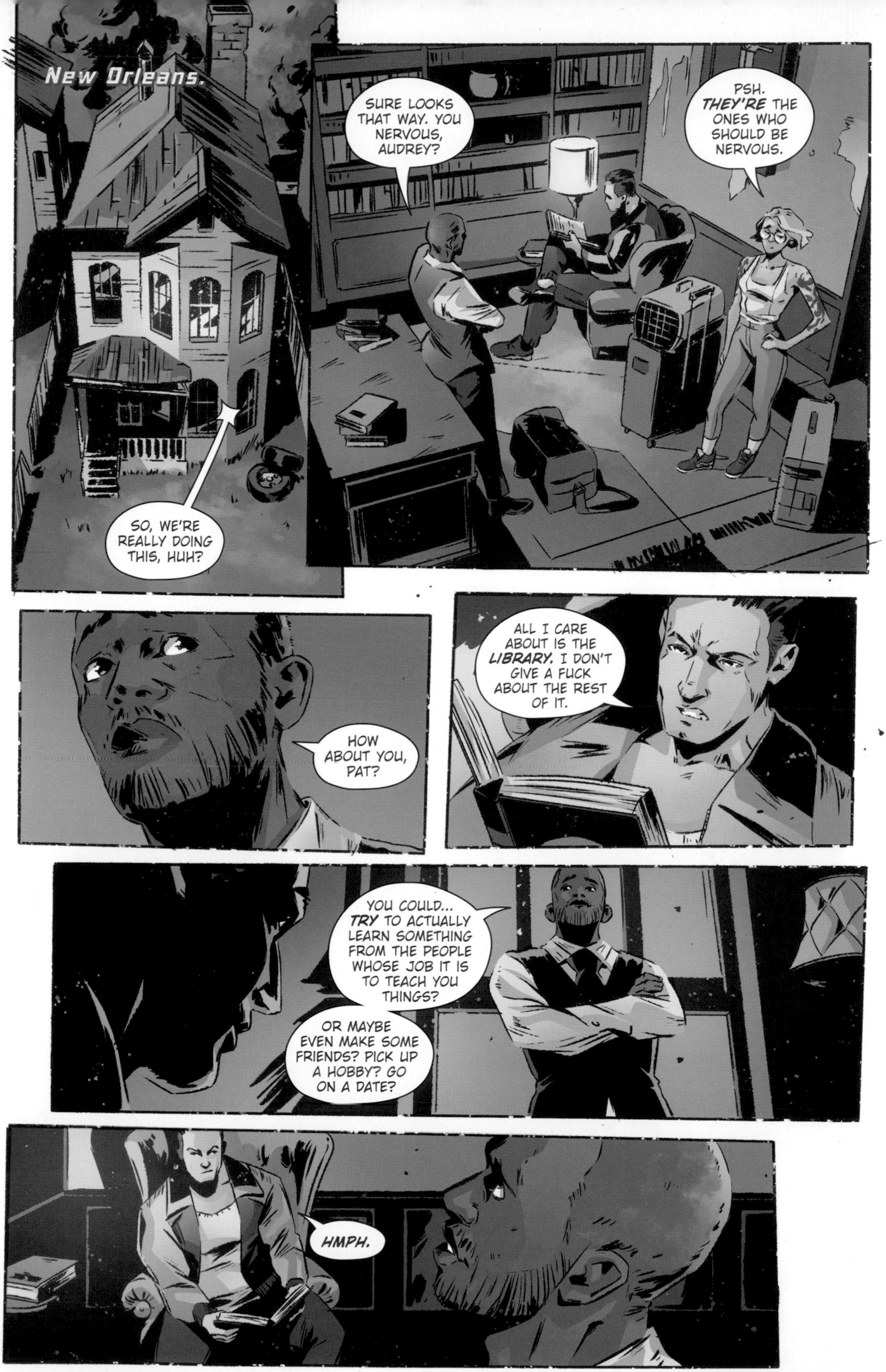
New Orleans.
So, we're really doing this, huh?
Sure looks that way. You nervous, Audrey?
Psh. *They're* the ones who should be nervous.
How about you, Pat?
All I care about is the *library.* I don't give a fuck about the rest of it.
You could... *try* to actually learn something from the people whose job it is to teach you things?
Or maybe even make some friends? Pick up a hobby? Go on a date?
Hmph.

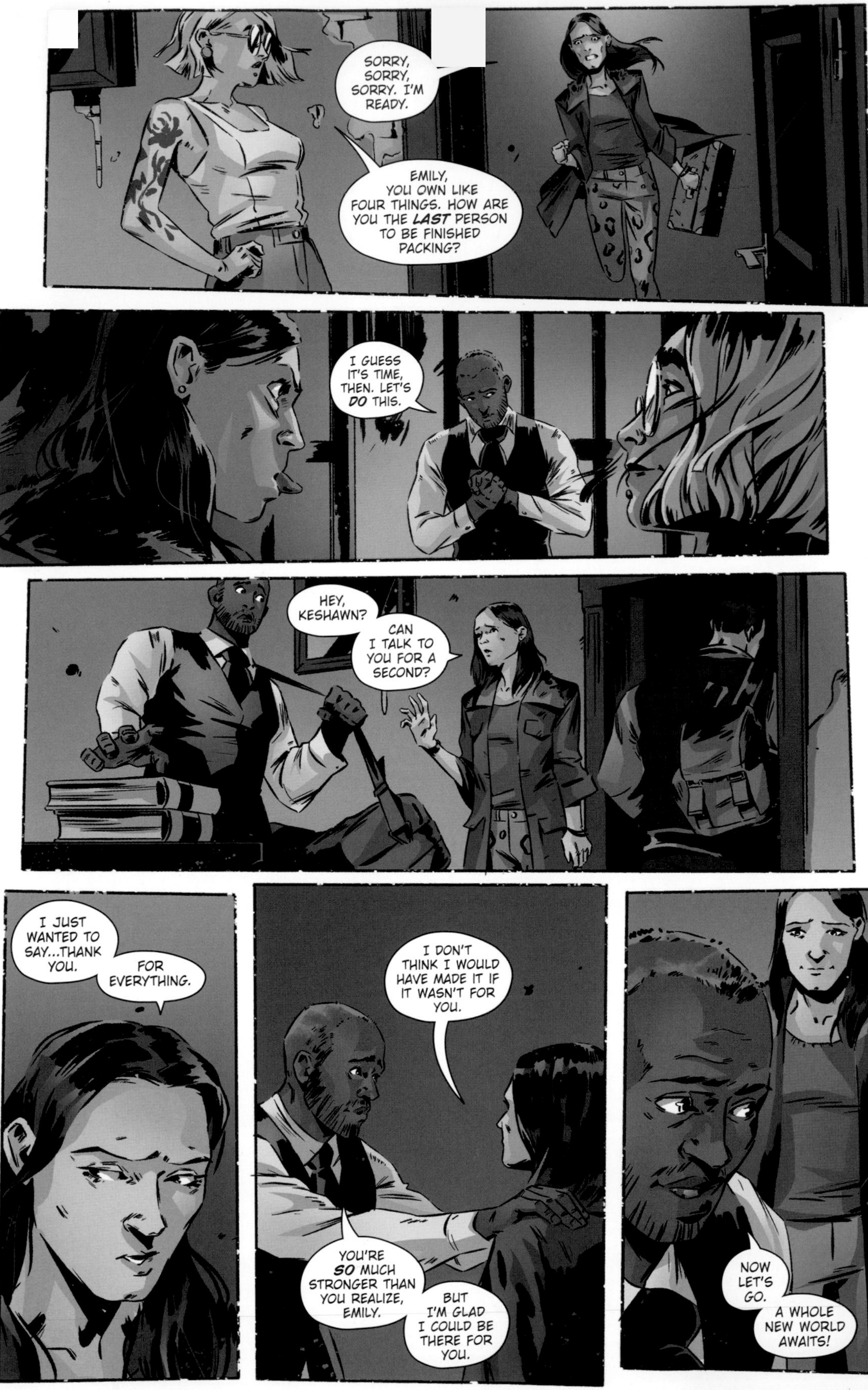
SORRY, SORRY, SORRY. I'M READY.
EMILY, YOU OWN LIKE FOUR THINGS. HOW ARE YOU THE LAST PERSON TO BE FINISHED PACKING?
I GUESS IT'S TIME, THEN. LET'S DO THIS.
HEY, KESHAWN?
CAN I TALK TO YOU FOR A SECOND?
I JUST WANTED TO SAY...THANK YOU.
FOR EVERYTHING.
I DON'T THINK I WOULD HAVE MADE IT IF IT WASN'T FOR YOU.
YOU'RE SO MUCH STRONGER THAN YOU REALIZE, EMILY.
BUT I'M GLAD I COULD BE THERE FOR YOU.
NOW LET'S GO.
A WHOLE NEW WORLD AWAITS!

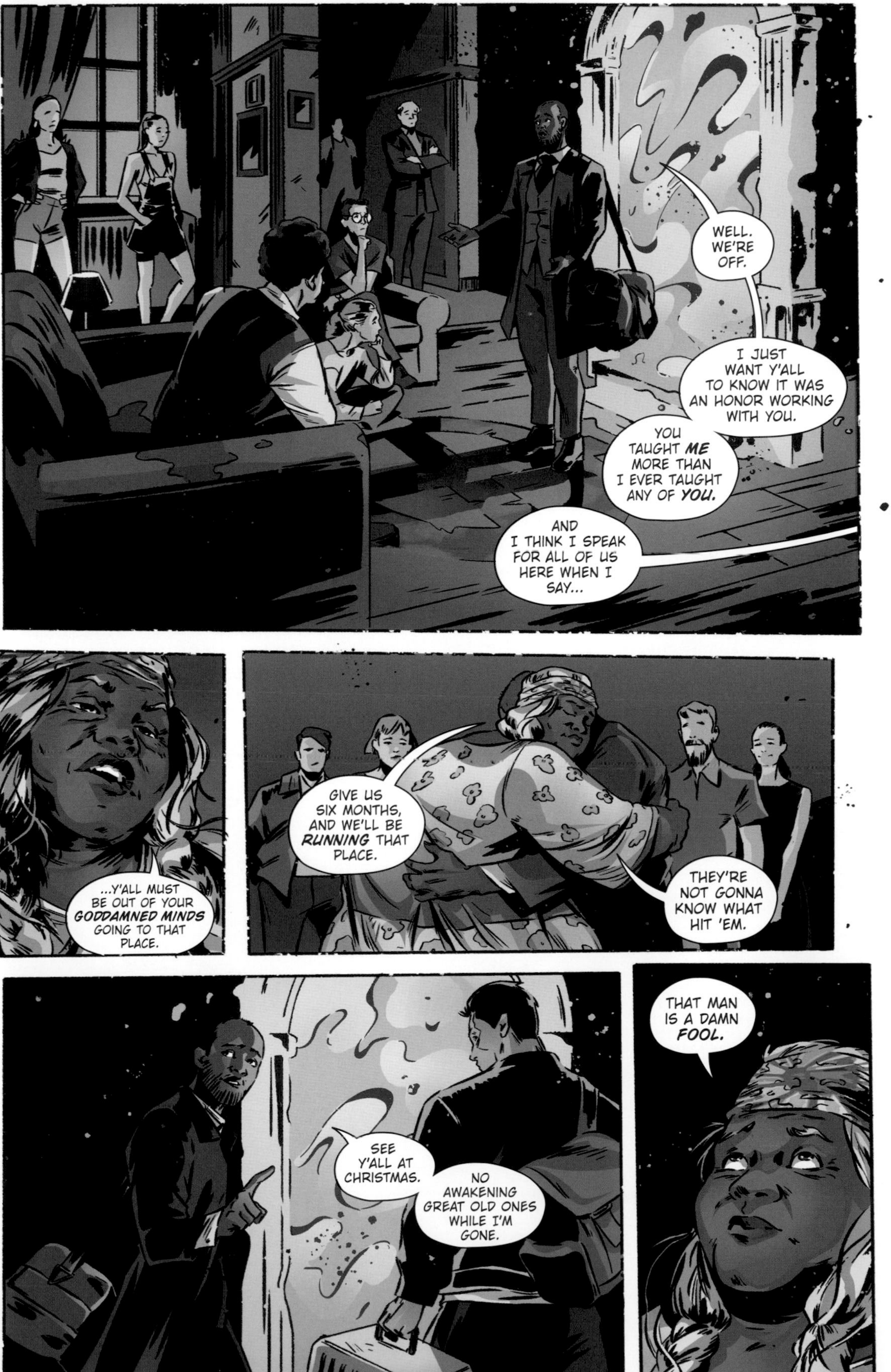
WELL. WE'RE OFF.
I JUST WANT Y'ALL TO KNOW IT WAS AN HONOR WORKING WITH YOU.
YOU TAUGHT ***ME*** MORE THAN I EVER TAUGHT ANY OF ***YOU.***
AND I THINK I SPEAK FOR ALL OF US HERE WHEN I SAY...
...Y'ALL MUST BE OUT OF YOUR ***GODDAMNED MINDS*** GOING TO THAT PLACE.
GIVE US SIX MONTHS, AND WE'LL BE ***RUNNING*** THAT PLACE.
THEY'RE NOT GONNA KNOW WHAT HIT 'EM.
SEE Y'ALL AT CHRISTMAS.
NO AWAKENING GREAT OLD ONES WHILE I'M GONE.
THAT MAN IS A DAMN ***FOOL.***

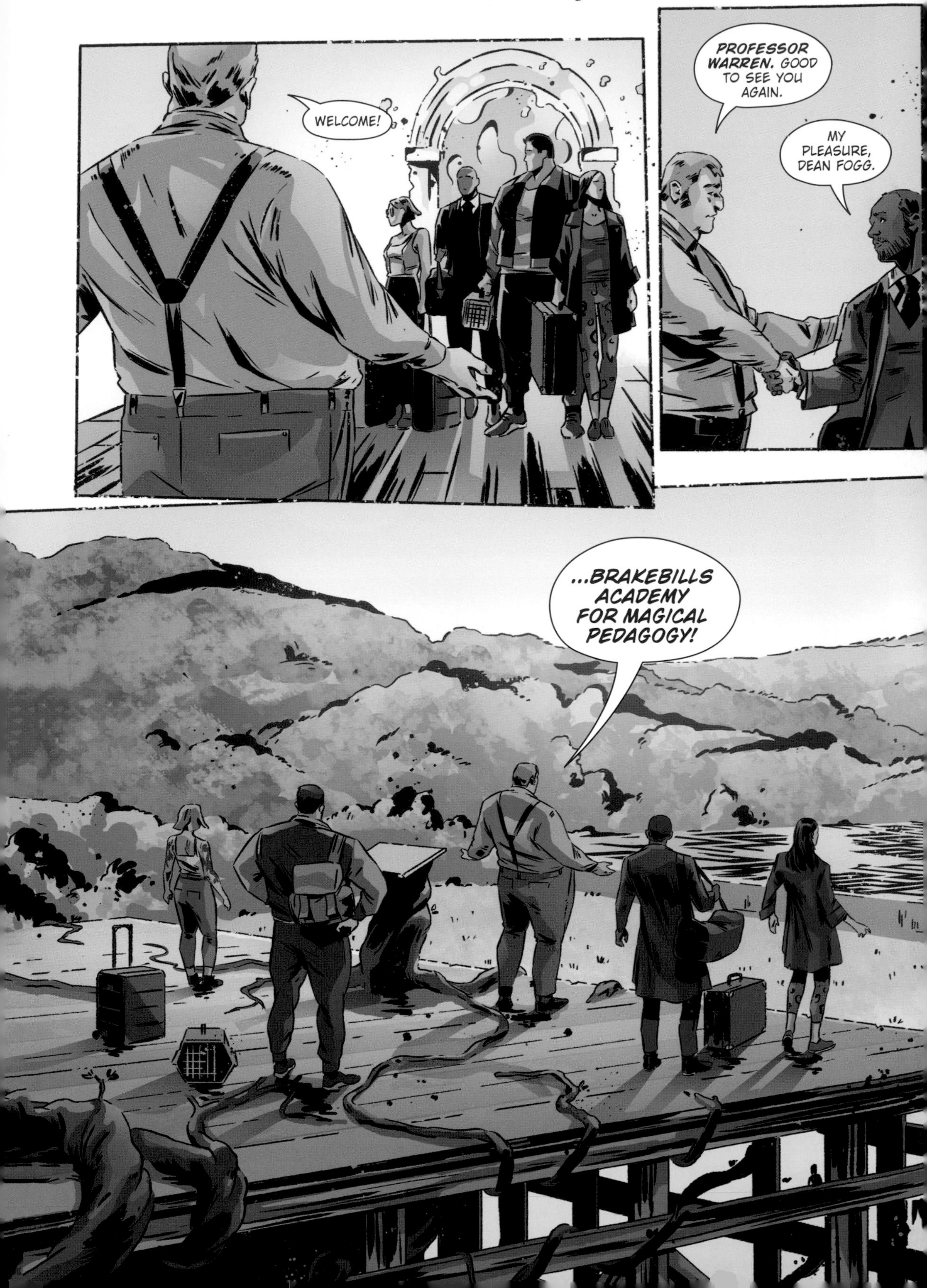
WELCOME!
PROFESSOR WARREN. GOOD TO SEE YOU AGAIN.
MY PLEASURE, DEAN FOGG.
...BRAKEBILLS ACADEMY FOR MAGICAL PEDAGOGY!

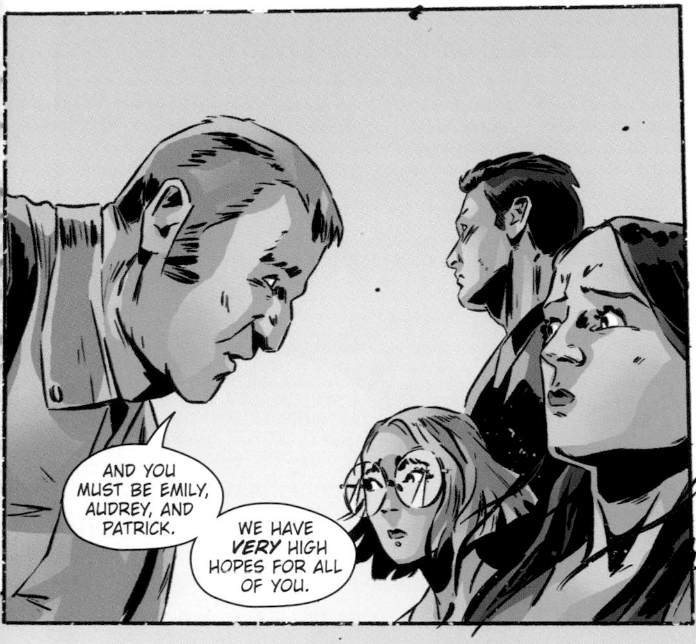
AND YOU MUST BE EMILY, AUDREY, AND PATRICK.
WE HAVE **VERY** HIGH HOPES FOR ALL OF YOU.

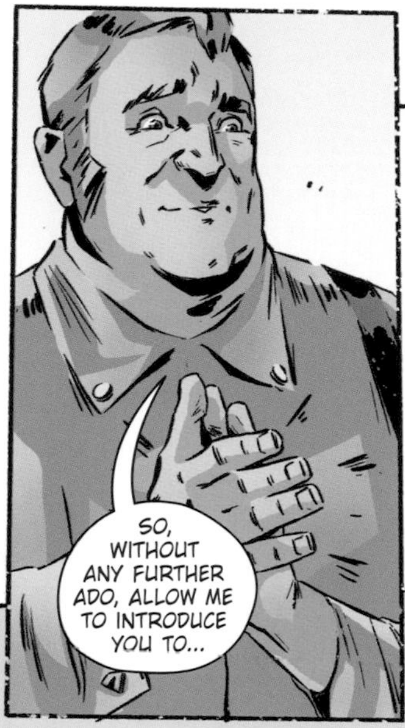
SO, WITHOUT ANY FURTHER ADO, ALLOW ME TO INTRODUCE YOU TO...

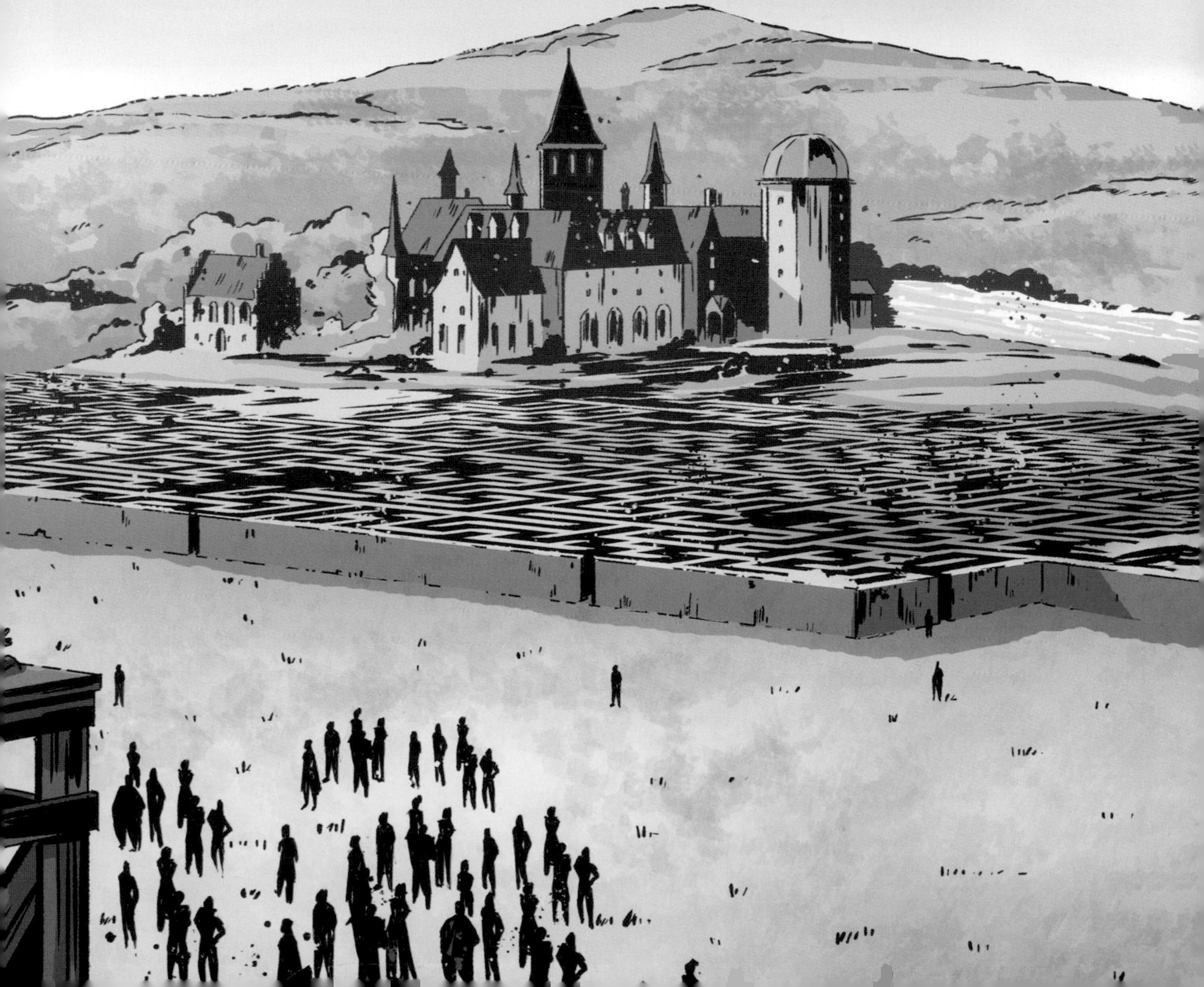

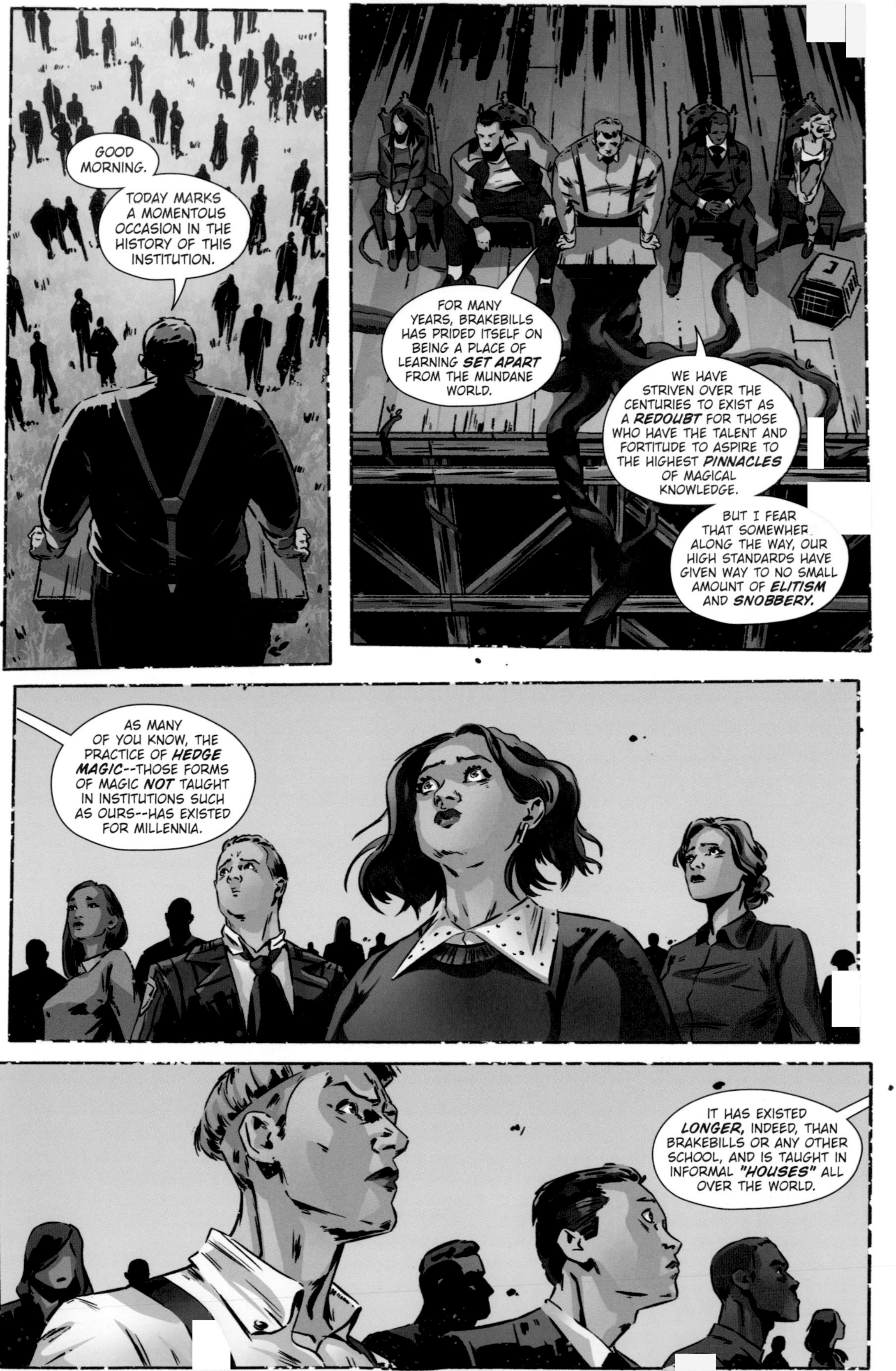
GOOD MORNING.
TODAY MARKS A MOMENTOUS OCCASION IN THE HISTORY OF THIS INSTITUTION.
FOR MANY YEARS, BRAKEBILLS HAS PRIDED ITSELF ON BEING A PLACE OF LEARNING SET APART FROM THE MUNDANE WORLD.
WE HAVE STRIVEN OVER THE CENTURIES TO EXIST AS A REDOUBT FOR THOSE WHO HAVE THE TALENT AND FORTITUDE TO ASPIRE TO THE HIGHEST PINNACLES OF MAGICAL KNOWLEDGE.
BUT I FEAR THAT SOMEWHERE ALONG THE WAY, OUR HIGH STANDARDS HAVE GIVEN WAY TO NO SMALL AMOUNT OF ELITISM AND SNOBBERY.
AS MANY OF YOU KNOW, THE PRACTICE OF HEDGE MAGIC--THOSE FORMS OF MAGIC NOT TAUGHT IN INSTITUTIONS SUCH AS OURS--HAS EXISTED FOR MILLENNIA.
IT HAS EXISTED LONGER, INDEED, THAN BRAKEBILLS OR ANY OTHER SCHOOL, AND IS TAUGHT IN INFORMAL "HOUSES" ALL OVER THE WORLD.

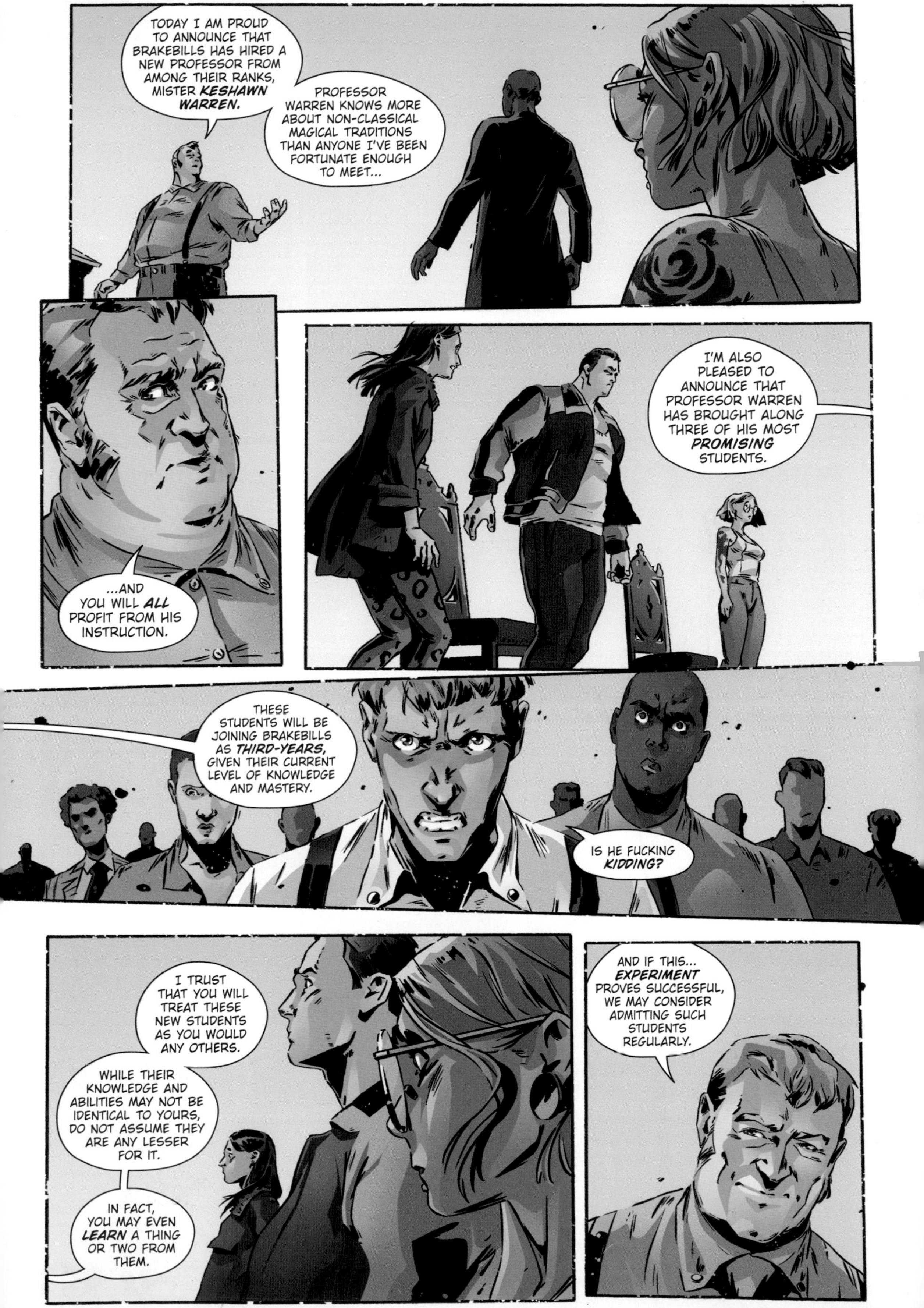
TODAY I AM PROUD TO ANNOUNCE THAT BRAKEBILLS HAS HIRED A NEW PROFESSOR FROM AMONG THEIR RANKS, MISTER KESHAWN WARREN.
PROFESSOR WARREN KNOWS MORE ABOUT NON-CLASSICAL MAGICAL TRADITIONS THAN ANYONE I'VE BEEN FORTUNATE ENOUGH TO MEET...
...AND YOU WILL ALL PROFIT FROM HIS INSTRUCTION.
I'M ALSO PLEASED TO ANNOUNCE THAT PROFESSOR WARREN HAS BROUGHT ALONG THREE OF HIS MOST PROMISING STUDENTS.
THESE STUDENTS WILL BE JOINING BRAKEBILLS AS THIRD-YEARS, GIVEN THEIR CURRENT LEVEL OF KNOWLEDGE AND MASTERY.
IS HE FUCKING KIDDING?
I TRUST THAT YOU WILL TREAT THESE NEW STUDENTS AS YOU WOULD ANY OTHERS.
WHILE THEIR KNOWLEDGE AND ABILITIES MAY NOT BE IDENTICAL TO YOURS, DO NOT ASSUME THEY ARE ANY LESSER FOR IT.
IN FACT, YOU MAY EVEN LEARN A THING OR TWO FROM THEM.
AND IF THIS... EXPERIMENT PROVES SUCCESSFUL, WE MAY CONSIDER ADMITTING SUCH STUDENTS REGULARLY.

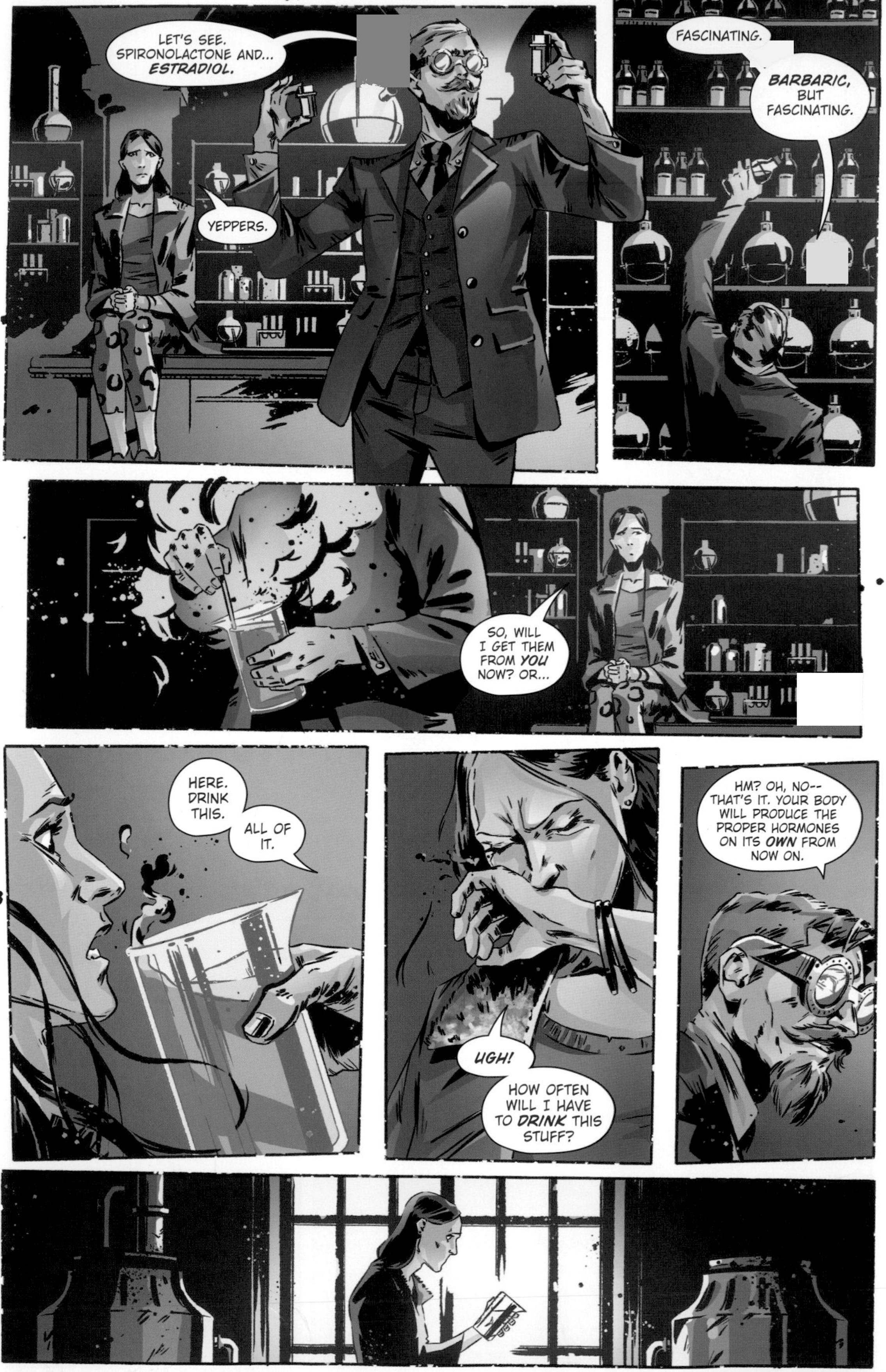
LET'S SEE. SPIRONOLACTONE AND... ESTRADIOL.
YEPPERS.
FASCINATING.
BARBARIC, BUT FASCINATING.
SO, WILL I GET THEM FROM YOU NOW? OR...
HERE. DRINK THIS.
ALL OF IT.
UGH!
HOW OFTEN WILL I HAVE TO DRINK THIS STUFF?
HM? OH, NO-- THAT'S IT. YOUR BODY WILL PRODUCE THE PROPER HORMONES ON ITS OWN FROM NOW ON.

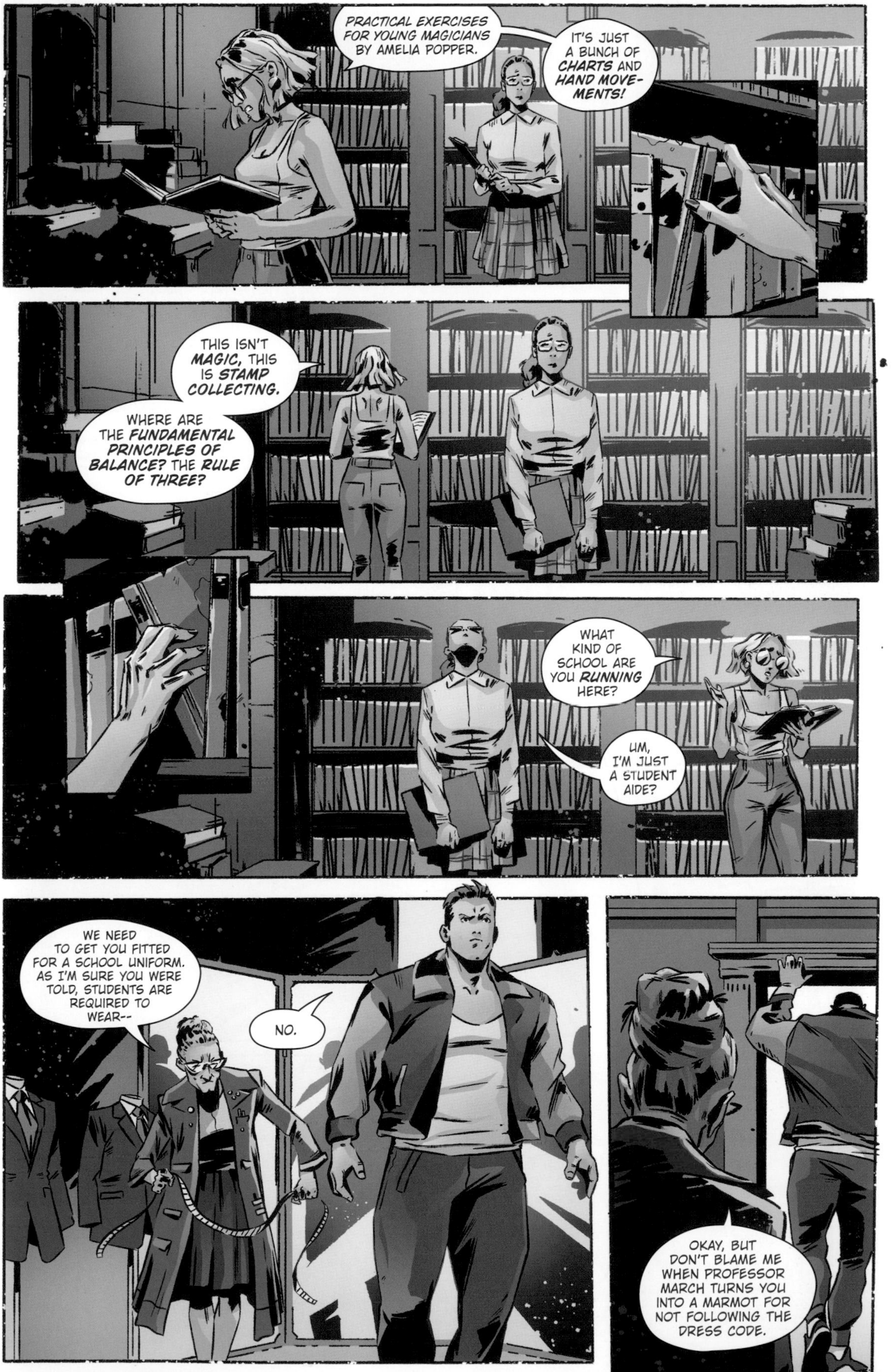
PRACTICAL EXERCISES FOR YOUNG MAGICIANS BY AMELIA POPPER.
IT'S JUST A BUNCH OF CHARTS AND HAND MOVEMENTS!
THIS ISN'T MAGIC, THIS IS STAMP COLLECTING.
WHERE ARE THE FUNDAMENTAL PRINCIPLES OF BALANCE? THE RULE OF THREE?
WHAT KIND OF SCHOOL ARE YOU RUNNING HERE?
UM, I'M JUST A STUDENT AIDE?
WE NEED TO GET YOU FITTED FOR A SCHOOL UNIFORM. AS I'M SURE YOU WERE TOLD, STUDENTS ARE REQUIRED TO WEAR--
NO.
OKAY, BUT DON'T BLAME ME WHEN PROFESSOR MARCH TURNS YOU INTO A MARMOT FOR NOT FOLLOWING THE DRESS CODE.

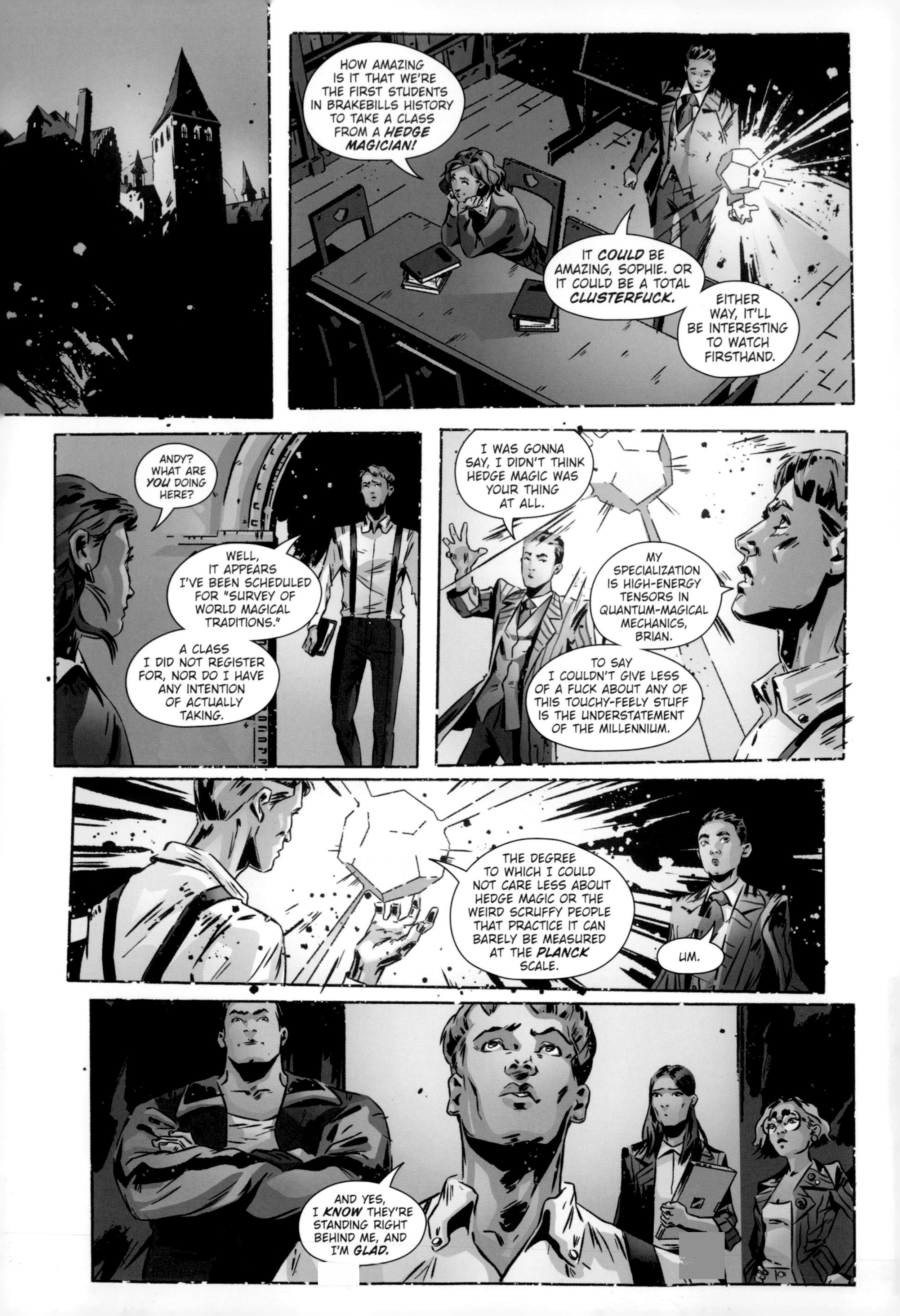

HOW AMAZING IS IT THAT WE'RE THE FIRST STUDENTS IN BRAKEBILLS HISTORY TO TAKE A CLASS FROM A *HEDGE MAGICIAN!*
IT *COULD* BE AMAZING, SOPHIE. OR IT COULD BE A TOTAL *CLUSTERFUCK.*
EITHER WAY, IT'LL BE INTERESTING TO WATCH FIRSTHAND.
ANDY? WHAT ARE *YOU* DOING HERE?
WELL, IT APPEARS I'VE BEEN SCHEDULED FOR "SURVEY OF WORLD MAGICAL TRADITIONS."
A CLASS I DID NOT REGISTER FOR, NOR DO I HAVE ANY INTENTION OF ACTUALLY TAKING.
I WAS GONNA SAY, I DIDN'T THINK HEDGE MAGIC WAS YOUR THING AT ALL.
MY SPECIALIZATION IS HIGH-ENERGY TENSORS IN QUANTUM-MAGICAL MECHANICS, BRIAN.
TO SAY I COULDN'T GIVE LESS OF A FUCK ABOUT ANY OF THIS TOUCHY-FEELY STUFF IS THE UNDERSTATEMENT OF THE MILLENNIUM.
THE DEGREE TO WHICH I COULD NOT CARE LESS ABOUT HEDGE MAGIC OR THE WEIRD SCRUFFY PEOPLE THAT PRACTICE IT CAN BARELY BE MEASURED AT THE *PLANCK* SCALE.
UM.
AND YES, I *KNOW* THEY'RE STANDING RIGHT BEHIND ME, AND I'M *GLAD.*

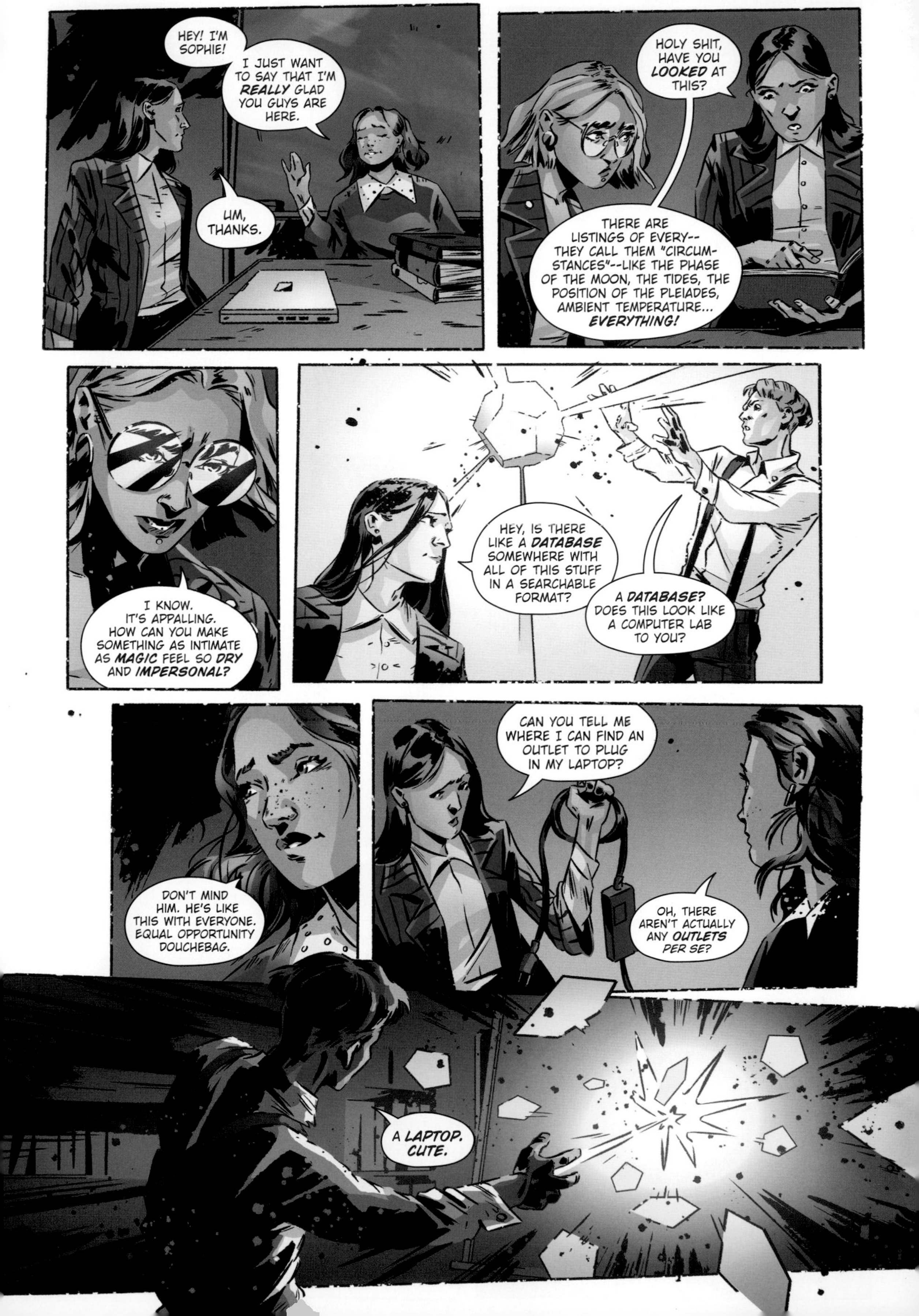
HEY! I'M SOPHIE!
I JUST WANT TO SAY THAT I'M REALLY GLAD YOU GUYS ARE HERE.
UM, THANKS.
HOLY SHIT, HAVE YOU LOOKED AT THIS?
THERE ARE LISTINGS OF EVERY-- THEY CALL THEM "CIRCUM-STANCES"--LIKE THE PHASE OF THE MOON, THE TIDES, THE POSITION OF THE PLEIADES, AMBIENT TEMPERATURE... EVERYTHING!
I KNOW. IT'S APPALLING. HOW CAN YOU MAKE SOMETHING AS INTIMATE AS MAGIC FEEL SO DRY AND IMPERSONAL?
HEY, IS THERE LIKE A DATABASE SOMEWHERE WITH ALL OF THIS STUFF IN A SEARCHABLE FORMAT?
A DATABASE? DOES THIS LOOK LIKE A COMPUTER LAB TO YOU?
DON'T MIND HIM. HE'S LIKE THIS WITH EVERYONE. EQUAL OPPORTUNITY DOUCHEBAG.
CAN YOU TELL ME WHERE I CAN FIND AN OUTLET TO PLUG IN MY LAPTOP?
OH, THERE AREN'T ACTUALLY ANY OUTLETS PER SE?
A LAPTOP. CUTE.

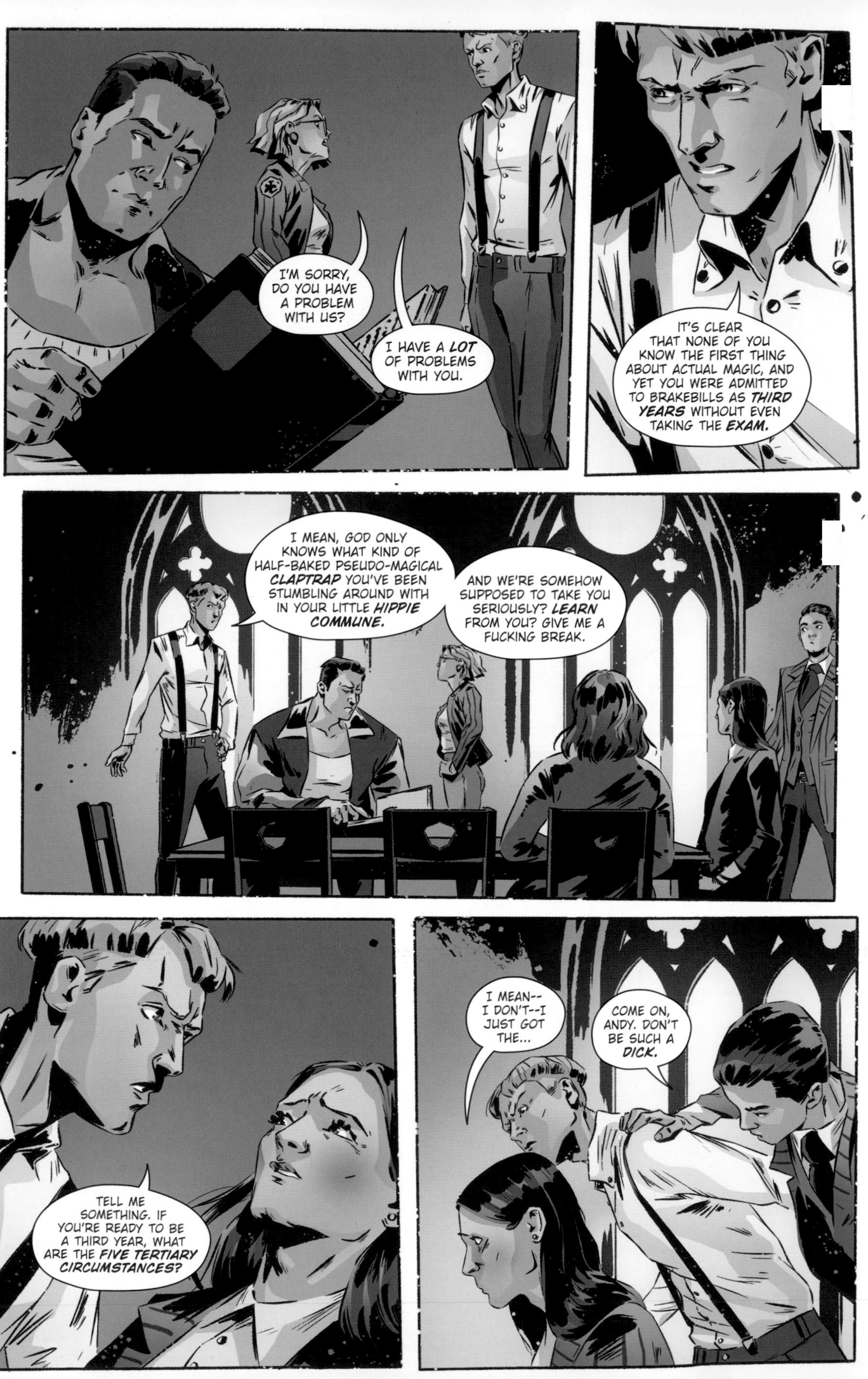

I'M SORRY, DO YOU HAVE A PROBLEM WITH US?
I HAVE A *LOT* OF PROBLEMS WITH YOU.
IT'S CLEAR THAT NONE OF YOU KNOW THE FIRST THING ABOUT ACTUAL MAGIC, AND YET YOU WERE ADMITTED TO BRAKEBILLS AS *THIRD YEARS* WITHOUT EVEN TAKING THE *EXAM.*
I MEAN, GOD ONLY KNOWS WHAT KIND OF HALF-BAKED PSEUDO-MAGICAL *CLAPTRAP* YOU'VE BEEN STUMBLING AROUND WITH IN YOUR LITTLE *HIPPIE COMMUNE.*
AND WE'RE SOMEHOW SUPPOSED TO TAKE YOU SERIOUSLY? *LEARN* FROM YOU? GIVE ME A FUCKING BREAK.
TELL ME SOMETHING. IF YOU'RE READY TO BE A THIRD YEAR, WHAT ARE THE *FIVE TERTIARY CIRCUMSTANCES?*
I MEAN-- I DON'T--I JUST GOT THE...
COME ON, ANDY. DON'T BE SUCH A *DICK.*

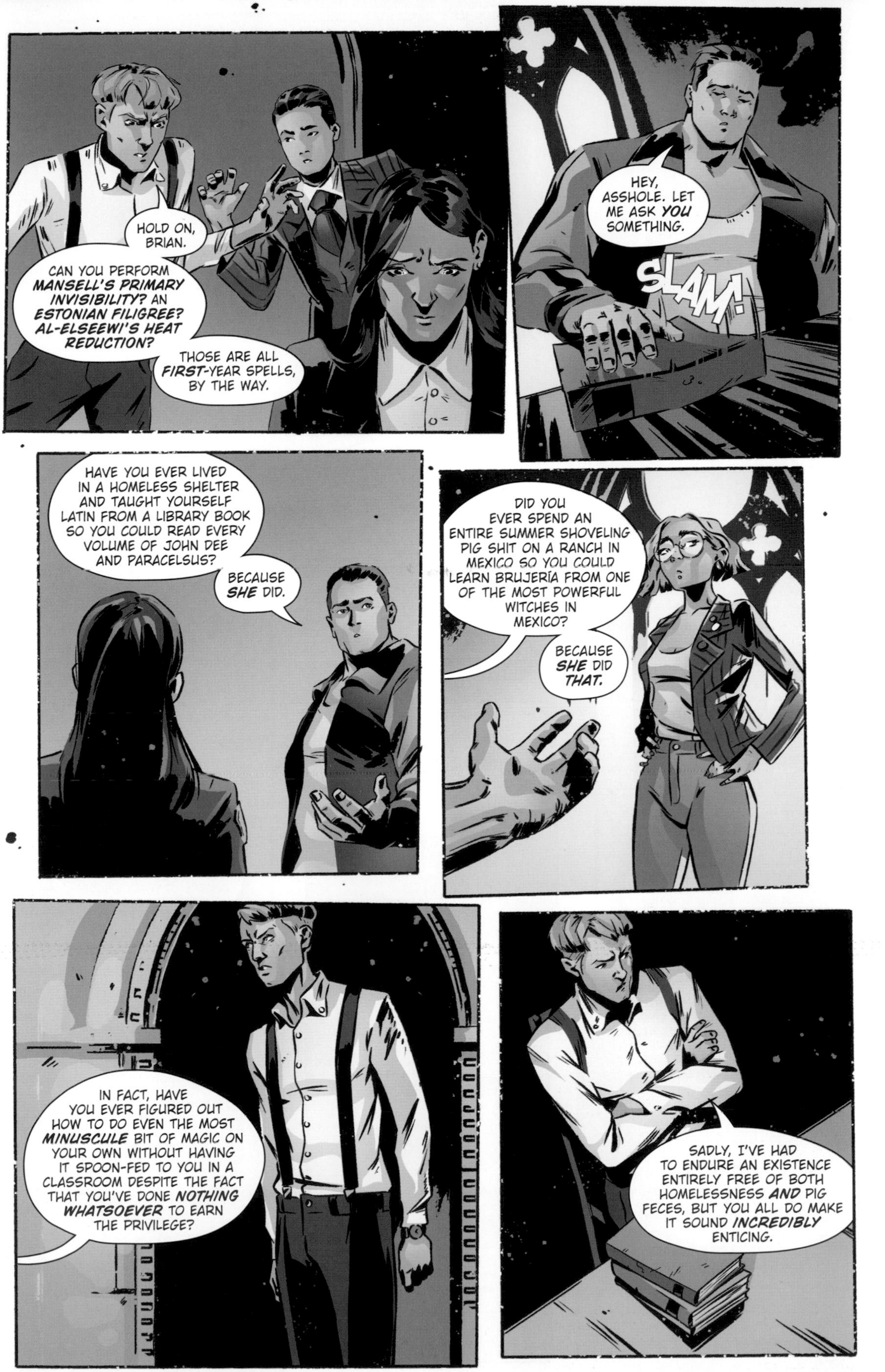
HOLD ON, BRIAN.
CAN YOU PERFORM **MANSELL'S PRIMARY INVISIBILITY?** AN **ESTONIAN FILIGREE? AL-ELSEEWI'S HEAT REDUCTION?**
THOSE ARE ALL **FIRST**-YEAR SPELLS, BY THE WAY.
HEY, ASSHOLE. LET ME ASK **YOU** SOMETHING.
SLAM!
HAVE YOU EVER LIVED IN A HOMELESS SHELTER AND TAUGHT YOURSELF LATIN FROM A LIBRARY BOOK SO YOU COULD READ EVERY VOLUME OF JOHN DEE AND PARACELSUS?
BECAUSE **SHE** DID.
DID YOU EVER SPEND AN ENTIRE SUMMER SHOVELING PIG SHIT ON A RANCH IN MEXICO SO YOU COULD LEARN BRUJERÍA FROM ONE OF THE MOST POWERFUL WITCHES IN MEXICO?
BECAUSE **SHE** DID **THAT.**
IN FACT, HAVE YOU EVER FIGURED OUT HOW TO DO EVEN THE MOST **MINUSCULE** BIT OF MAGIC ON YOUR OWN WITHOUT HAVING IT SPOON-FED TO YOU IN A CLASSROOM DESPITE THE FACT THAT YOU'VE DONE **NOTHING WHATSOEVER** TO EARN THE PRIVILEGE?
SADLY, I'VE HAD TO ENDURE AN EXISTENCE ENTIRELY FREE OF BOTH HOMELESSNESS **AND** PIG FECES, BUT YOU ALL DO MAKE IT SOUND **INCREDIBLY** ENTICING.

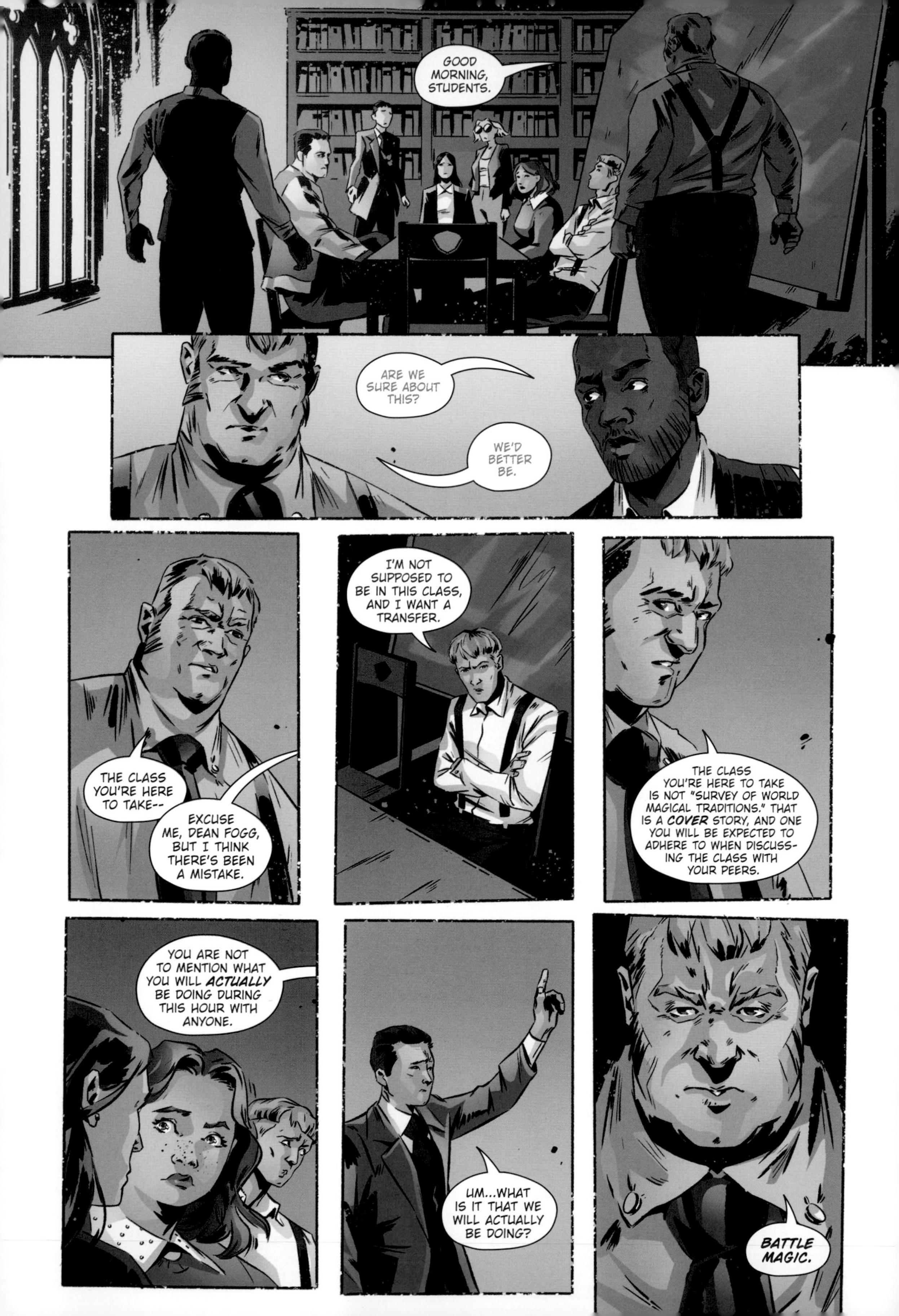
GOOD MORNING, STUDENTS.
ARE WE SURE ABOUT THIS?
WE'D BETTER BE.
THE CLASS YOU'RE HERE TO TAKE--
EXCUSE ME, DEAN FOGG, BUT I THINK THERE'S BEEN A MISTAKE.
I'M NOT SUPPOSED TO BE IN THIS CLASS, AND I WANT A TRANSFER.
THE CLASS YOU'RE HERE TO TAKE IS NOT "SURVEY OF WORLD MAGICAL TRADITIONS." THAT IS A ***COVER*** STORY, AND ONE YOU WILL BE EXPECTED TO ADHERE TO WHEN DISCUSSING THE CLASS WITH YOUR PEERS.
YOU ARE NOT TO MENTION WHAT YOU WILL ***ACTUALLY*** BE DOING DURING THIS HOUR WITH ANYONE.
UM...WHAT IS IT THAT WE WILL ACTUALLY BE DOING?
BATTLE MAGIC.

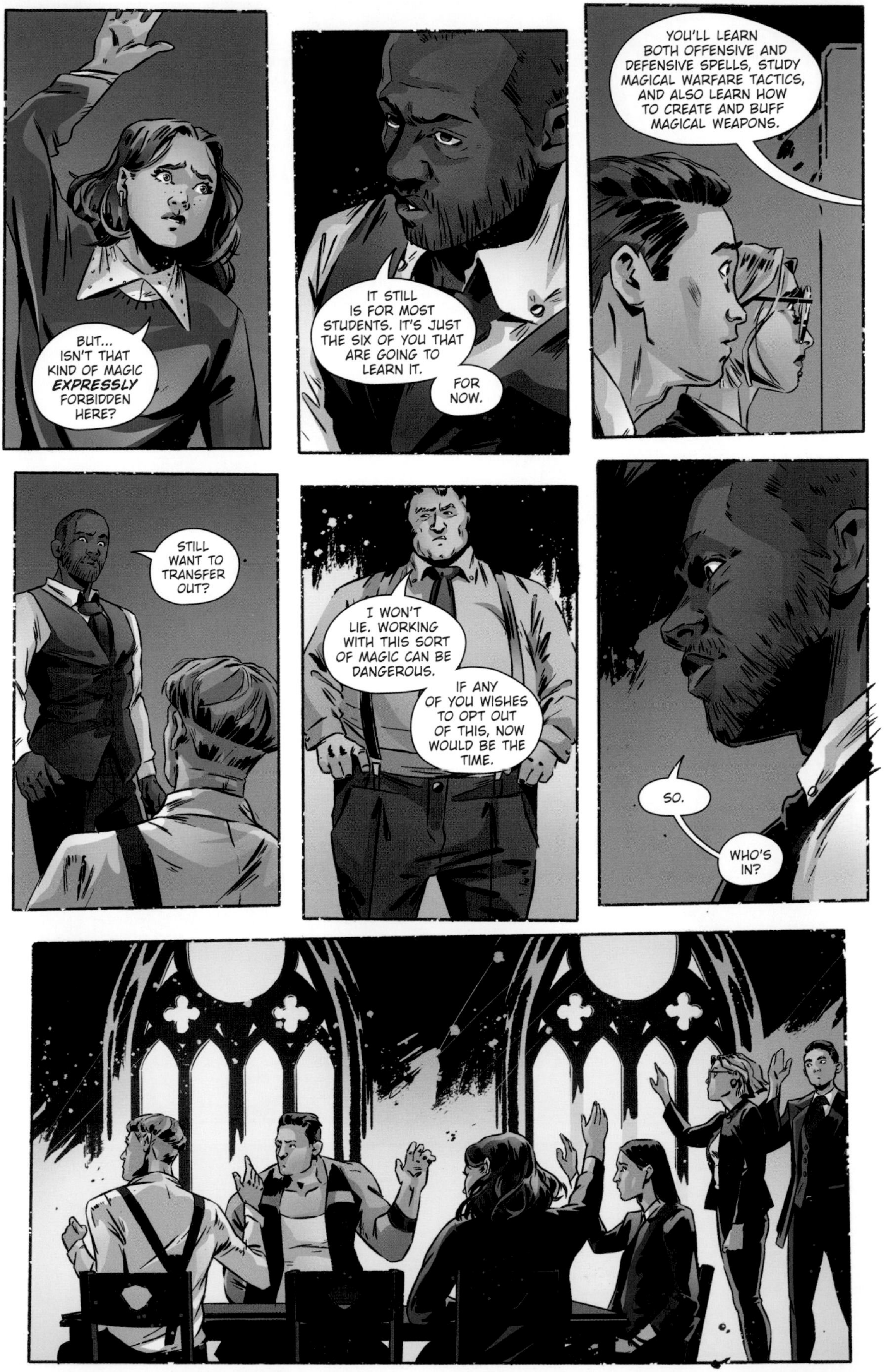
BUT... ISN'T THAT KIND OF MAGIC *EXPRESSLY* FORBIDDEN HERE?
IT STILL IS FOR MOST STUDENTS. IT'S JUST THE SIX OF YOU THAT ARE GOING TO LEARN IT.
FOR NOW.
YOU'LL LEARN BOTH OFFENSIVE AND DEFENSIVE SPELLS, STUDY MAGICAL WARFARE TACTICS, AND ALSO LEARN HOW TO CREATE AND BUFF MAGICAL WEAPONS.
STILL WANT TO TRANSFER OUT?
I WON'T LIE. WORKING WITH THIS SORT OF MAGIC CAN BE DANGEROUS.
IF ANY OF YOU WISHES TO OPT OUT OF THIS, NOW WOULD BE THE TIME.
SO.
WHO'S IN?

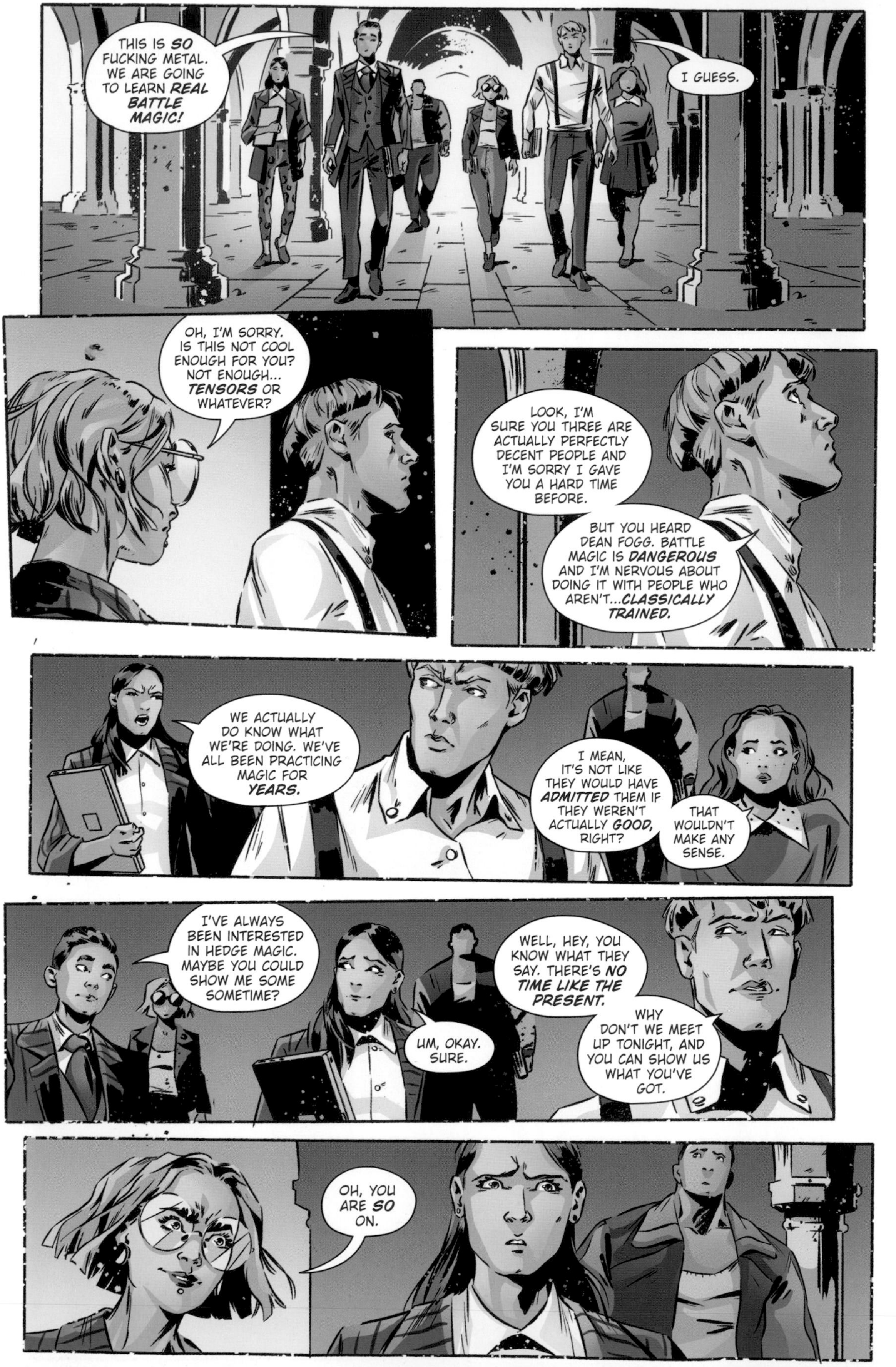
THIS IS SO FUCKING METAL. WE ARE GOING TO LEARN REAL BATTLE MAGIC!
I GUESS.
OH, I'M SORRY. IS THIS NOT COOL ENOUGH FOR YOU? NOT ENOUGH... TENSORS OR WHATEVER?
LOOK, I'M SURE YOU THREE ARE ACTUALLY PERFECTLY DECENT PEOPLE AND I'M SORRY I GAVE YOU A HARD TIME BEFORE.
BUT YOU HEARD DEAN FOGG. BATTLE MAGIC IS DANGEROUS AND I'M NERVOUS ABOUT DOING IT WITH PEOPLE WHO AREN'T...CLASSICALLY TRAINED.
WE ACTUALLY DO KNOW WHAT WE'RE DOING. WE'VE ALL BEEN PRACTICING MAGIC FOR YEARS.
I MEAN, IT'S NOT LIKE THEY WOULD HAVE ADMITTED THEM IF THEY WEREN'T ACTUALLY GOOD, RIGHT?
THAT WOULDN'T MAKE ANY SENSE.
I'VE ALWAYS BEEN INTERESTED IN HEDGE MAGIC. MAYBE YOU COULD SHOW ME SOME SOMETIME?
UM, OKAY. SURE.
WELL, HEY, YOU KNOW WHAT THEY SAY. THERE'S NO TIME LIKE THE PRESENT.
WHY DON'T WE MEET UP TONIGHT, AND YOU CAN SHOW US WHAT YOU'VE GOT.
OH, YOU ARE SO ON.

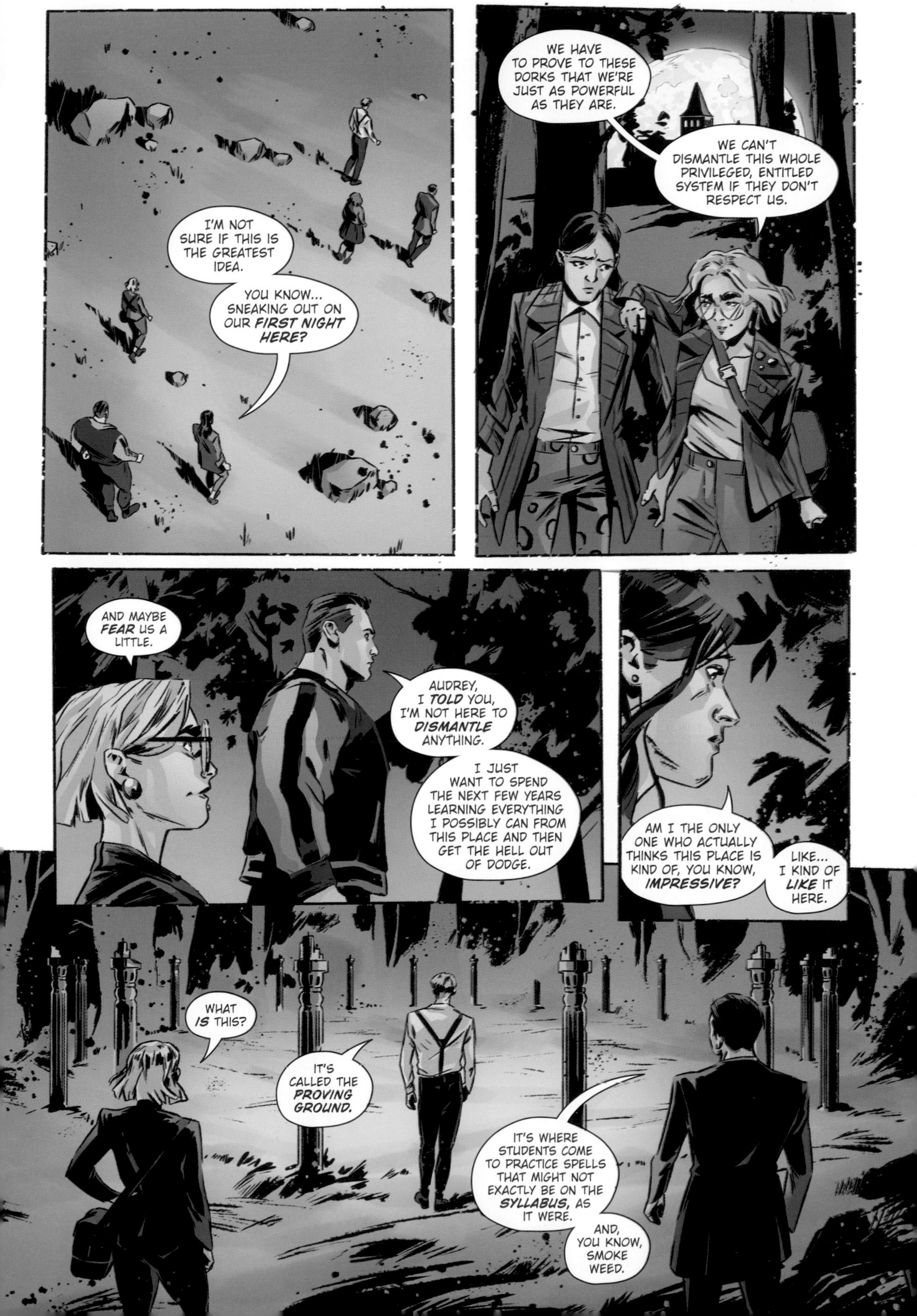
I'M NOT SURE IF THIS IS THE GREATEST IDEA.
YOU KNOW... SNEAKING OUT ON OUR FIRST NIGHT HERE?
WE HAVE TO PROVE TO THESE DORKS THAT WE'RE JUST AS POWERFUL AS THEY ARE.
WE CAN'T DISMANTLE THIS WHOLE PRIVILEGED, ENTITLED SYSTEM IF THEY DON'T RESPECT US.
AND MAYBE FEAR US A LITTLE.
AUDREY, I TOLD YOU, I'M NOT HERE TO DISMANTLE ANYTHING.
I JUST WANT TO SPEND THE NEXT FEW YEARS LEARNING EVERYTHING I POSSIBLY CAN FROM THIS PLACE AND THEN GET THE HELL OUT OF DODGE.
AM I THE ONLY ONE WHO ACTUALLY THINKS THIS PLACE IS KIND OF, YOU KNOW, IMPRESSIVE?
LIKE... I KIND OF LIKE IT HERE.
WHAT IS THIS?
IT'S CALLED THE PROVING GROUND.
IT'S WHERE STUDENTS COME TO PRACTICE SPELLS THAT MIGHT NOT EXACTLY BE ON THE SYLLABUS, AS IT WERE.
AND, YOU KNOW, SMOKE WEED.

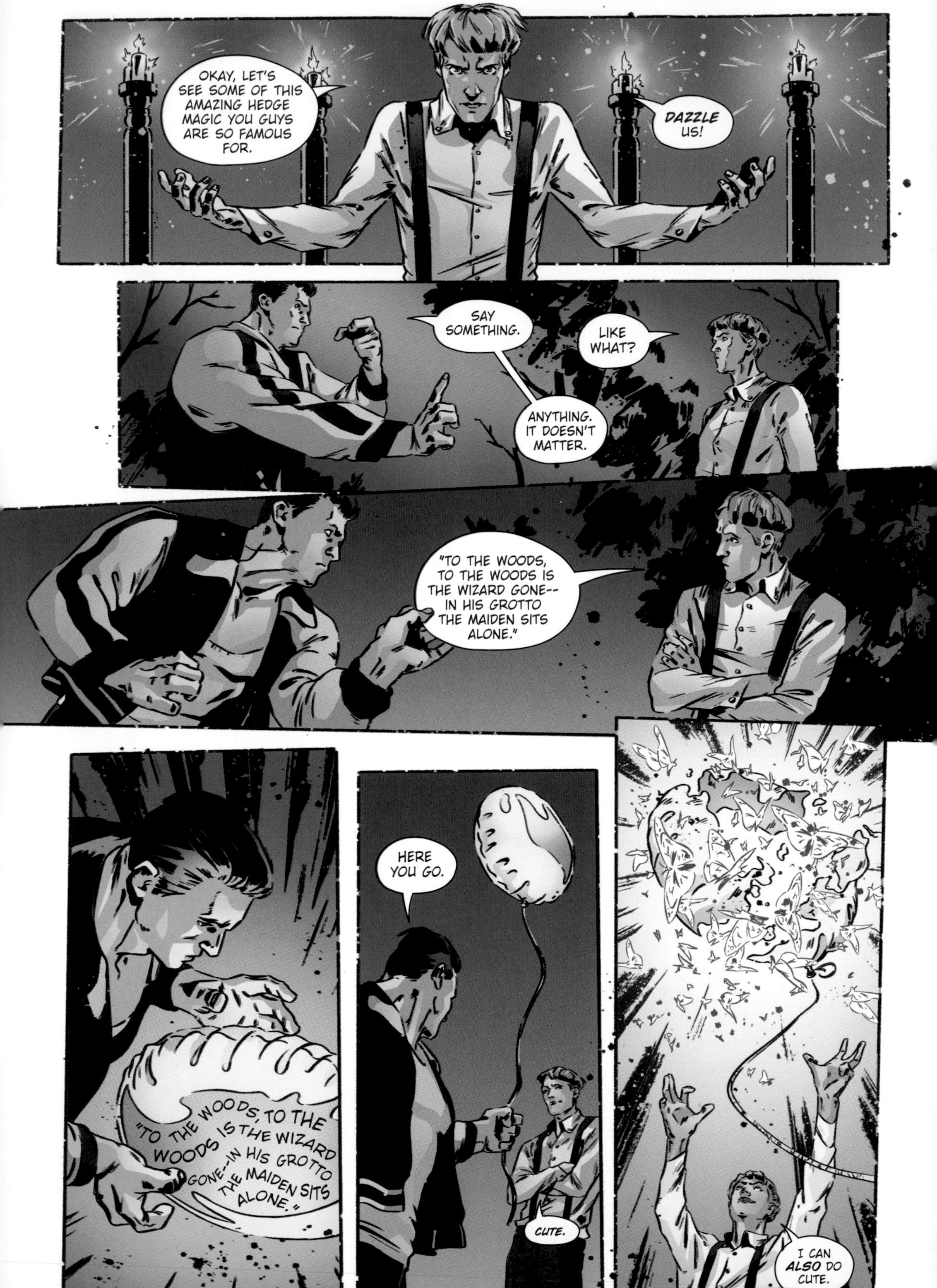

OKAY, LET'S SEE SOME OF THIS AMAZING HEDGE MAGIC YOU GUYS ARE SO FAMOUS FOR.
DAZZLE US!
SAY SOMETHING.
LIKE WHAT?
ANYTHING. IT DOESN'T MATTER.
"TO THE WOODS, TO THE WOODS IS THE WIZARD GONE-- IN HIS GROTTO THE MAIDEN SITS ALONE."
"TO THE WOODS, TO THE WOODS IS THE WIZARD GONE--IN HIS GROTTO THE MAIDEN SITS ALONE."
HERE YOU GO.
CUTE.
I CAN *ALSO* DO CUTE.

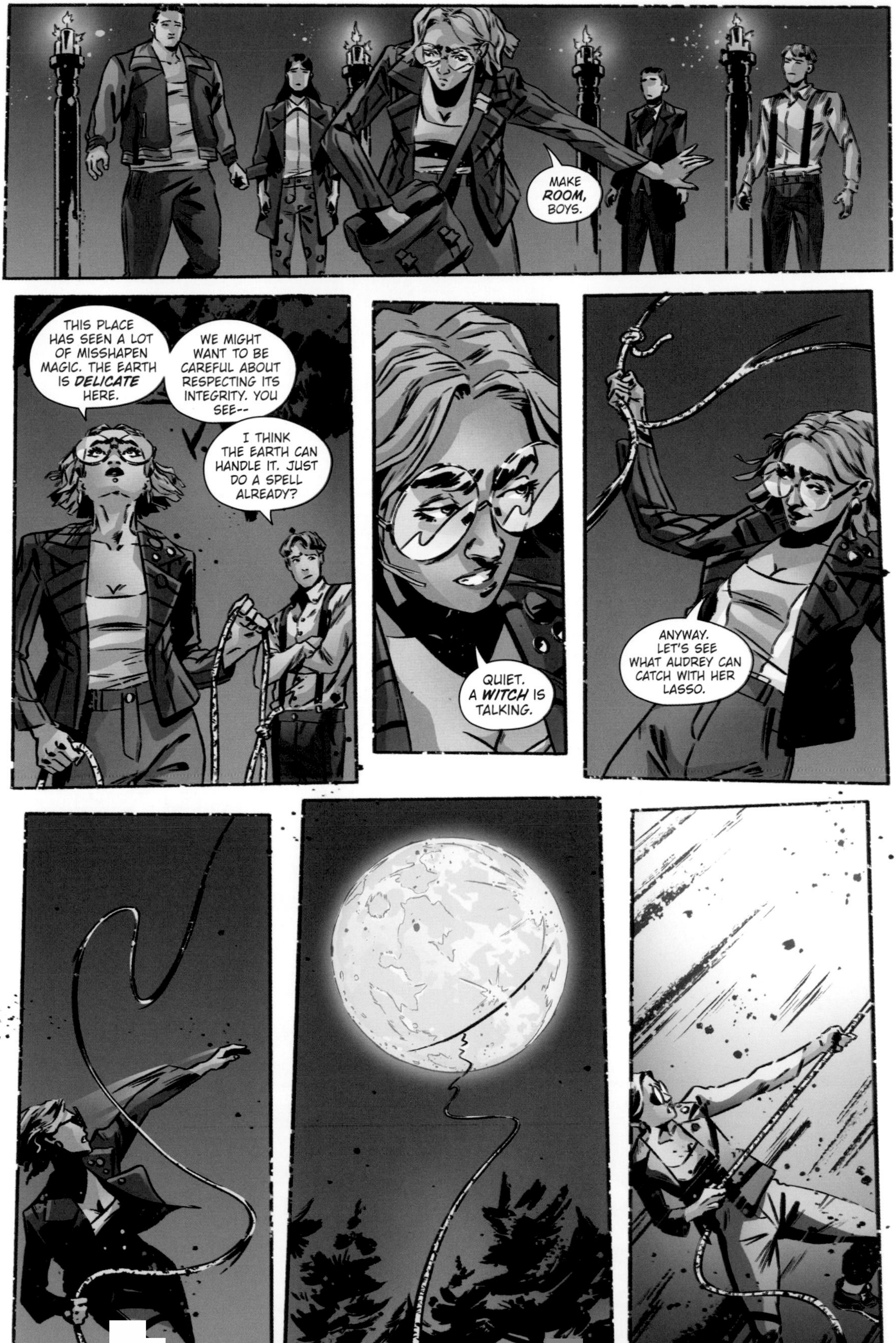
MAKE ROOM, BOYS.
THIS PLACE HAS SEEN A LOT OF MISSHAPEN MAGIC. THE EARTH IS DELICATE HERE.
WE MIGHT WANT TO BE CAREFUL ABOUT RESPECTING ITS INTEGRITY. YOU SEE--
I THINK THE EARTH CAN HANDLE IT. JUST DO A SPELL ALREADY?
QUIET. A WITCH IS TALKING.
ANYWAY. LET'S SEE WHAT AUDREY CAN CATCH WITH HER LASSO.

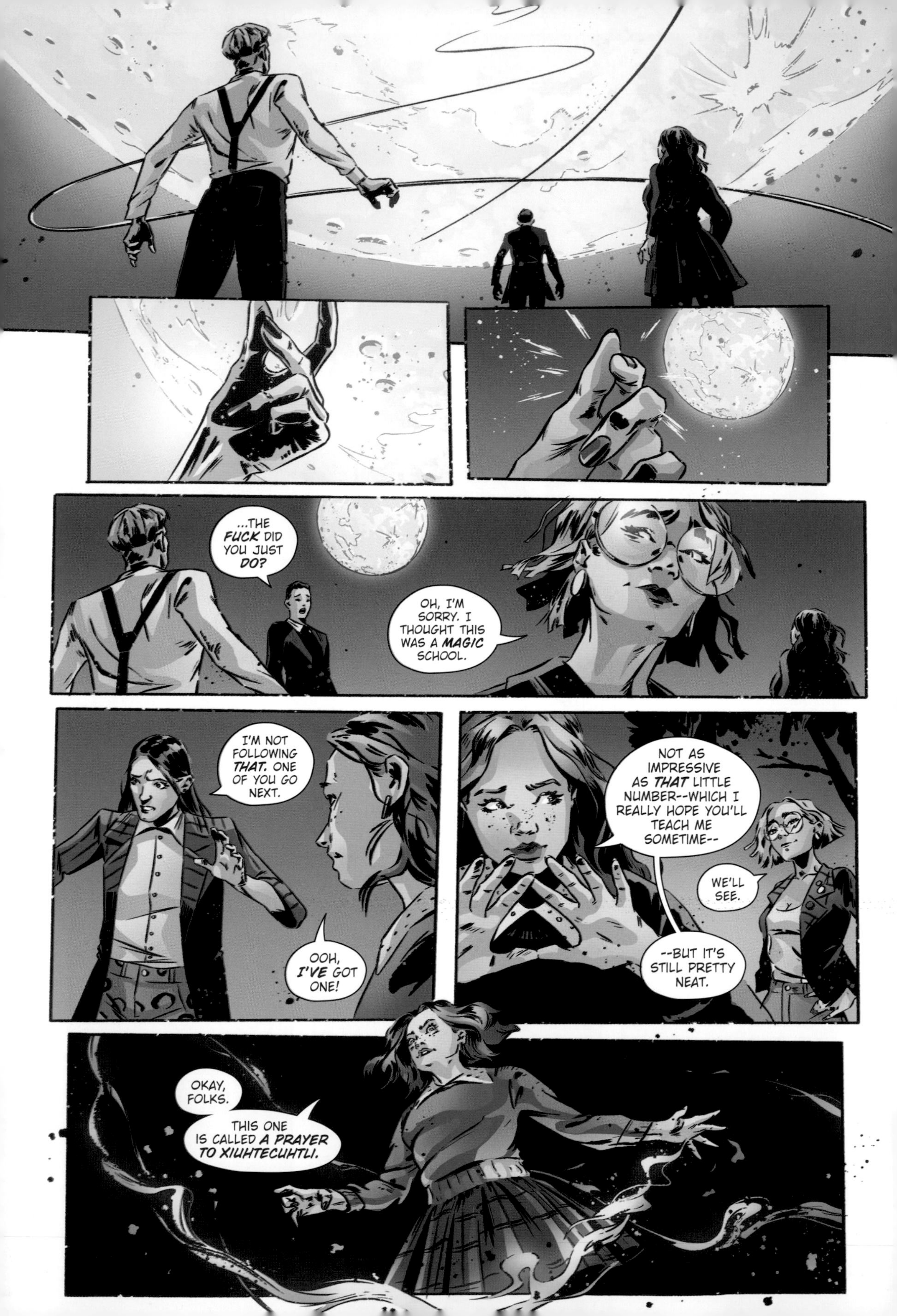
...THE FUCK DID YOU JUST DO?
OH, I'M SORRY. I THOUGHT THIS WAS A MAGIC SCHOOL.
I'M NOT FOLLOWING THAT. ONE OF YOU GO NEXT.
OOH, I'VE GOT ONE!
NOT AS IMPRESSIVE AS THAT LITTLE NUMBER--WHICH I REALLY HOPE YOU'LL TEACH ME SOMETIME--
WE'LL SEE.
--BUT IT'S STILL PRETTY NEAT.
OKAY, FOLKS.
THIS ONE IS CALLED A PRAYER TO XIUHTECUHTLI.

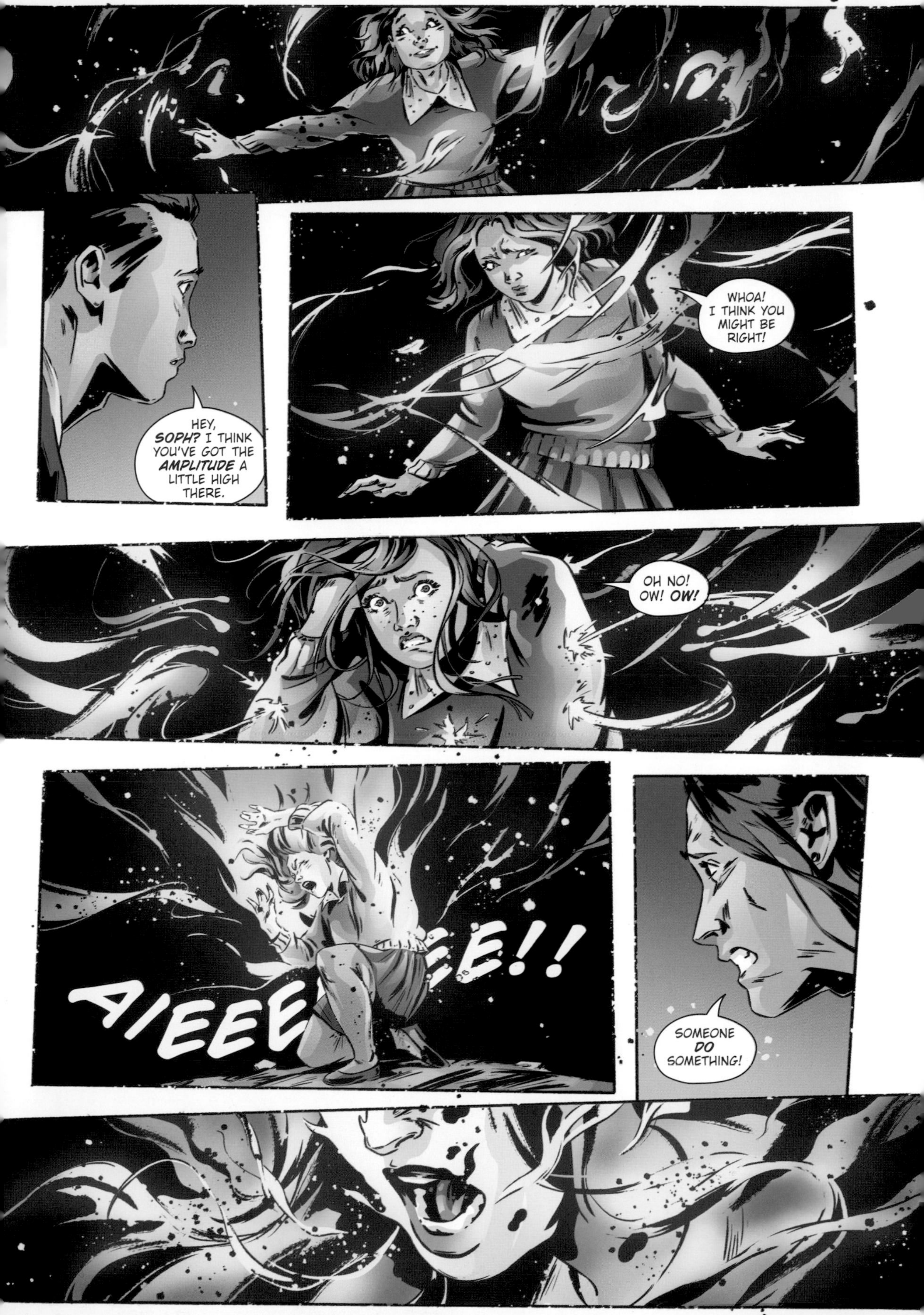
HEY, SOPH? I THINK YOU'VE GOT THE AMPLITUDE A LITTLE HIGH THERE.
WHOA! I THINK YOU MIGHT BE RIGHT!
OH NO! OW! OW!
AIEEEEEE!!
SOMEONE DO SOMETHING!

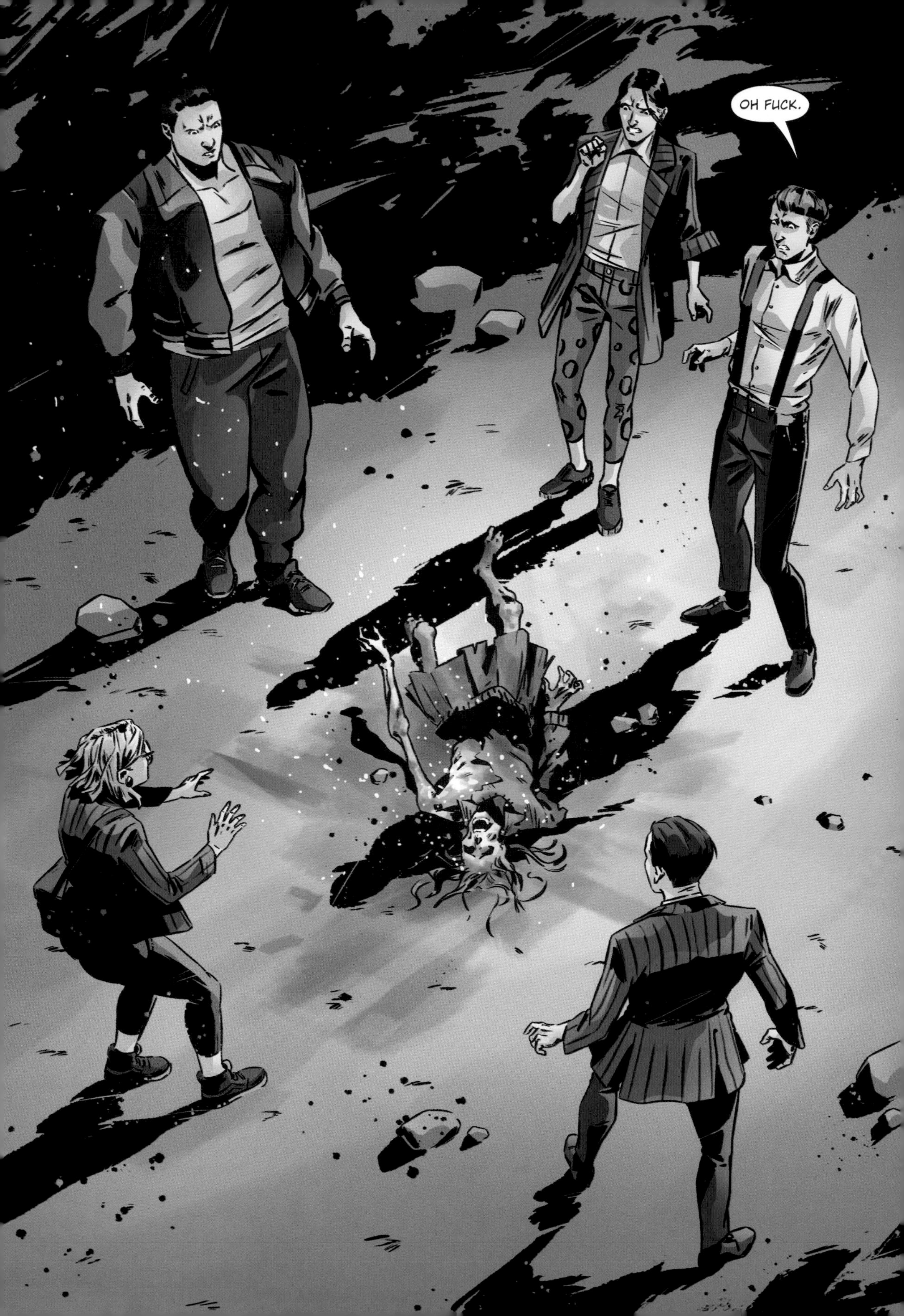
OH FUCK.

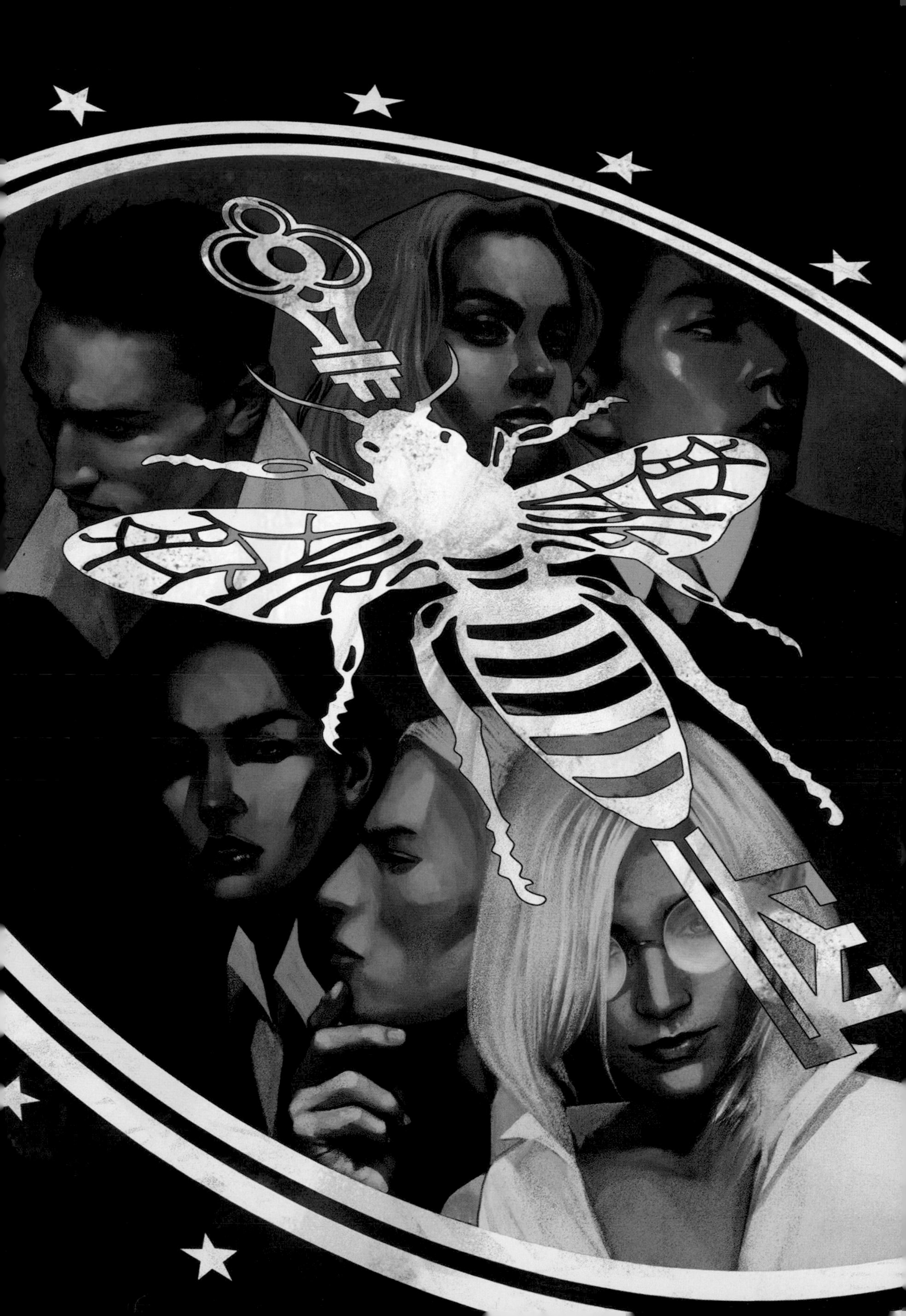

CHAPTER
TWO

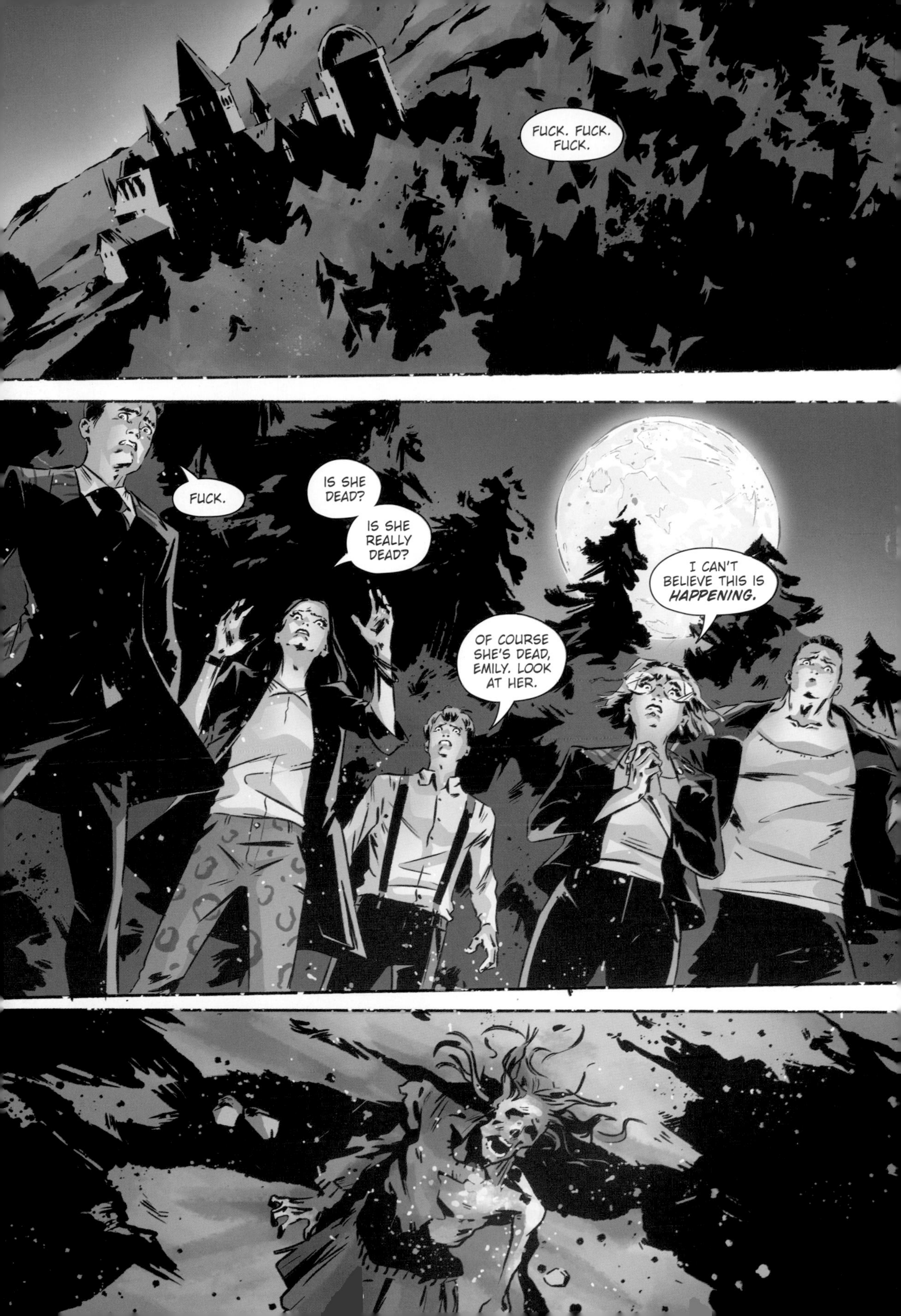
FUCK. FUCK. FUCK.
FUCK.
IS SHE DEAD?
IS SHE REALLY DEAD?
OF COURSE SHE'S DEAD, EMILY. LOOK AT HER.
I CAN'T BELIEVE THIS IS *HAPPENING.*

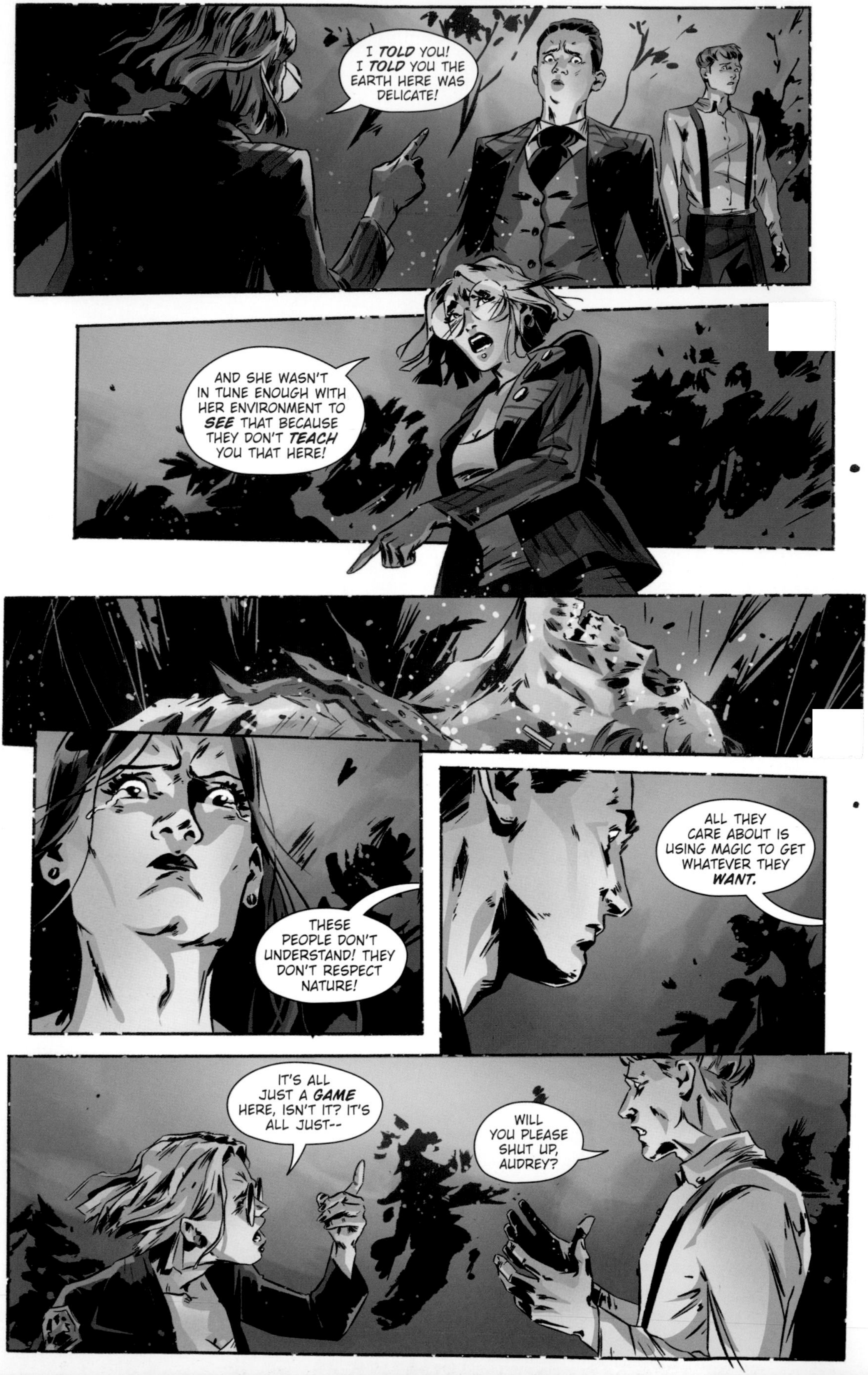
I TOLD YOU! I TOLD YOU THE EARTH HERE WAS DELICATE!
AND SHE WASN'T IN TUNE ENOUGH WITH HER ENVIRONMENT TO SEE THAT BECAUSE THEY DON'T TEACH YOU THAT HERE!
THESE PEOPLE DON'T UNDERSTAND! THEY DON'T RESPECT NATURE!
ALL THEY CARE ABOUT IS USING MAGIC TO GET WHATEVER THEY WANT.
IT'S ALL JUST A GAME HERE, ISN'T IT? IT'S ALL JUST--
WILL YOU PLEASE SHUT UP, AUDREY?

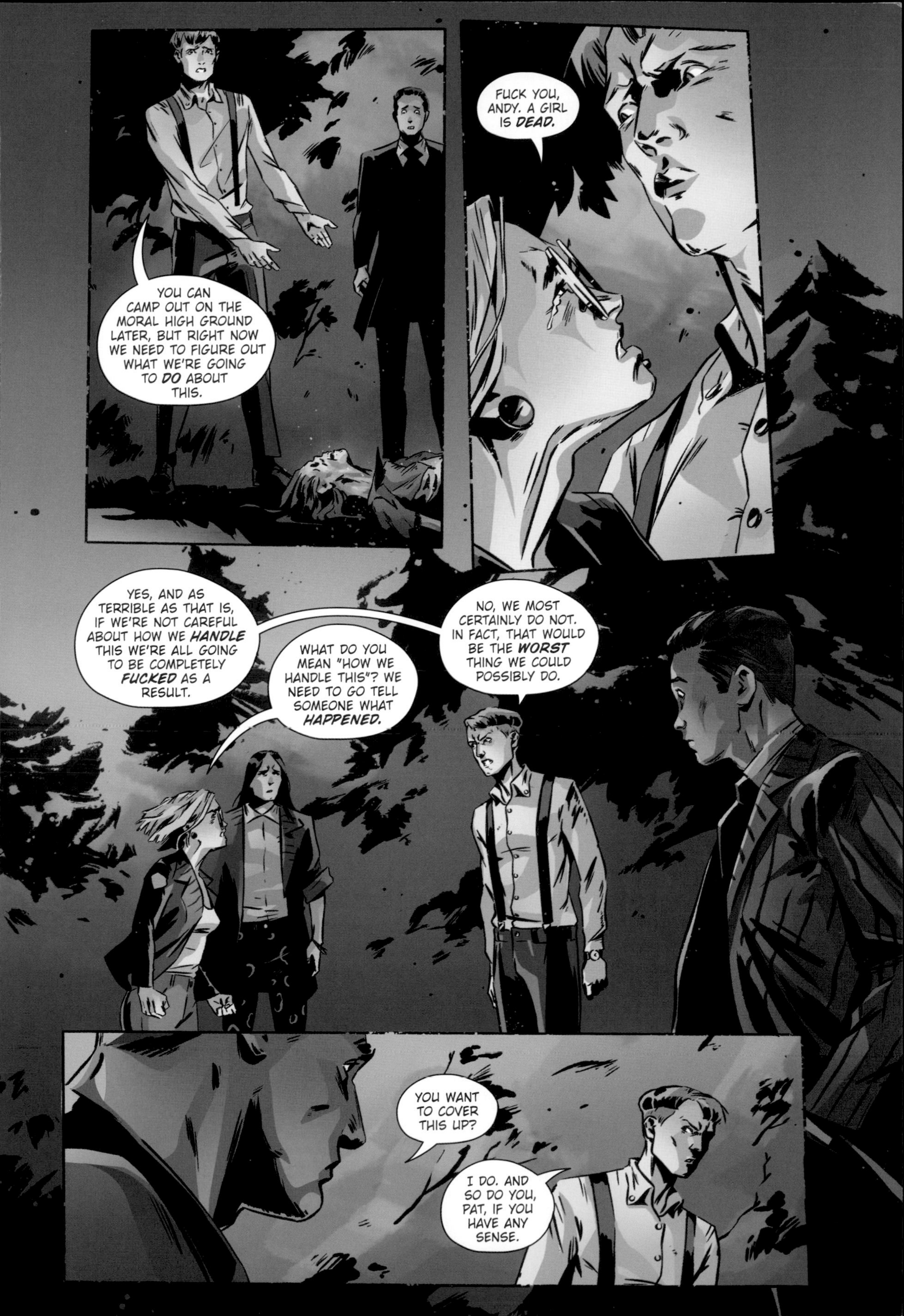
YOU CAN CAMP OUT ON THE MORAL HIGH GROUND LATER, BUT RIGHT NOW WE NEED TO FIGURE OUT WHAT WE'RE GOING TO DO ABOUT THIS.
FUCK YOU, ANDY. A GIRL IS DEAD.
YES, AND AS TERRIBLE AS THAT IS, IF WE'RE NOT CAREFUL ABOUT HOW WE HANDLE THIS WE'RE ALL GOING TO BE COMPLETELY FUCKED AS A RESULT.
WHAT DO YOU MEAN "HOW WE HANDLE THIS"? WE NEED TO GO TELL SOMEONE WHAT HAPPENED.
NO, WE MOST CERTAINLY DO NOT. IN FACT, THAT WOULD BE THE WORST THING WE COULD POSSIBLY DO.
YOU WANT TO COVER THIS UP?
I DO. AND SO DO YOU, PAT, IF YOU HAVE ANY SENSE.

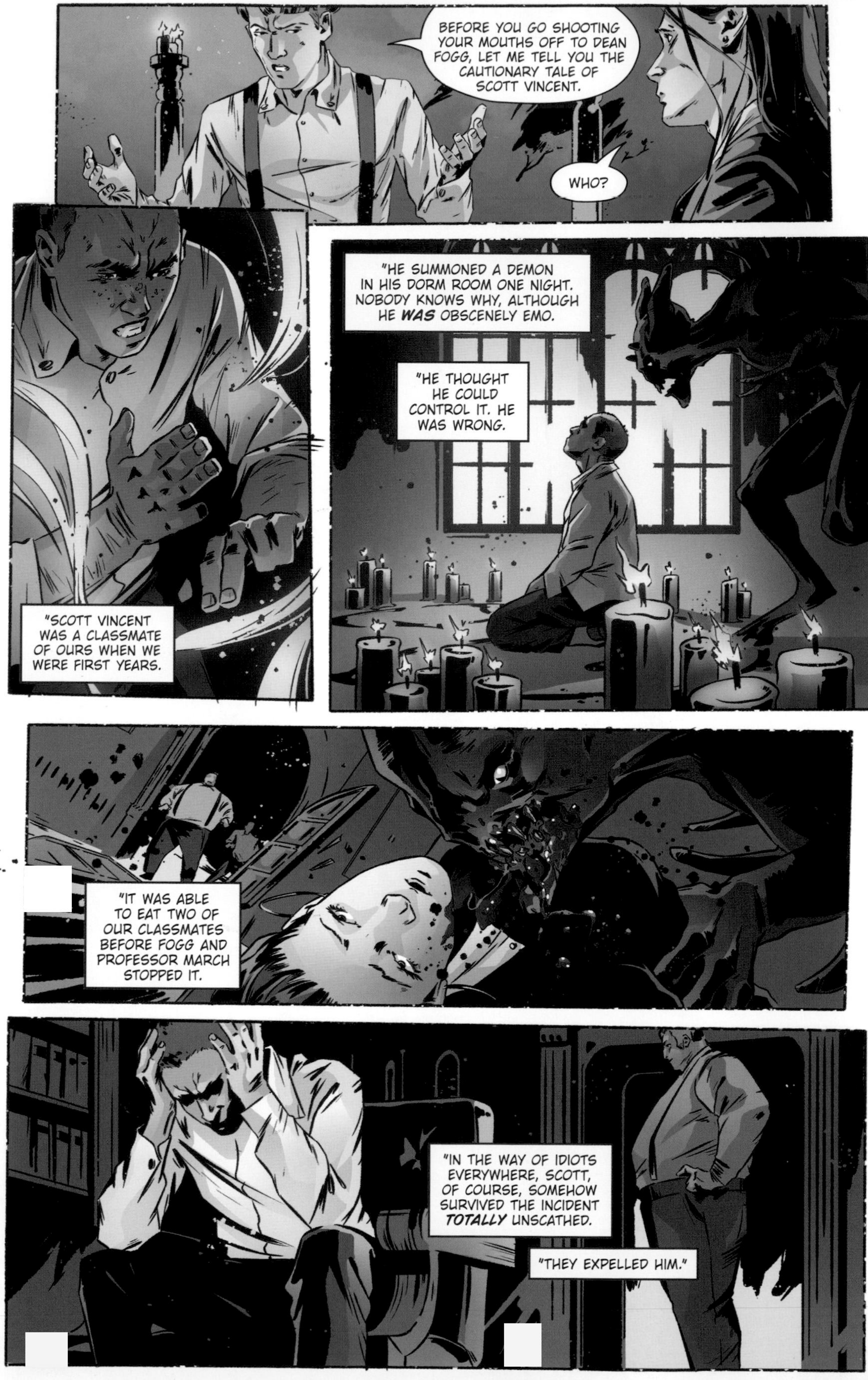
BEFORE YOU GO SHOOTING YOUR MOUTHS OFF TO DEAN FOGG, LET ME TELL YOU THE CAUTIONARY TALE OF SCOTT VINCENT.
WHO?
"SCOTT VINCENT WAS A CLASSMATE OF OURS WHEN WE WERE FIRST YEARS.
"HE SUMMONED A DEMON IN HIS DORM ROOM ONE NIGHT. NOBODY KNOWS WHY, ALTHOUGH HE *WAS* OBSCENELY EMO.
"HE THOUGHT HE COULD CONTROL IT. HE WAS WRONG.
"IT WAS ABLE TO EAT TWO OF OUR CLASSMATES BEFORE FOGG AND PROFESSOR MARCH STOPPED IT.
"IN THE WAY OF IDIOTS EVERYWHERE, SCOTT, OF COURSE, SOMEHOW SURVIVED THE INCIDENT *TOTALLY* UNSCATHED.
"THEY EXPELLED HIM."

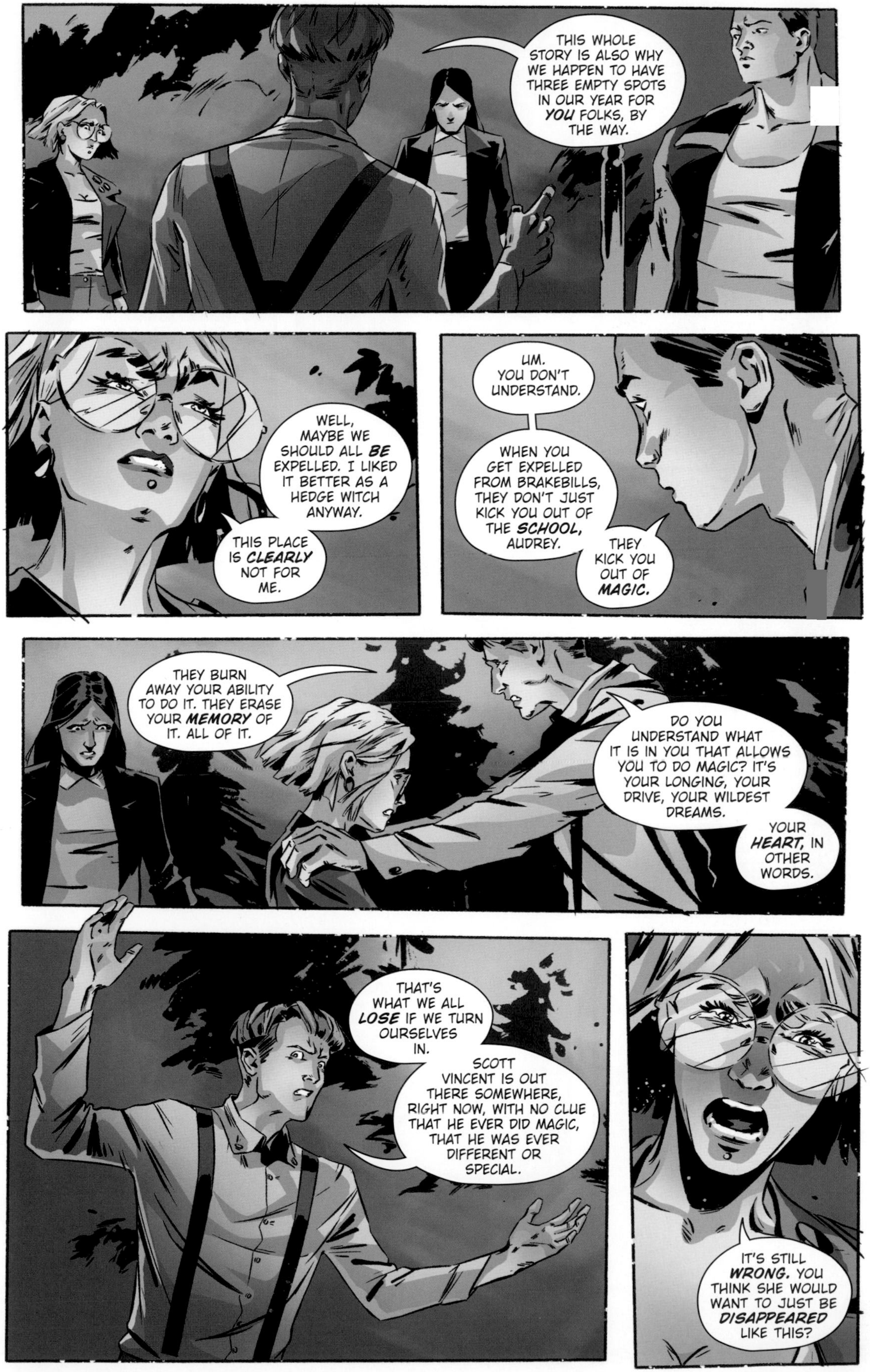

THIS WHOLE STORY IS ALSO WHY WE HAPPEN TO HAVE THREE EMPTY SPOTS IN OUR YEAR FOR *YOU* FOLKS, BY THE WAY.
WELL, MAYBE WE SHOULD ALL *BE* EXPELLED. I LIKED IT BETTER AS A HEDGE WITCH ANYWAY.
THIS PLACE IS *CLEARLY* NOT FOR ME.
UM. YOU DON'T UNDERSTAND.
WHEN YOU GET EXPELLED FROM BRAKEBILLS, THEY DON'T JUST KICK YOU OUT OF THE *SCHOOL,* AUDREY.
THEY KICK YOU OUT OF *MAGIC.*
THEY BURN AWAY YOUR ABILITY TO DO IT. THEY ERASE YOUR *MEMORY* OF IT. ALL OF IT.
DO YOU UNDERSTAND WHAT IT IS IN YOU THAT ALLOWS YOU TO DO MAGIC? IT'S YOUR LONGING, YOUR DRIVE, YOUR WILDEST DREAMS.
YOUR *HEART,* IN OTHER WORDS.
THAT'S WHAT WE ALL *LOSE* IF WE TURN OURSELVES IN.
SCOTT VINCENT IS OUT THERE SOMEWHERE, RIGHT NOW, WITH NO CLUE THAT HE EVER DID MAGIC, THAT HE WAS EVER DIFFERENT OR SPECIAL.
IT'S STILL *WRONG.* YOU THINK SHE WOULD WANT TO JUST BE *DISAPPEARED* LIKE THIS?

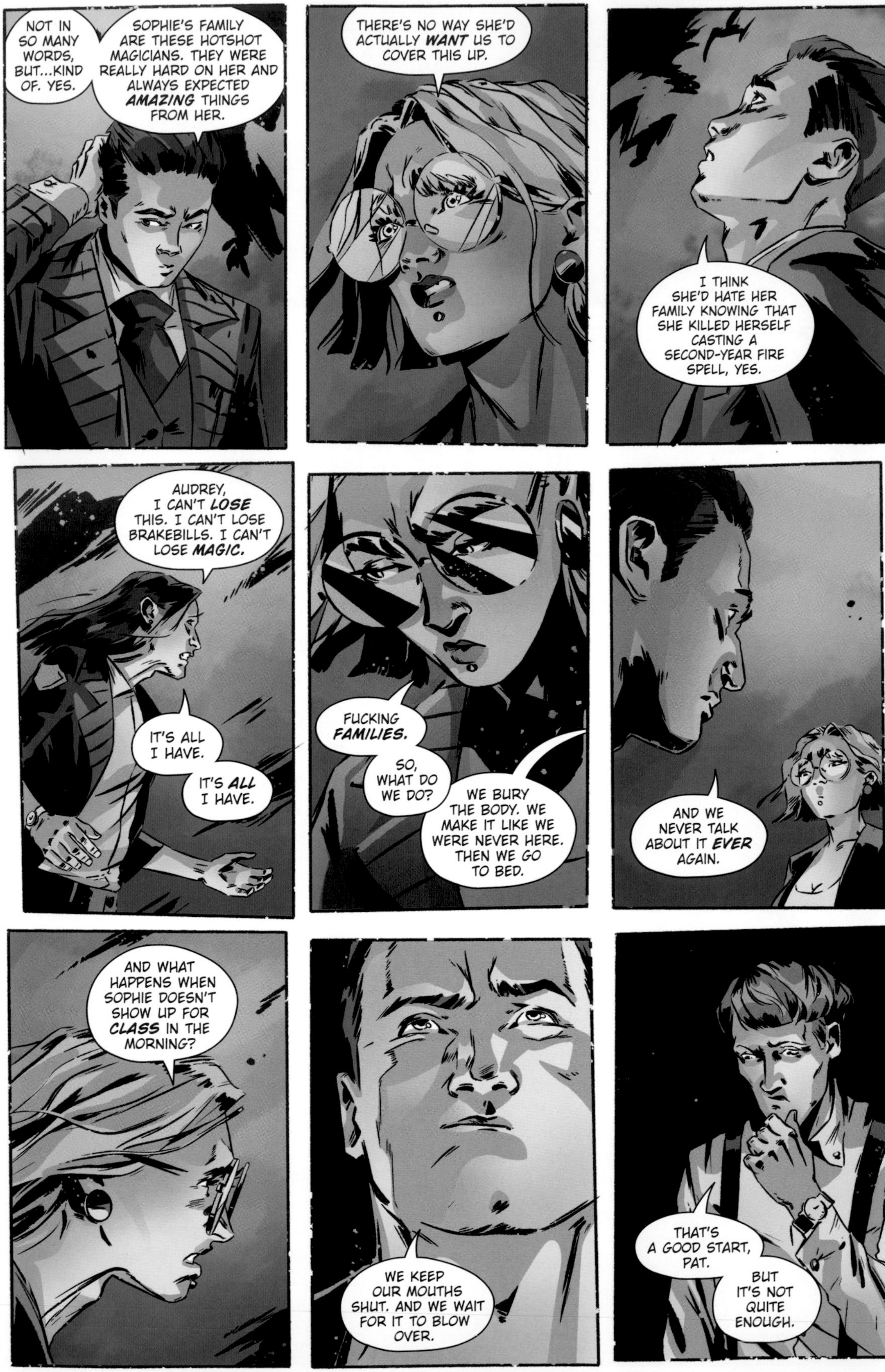
NOT IN SO MANY WORDS, BUT...KIND OF. YES.
SOPHIE'S FAMILY ARE THESE HOTSHOT MAGICIANS. THEY WERE REALLY HARD ON HER AND ALWAYS EXPECTED AMAZING THINGS FROM HER.
THERE'S NO WAY SHE'D ACTUALLY WANT US TO COVER THIS UP.
I THINK SHE'D HATE HER FAMILY KNOWING THAT SHE KILLED HERSELF CASTING A SECOND-YEAR FIRE SPELL, YES.
AUDREY, I CAN'T LOSE THIS. I CAN'T LOSE BRAKEBILLS. I CAN'T LOSE MAGIC.
IT'S ALL I HAVE.
IT'S ALL I HAVE.
FUCKING FAMILIES.
SO, WHAT DO WE DO?
WE BURY THE BODY. WE MAKE IT LIKE WE WERE NEVER HERE. THEN WE GO TO BED.
AND WE NEVER TALK ABOUT IT EVER AGAIN.
AND WHAT HAPPENS WHEN SOPHIE DOESN'T SHOW UP FOR CLASS IN THE MORNING?
WE KEEP OUR MOUTHS SHUT. AND WE WAIT FOR IT TO BLOW OVER.
THAT'S A GOOD START, PAT.
BUT IT'S NOT QUITE ENOUGH.

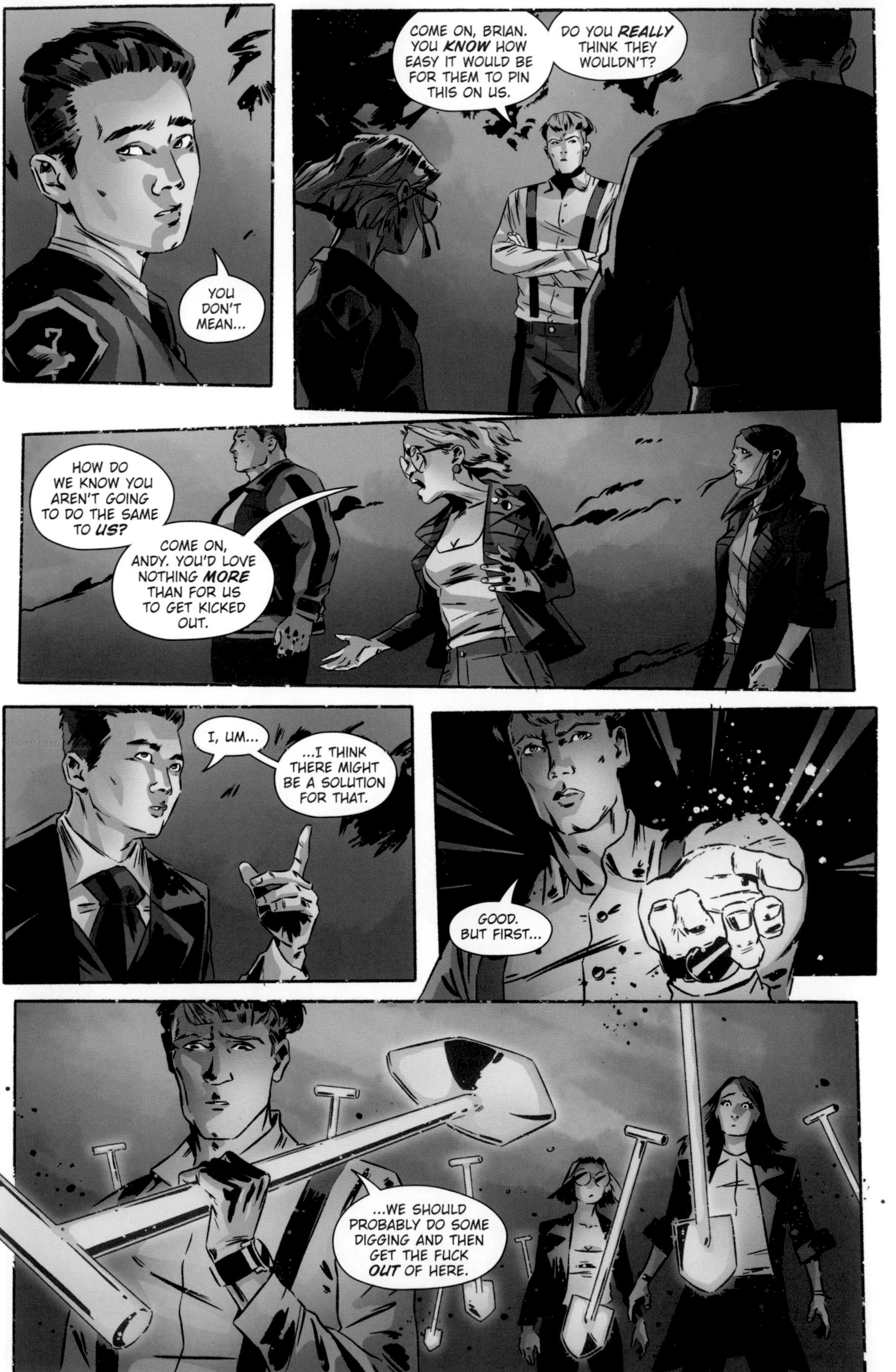
YOU DON'T MEAN...
COME ON, BRIAN. YOU **KNOW** HOW EASY IT WOULD BE FOR THEM TO PIN THIS ON US.
DO YOU **REALLY** THINK THEY WOULDN'T?
HOW DO WE KNOW YOU AREN'T GOING TO DO THE SAME TO **US?**
COME ON, ANDY. YOU'D LOVE NOTHING **MORE** THAN FOR US TO GET KICKED OUT.
I, UM...
...I THINK THERE MIGHT BE A SOLUTION FOR THAT.
GOOD. BUT FIRST...
...WE SHOULD PROBABLY DO SOME DIGGING AND THEN GET THE FUCK **OUT** OF HERE.

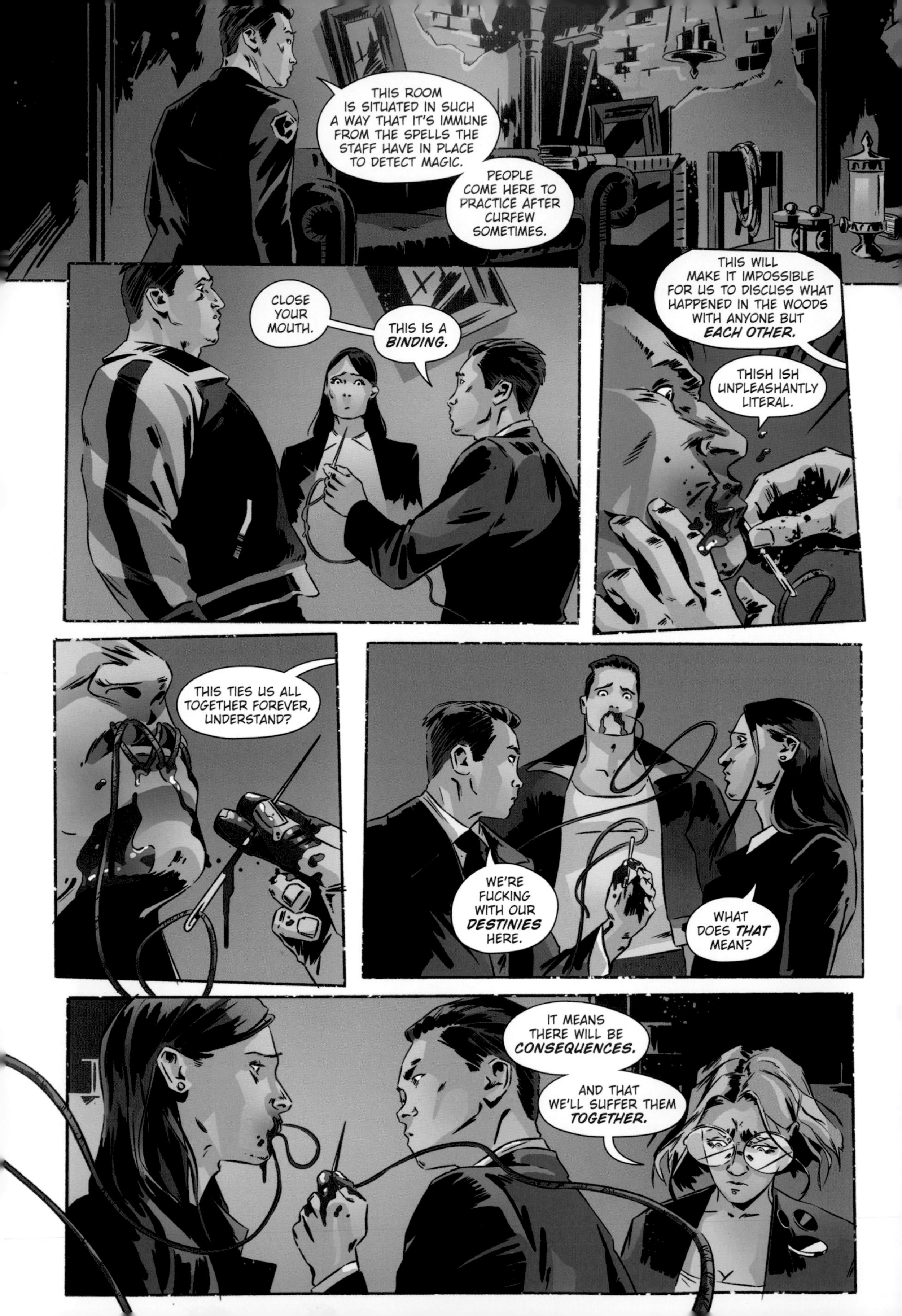
THIS ROOM IS SITUATED IN SUCH A WAY THAT IT'S IMMUNE FROM THE SPELLS THE STAFF HAVE IN PLACE TO DETECT MAGIC.
PEOPLE COME HERE TO PRACTICE AFTER CURFEW SOMETIMES.
CLOSE YOUR MOUTH.
THIS IS A *BINDING.*
THIS WILL MAKE IT IMPOSSIBLE FOR US TO DISCUSS WHAT HAPPENED IN THE WOODS WITH ANYONE BUT *EACH OTHER.*
THISH ISH UNPLEASHANTLY LITERAL.
THIS TIES US ALL TOGETHER FOREVER, UNDERSTAND?
WE'RE FUCKING WITH OUR *DESTINIES* HERE.
WHAT DOES *THAT* MEAN?
IT MEANS THERE WILL BE *CONSEQUENCES.*
AND THAT WE'LL SUFFER THEM *TOGETHER.*

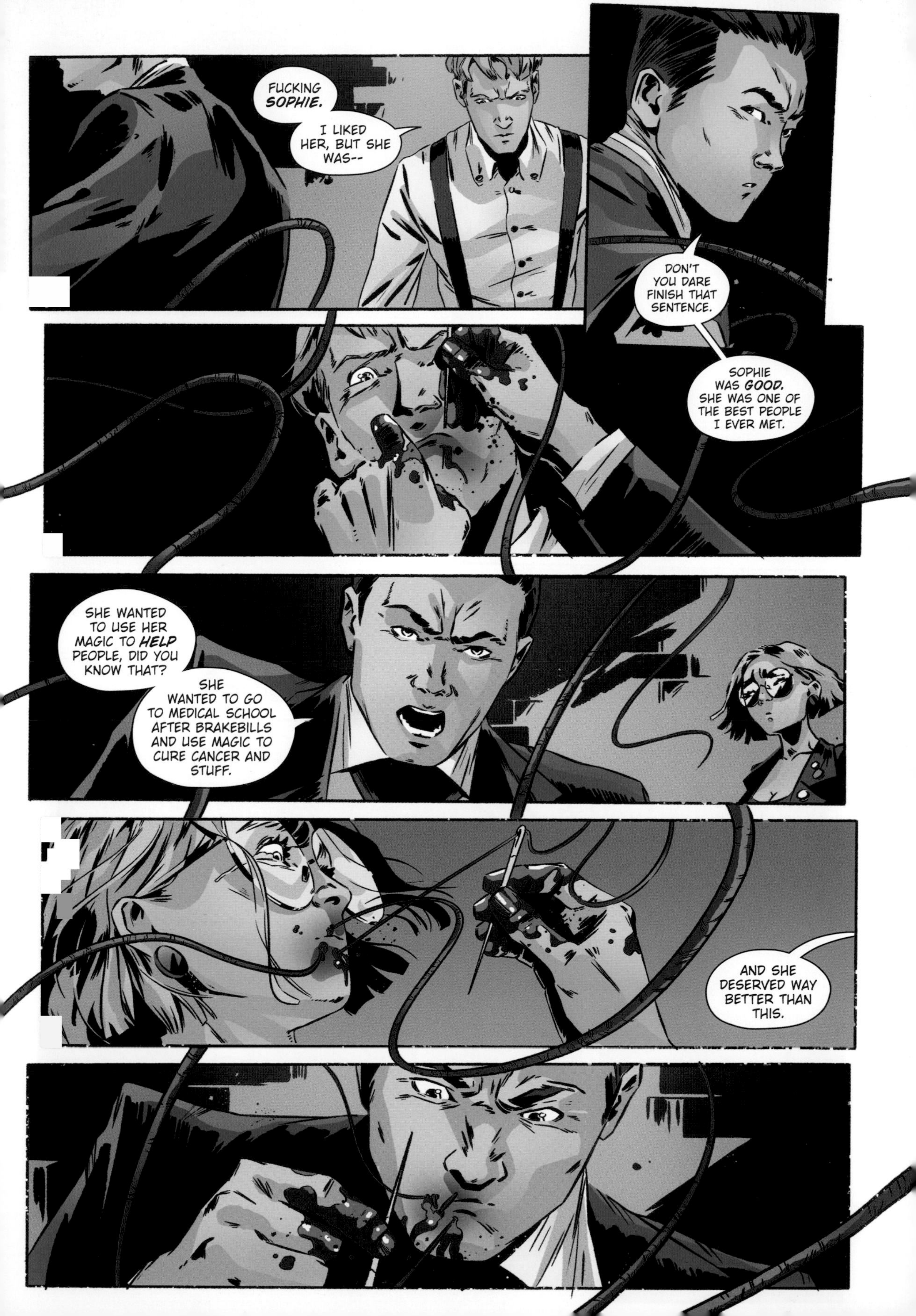
FUCKING **SOPHIE.**
I LIKED HER, BUT SHE WAS--
DON'T YOU DARE FINISH THAT SENTENCE.
SOPHIE WAS **GOOD.** SHE WAS ONE OF THE BEST PEOPLE I EVER MET.
SHE WANTED TO USE HER MAGIC TO **HELP** PEOPLE, DID YOU KNOW THAT?
SHE WANTED TO GO TO MEDICAL SCHOOL AFTER BRAKEBILLS AND USE MAGIC TO CURE CANCER AND STUFF.
AND SHE DESERVED WAY BETTER THAN THIS.

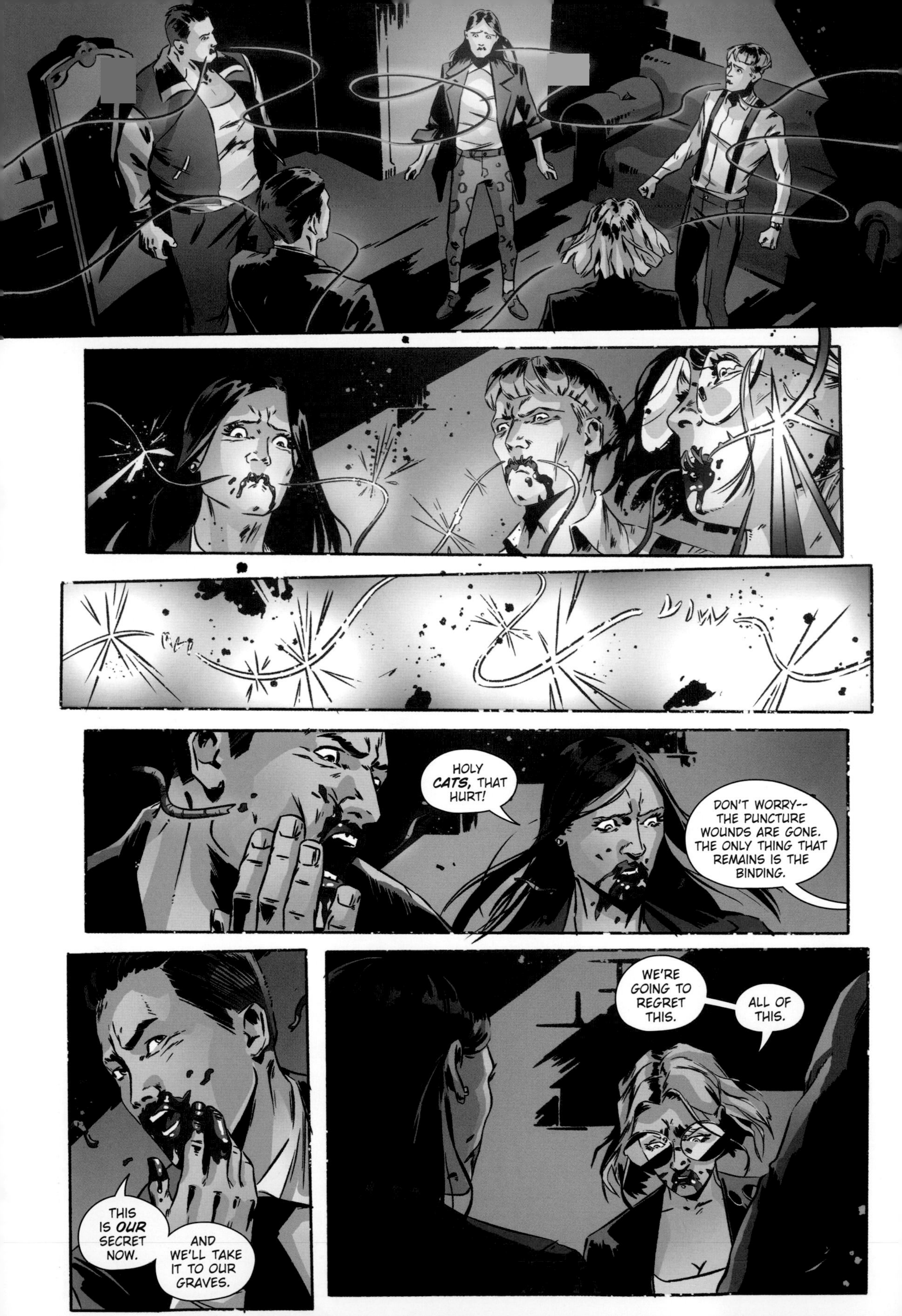
HOLY *CATS,* THAT HURT!
DON'T WORRY-- THE PUNCTURE WOUNDS ARE GONE. THE ONLY THING THAT REMAINS IS THE BINDING.
THIS IS *OUR* SECRET NOW.
AND WE'LL TAKE IT TO OUR GRAVES.
WE'RE GOING TO REGRET THIS.
ALL OF THIS.

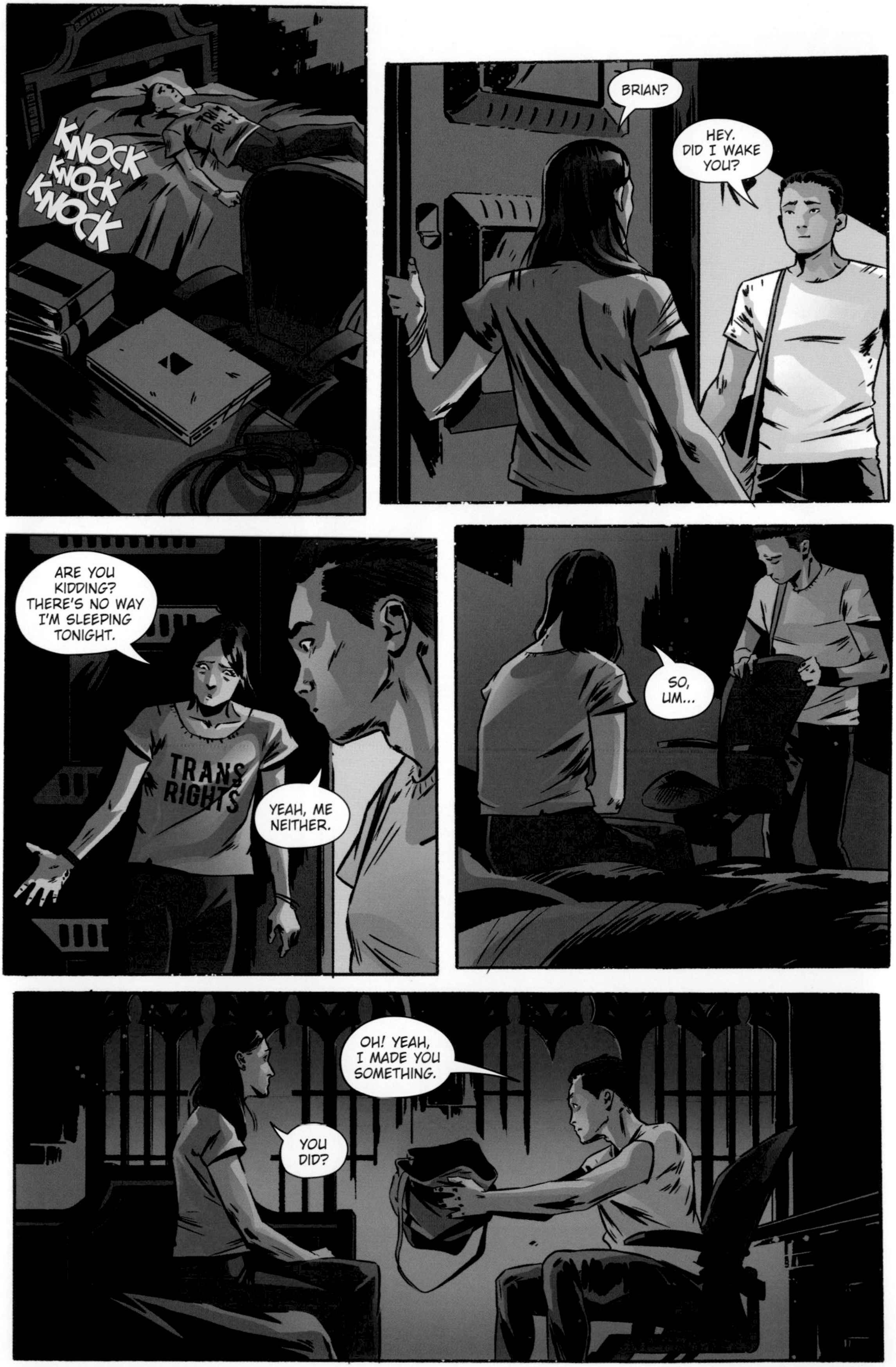

KNOCK KNOCK KNOCK
BRIAN?
HEY. DID I WAKE YOU?
ARE YOU KIDDING? THERE'S NO WAY I'M SLEEPING TONIGHT.
TRANS RIGHTS
YEAH, ME NEITHER.
SO, UM...
OH! YEAH, I MADE YOU SOMETHING.
YOU DID?

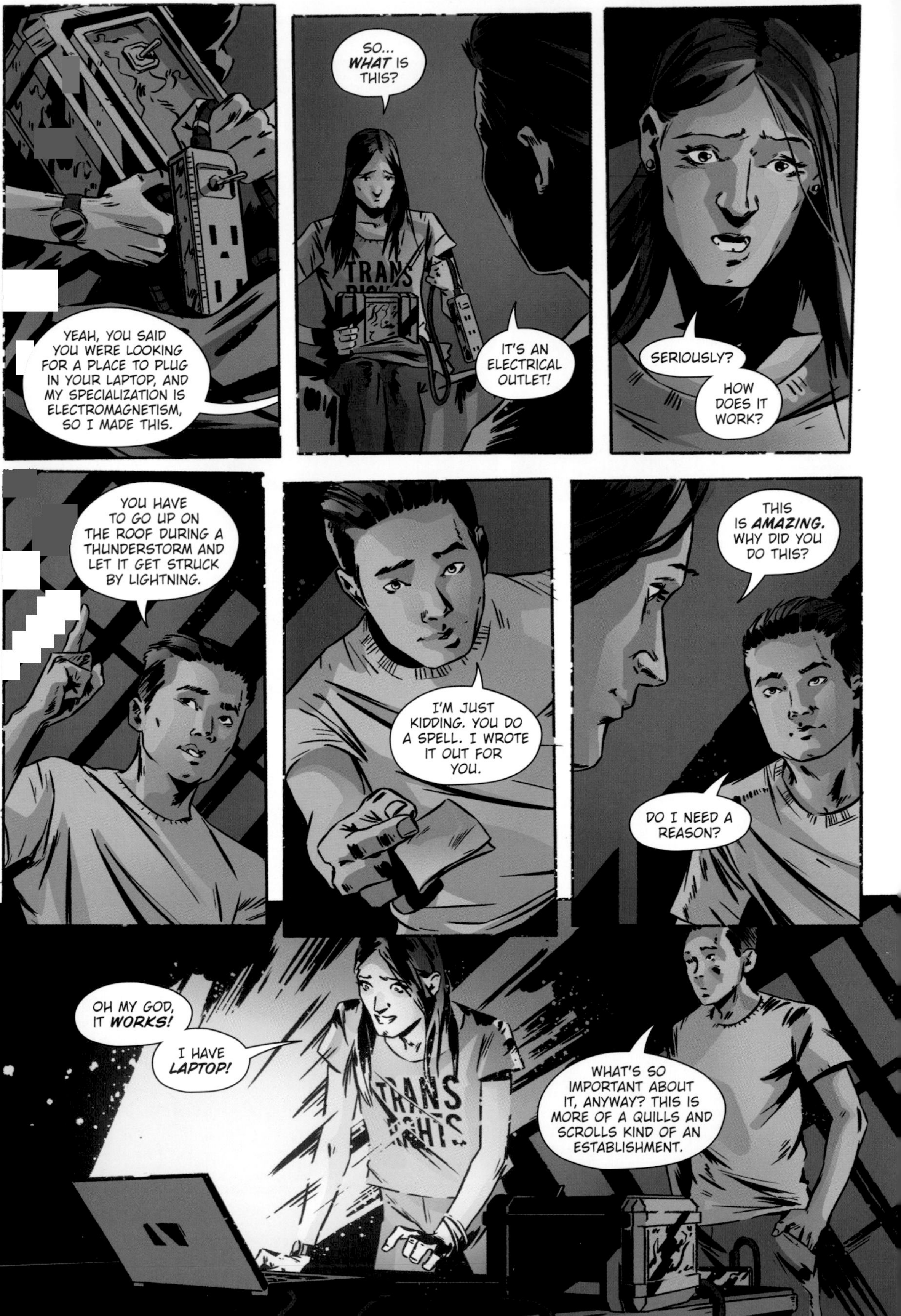

YEAH, YOU SAID YOU WERE LOOKING FOR A PLACE TO PLUG IN YOUR LAPTOP, AND MY SPECIALIZATION IS ELECTROMAGNETISM, SO I MADE THIS.
SO... WHAT IS THIS?
IT'S AN ELECTRICAL OUTLET!
SERIOUSLY?
HOW DOES IT WORK?
YOU HAVE TO GO UP ON THE ROOF DURING A THUNDERSTORM AND LET IT GET STRUCK BY LIGHTNING.
I'M JUST KIDDING. YOU DO A SPELL. I WROTE IT OUT FOR YOU.
THIS IS AMAZING. WHY DID YOU DO THIS?
DO I NEED A REASON?
OH MY GOD, IT WORKS!
I HAVE LAPTOP!
WHAT'S SO IMPORTANT ABOUT IT, ANYWAY? THIS IS MORE OF A QUILLS AND SCROLLS KIND OF AN ESTABLISHMENT.

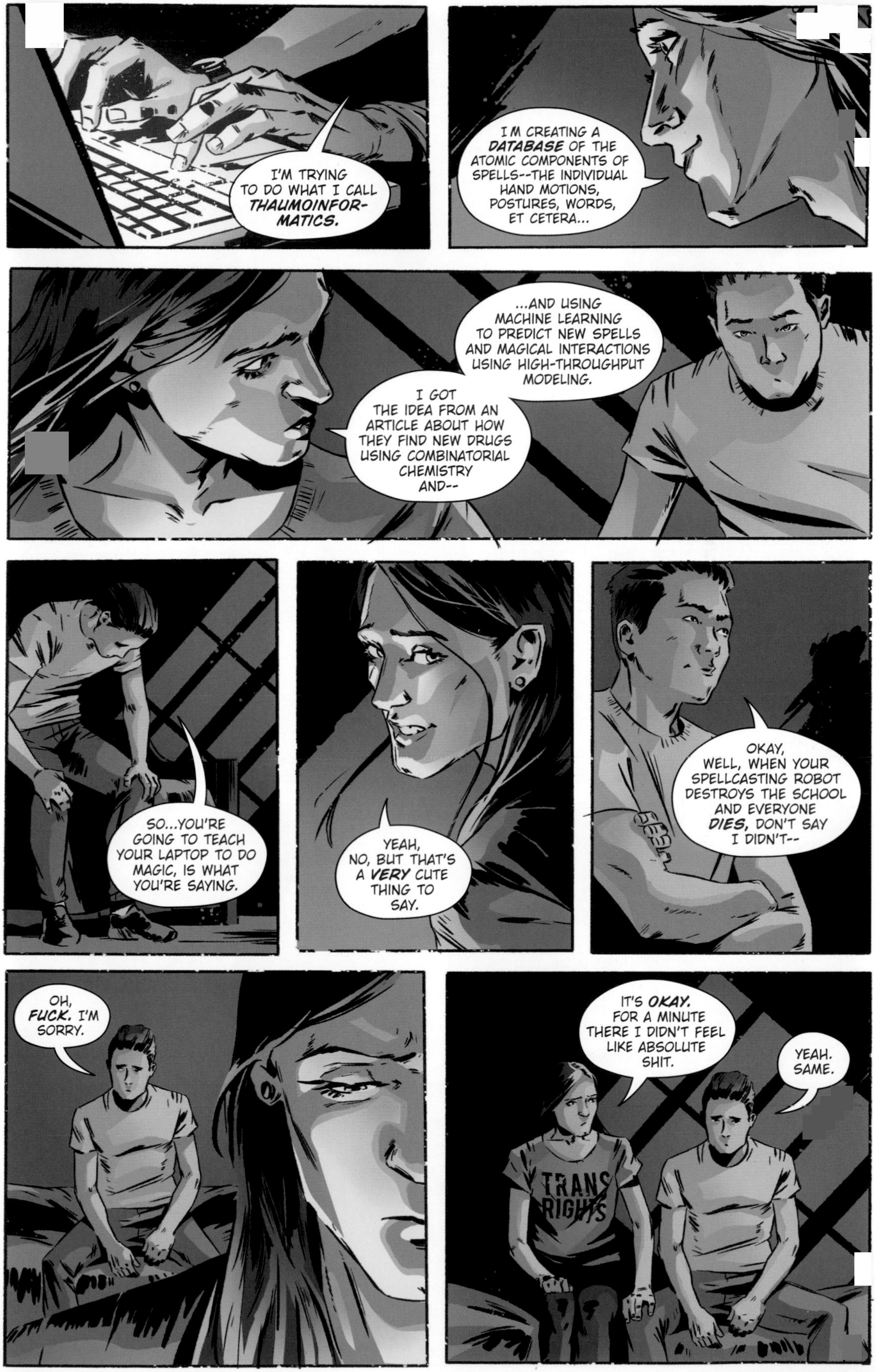
I'M TRYING TO DO WHAT I CALL THAUMOINFORMATICS.
I'M CREATING A DATABASE OF THE ATOMIC COMPONENTS OF SPELLS--THE INDIVIDUAL HAND MOTIONS, POSTURES, WORDS, ET CETERA...
...AND USING MACHINE LEARNING TO PREDICT NEW SPELLS AND MAGICAL INTERACTIONS USING HIGH-THROUGHPUT MODELING.
I GOT THE IDEA FROM AN ARTICLE ABOUT HOW THEY FIND NEW DRUGS USING COMBINATORIAL CHEMISTRY AND--
SO...YOU'RE GOING TO TEACH YOUR LAPTOP TO DO MAGIC, IS WHAT YOU'RE SAYING.
YEAH, NO, BUT THAT'S A VERY CUTE THING TO SAY.
OKAY, WELL, WHEN YOUR SPELLCASTING ROBOT DESTROYS THE SCHOOL AND EVERYONE DIES, DON'T SAY I DIDN'T--
OH, FUCK. I'M SORRY.
IT'S OKAY. FOR A MINUTE THERE I DIDN'T FEEL LIKE ABSOLUTE SHIT.
YEAH. SAME.
TRANS RIGHTS

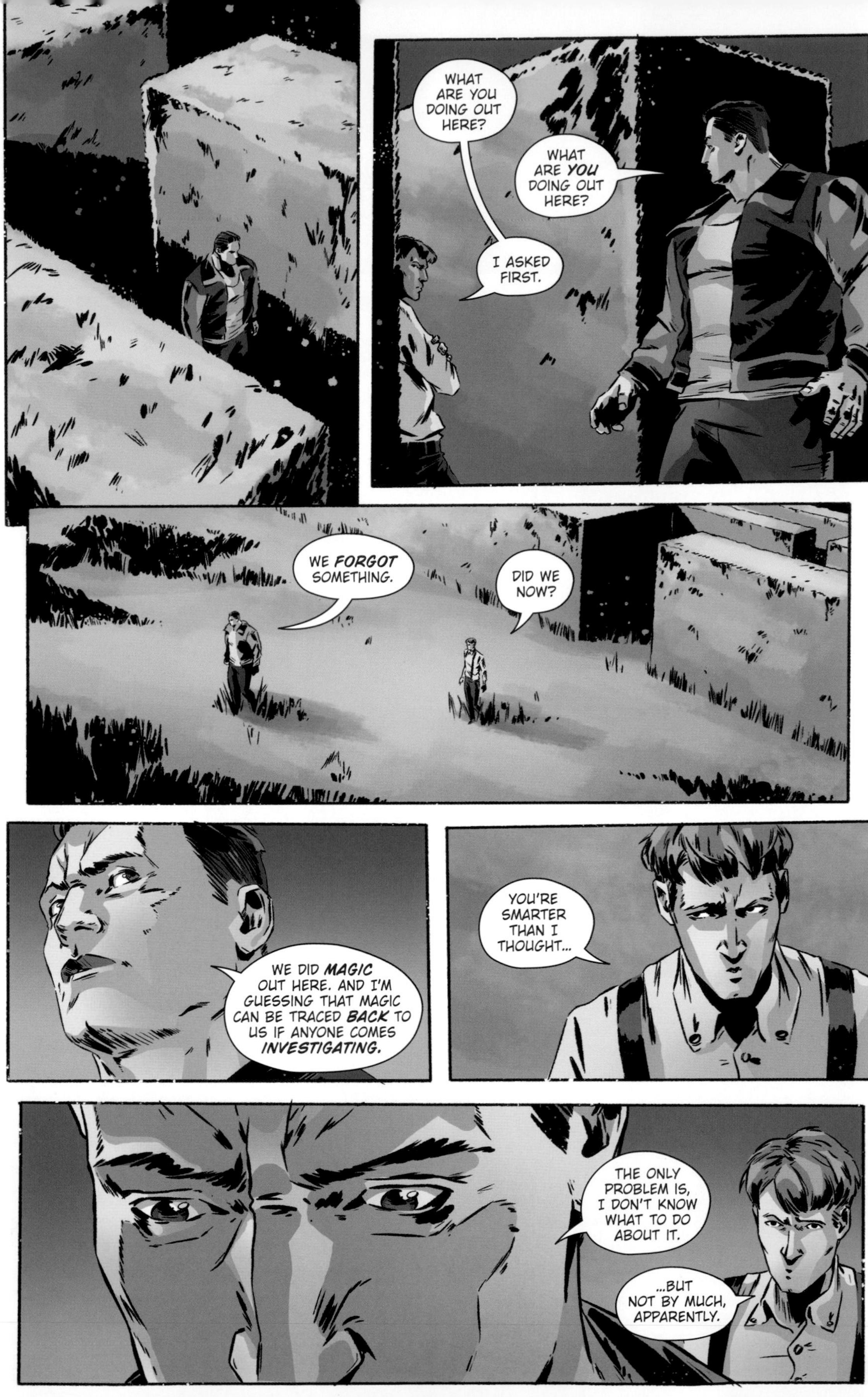
WHAT ARE YOU DOING OUT HERE?
WHAT ARE YOU DOING OUT HERE?
I ASKED FIRST.
WE FORGOT SOMETHING.
DID WE NOW?
WE DID MAGIC OUT HERE. AND I'M GUESSING THAT MAGIC CAN BE TRACED BACK TO US IF ANYONE COMES INVESTIGATING.
YOU'RE SMARTER THAN I THOUGHT...
THE ONLY PROBLEM IS, I DON'T KNOW WHAT TO DO ABOUT IT.
...BUT NOT BY MUCH, APPARENTLY.

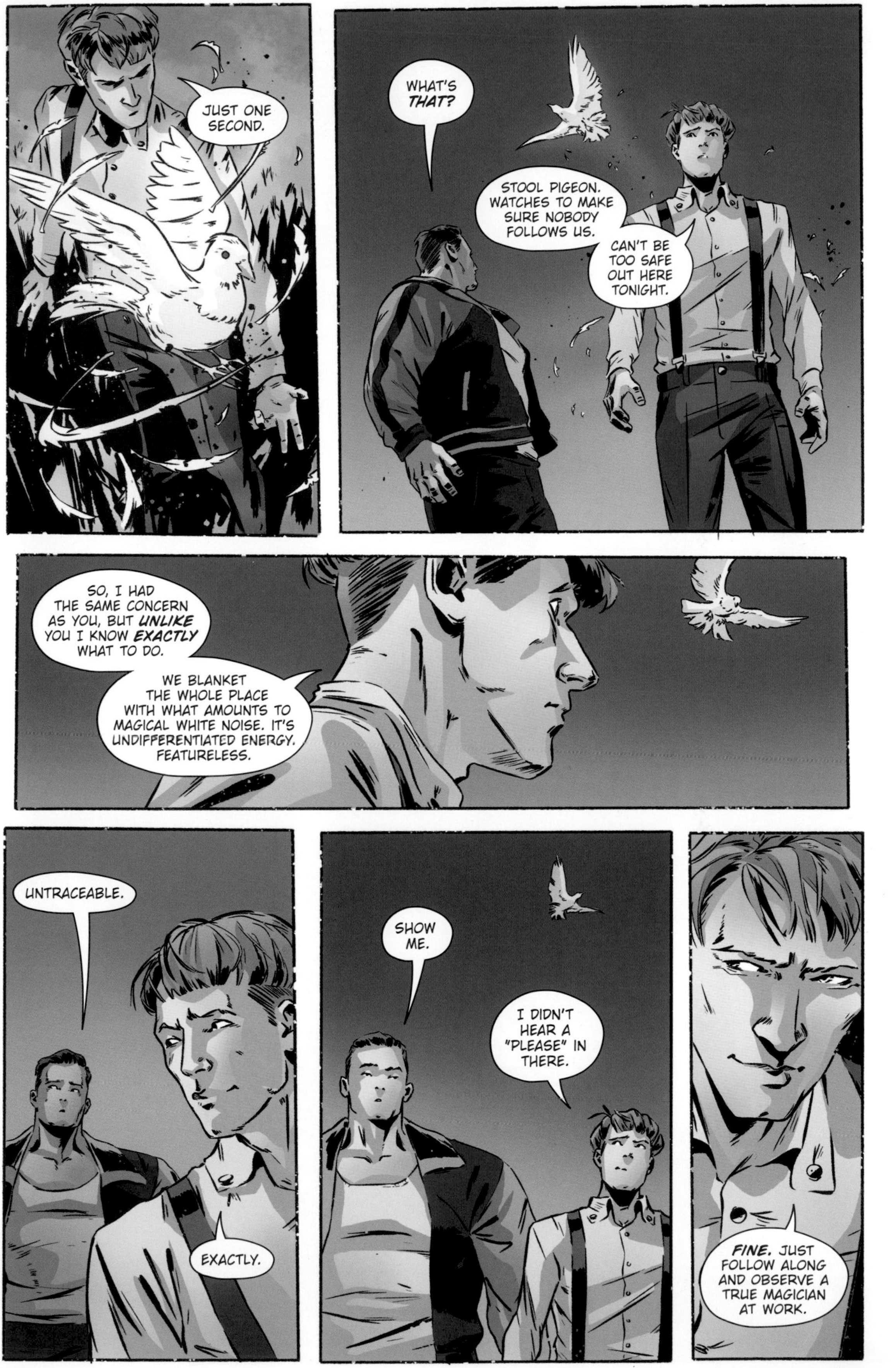
JUST ONE SECOND.
WHAT'S *THAT?*
STOOL PIGEON. WATCHES TO MAKE SURE NOBODY FOLLOWS US.
CAN'T BE TOO SAFE OUT HERE TONIGHT.
SO, I HAD THE SAME CONCERN AS YOU, BUT *UNLIKE* YOU I KNOW *EXACTLY* WHAT TO DO.
WE BLANKET THE WHOLE PLACE WITH WHAT AMOUNTS TO MAGICAL WHITE NOISE. IT'S UNDIFFERENTIATED ENERGY. FEATURELESS.
UNTRACEABLE.
EXACTLY.
SHOW ME.
I DIDN'T HEAR A "PLEASE" IN THERE.
FINE. JUST FOLLOW ALONG AND OBSERVE A TRUE MAGICIAN AT WORK.

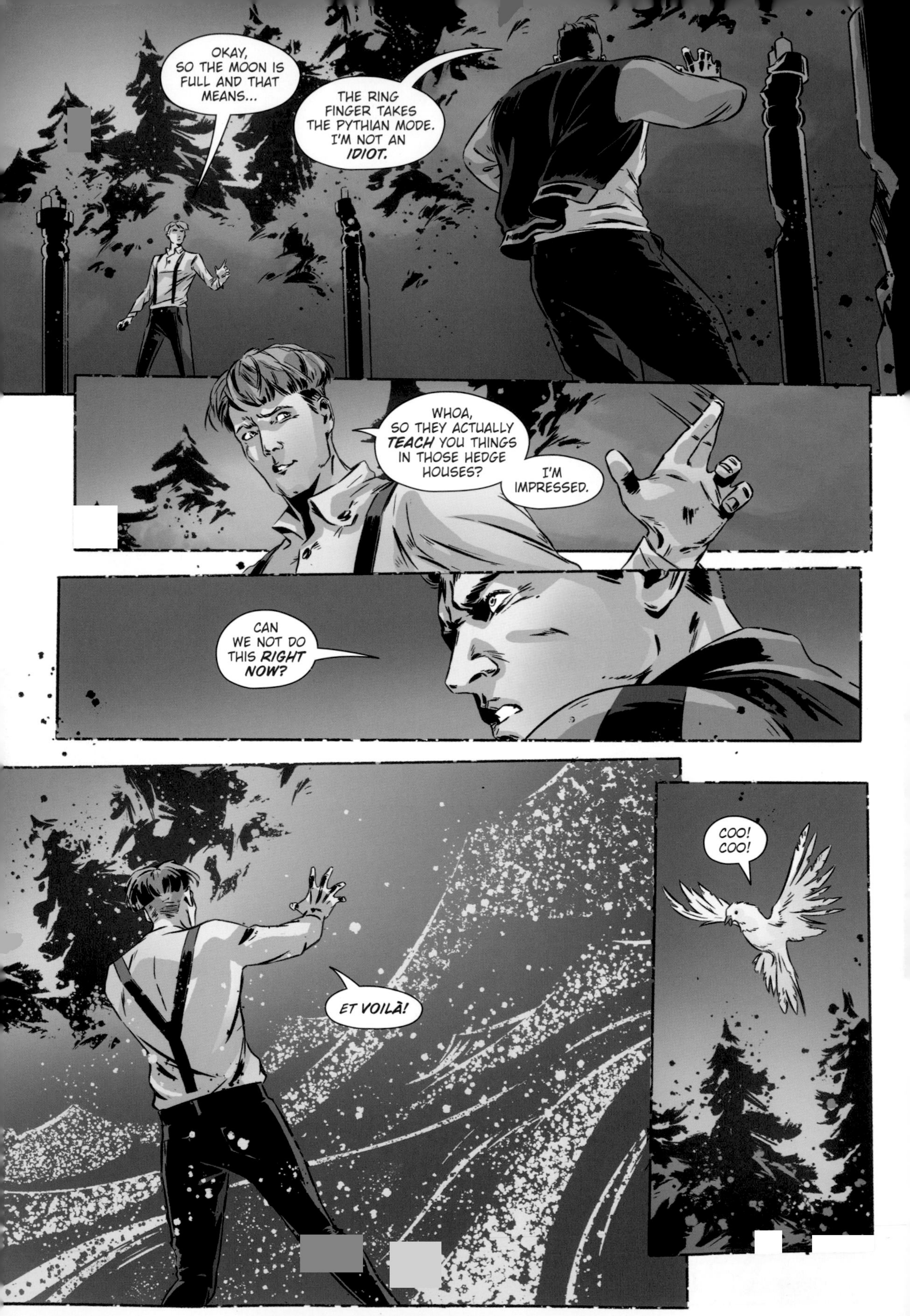
OKAY, SO THE MOON IS FULL AND THAT MEANS...
THE RING FINGER TAKES THE PYTHIAN MODE. I'M NOT AN IDIOT.
WHOA, SO THEY ACTUALLY TEACH YOU THINGS IN THOSE HEDGE HOUSES?
I'M IMPRESSED.
CAN WE NOT DO THIS RIGHT NOW?
ET VOILÀ!
COO! COO!

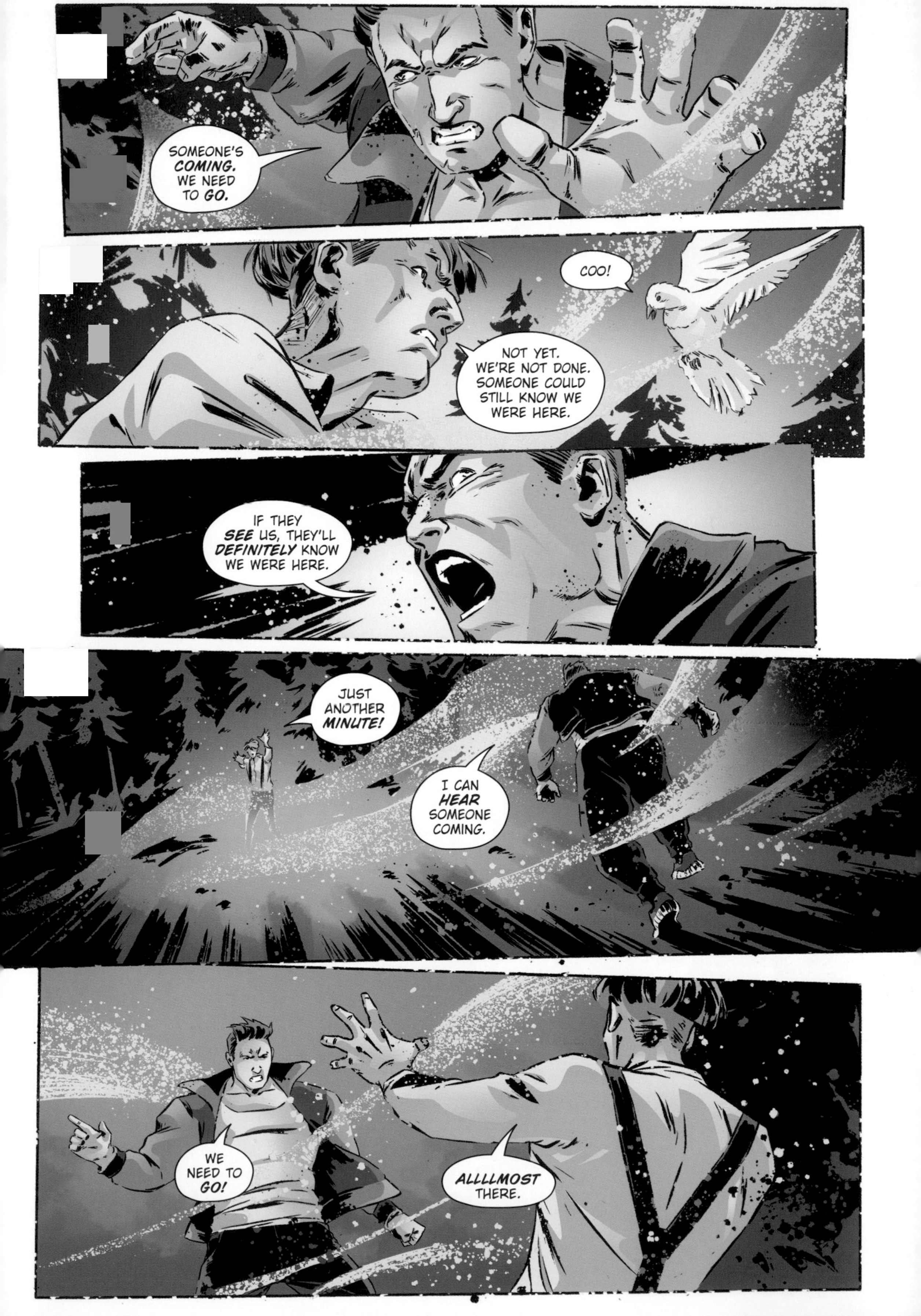
SOMEONE'S COMING. WE NEED TO GO.
NOT YET. WE'RE NOT DONE. SOMEONE COULD STILL KNOW WE WERE HERE.
COO!
IF THEY SEE US, THEY'LL DEFINITELY KNOW WE WERE HERE.
JUST ANOTHER MINUTE!
I CAN HEAR SOMEONE COMING.
WE NEED TO GO!
ALLLLMOST THERE.

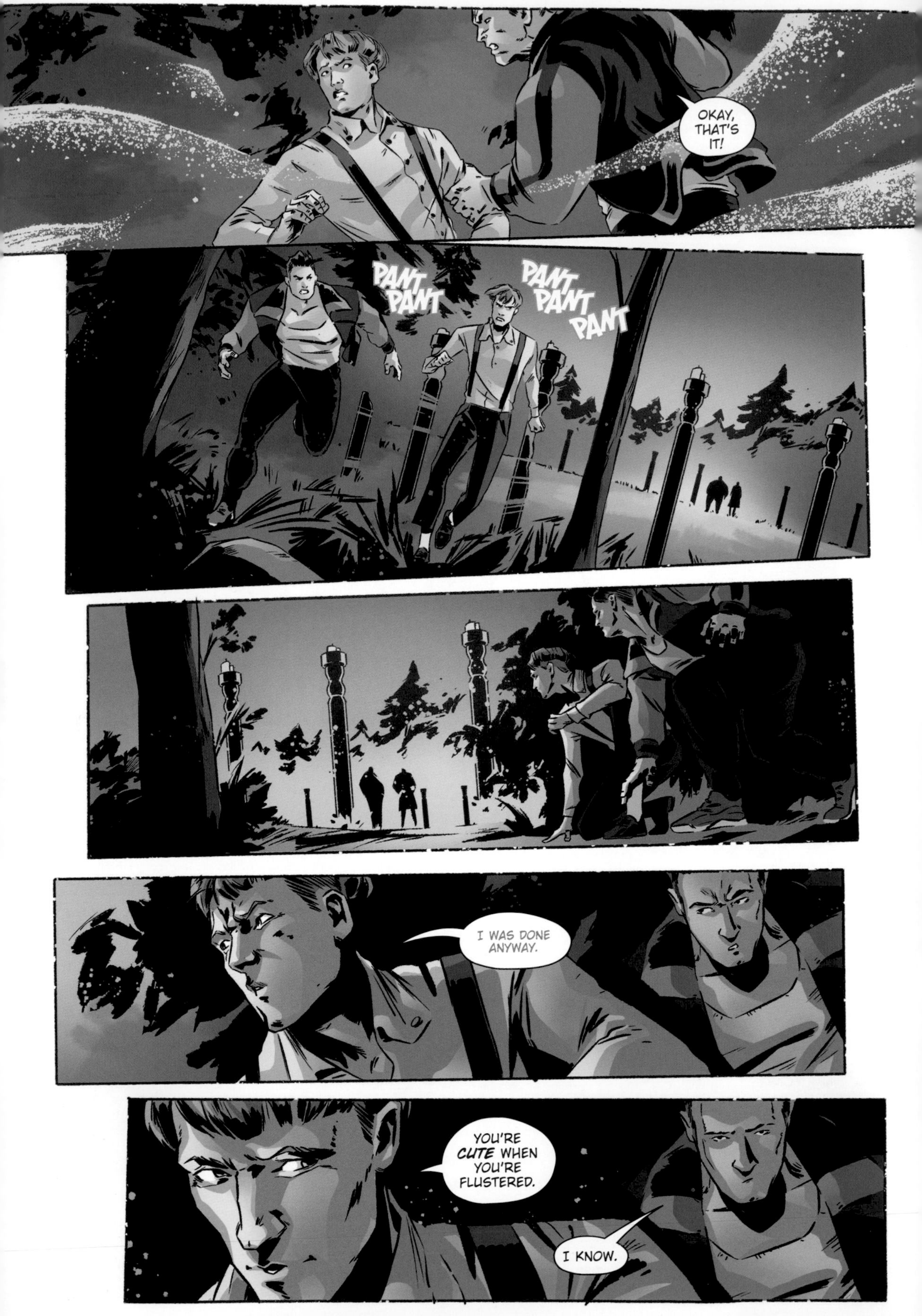
OKAY, THAT'S IT!
PANT PANT
PANT PANT PANT
I WAS DONE ANYWAY.
YOU'RE *CUTE* WHEN YOU'RE FLUSTERED.
I KNOW.

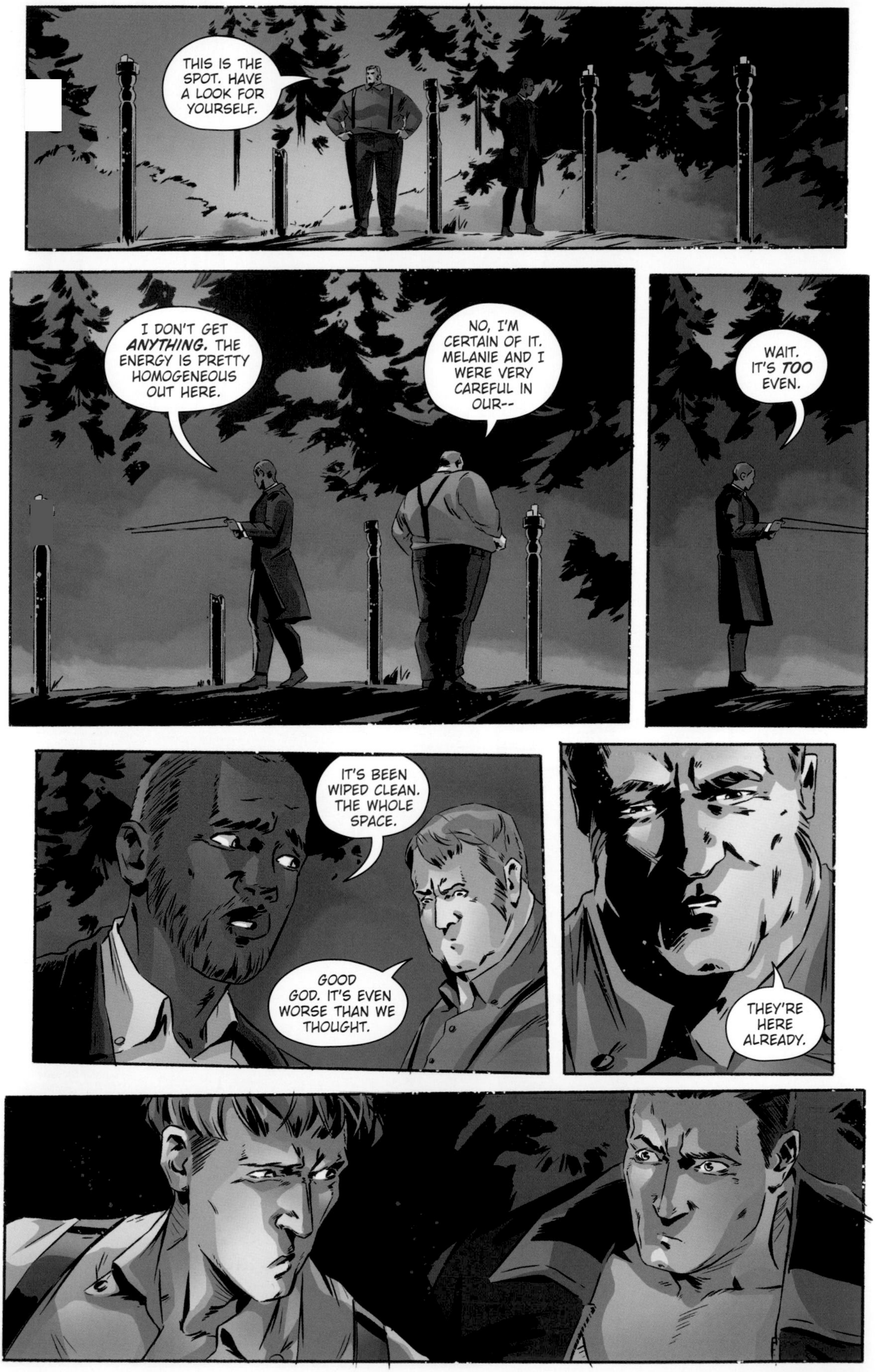
THIS IS THE SPOT. HAVE A LOOK FOR YOURSELF.
I DON'T GET *ANYTHING.* THE ENERGY IS PRETTY HOMOGENEOUS OUT HERE.
NO, I'M CERTAIN OF IT. MELANIE AND I WERE VERY CAREFUL IN OUR--
WAIT. IT'S *TOO* EVEN.
IT'S BEEN WIPED CLEAN. THE WHOLE SPACE.
GOOD GOD. IT'S EVEN WORSE THAN WE THOUGHT.
THEY'RE HERE ALREADY.

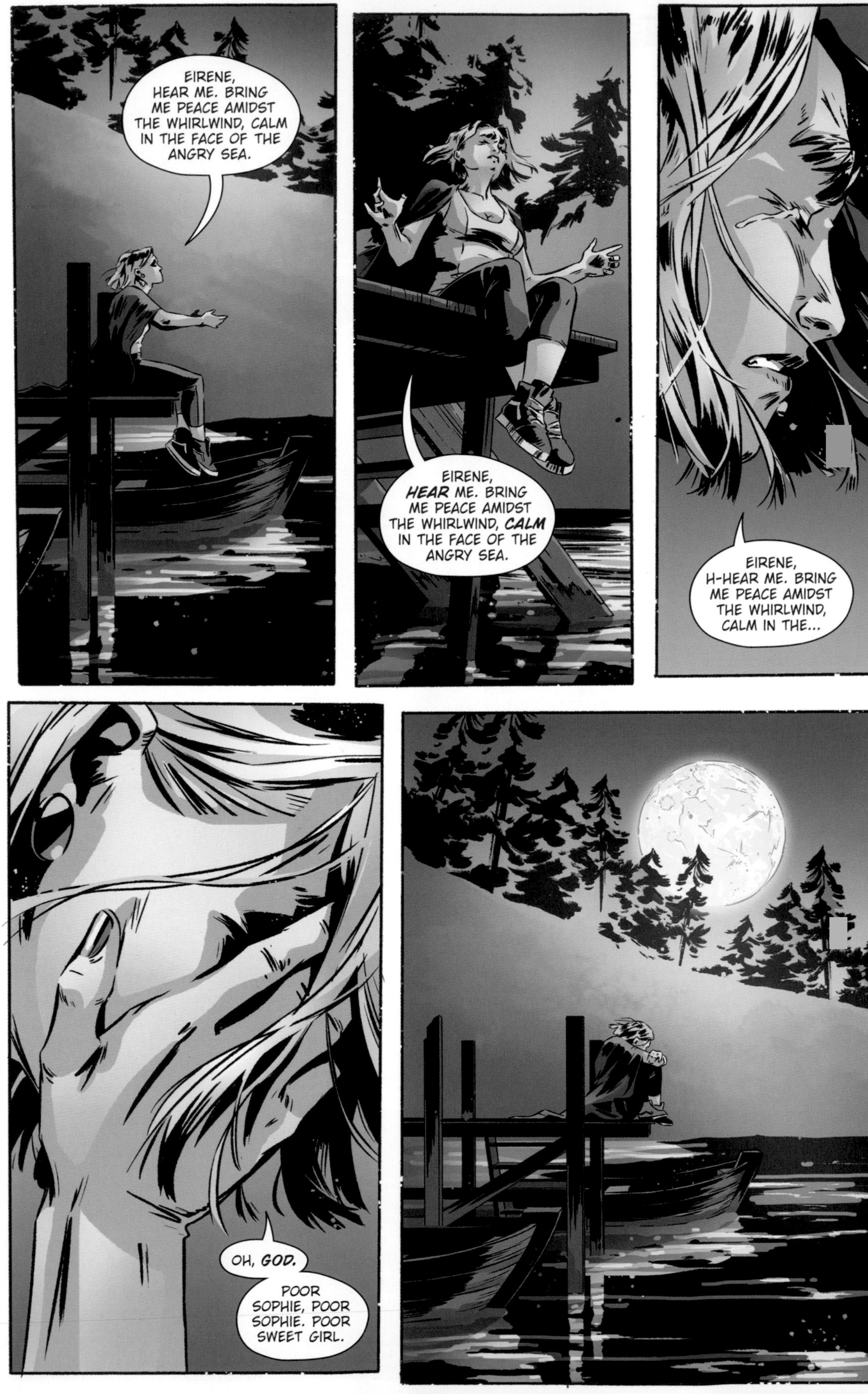
EIRENE, HEAR ME. BRING ME PEACE AMIDST THE WHIRLWIND, CALM IN THE FACE OF THE ANGRY SEA.
EIRENE, **HEAR** ME. BRING ME PEACE AMIDST THE WHIRLWIND, **CALM** IN THE FACE OF THE ANGRY SEA.
EIRENE, H-HEAR ME. BRING ME PEACE AMIDST THE WHIRLWIND, CALM IN THE...
OH, **GOD.**
POOR SOPHIE, POOR SOPHIE. POOR SWEET GIRL.

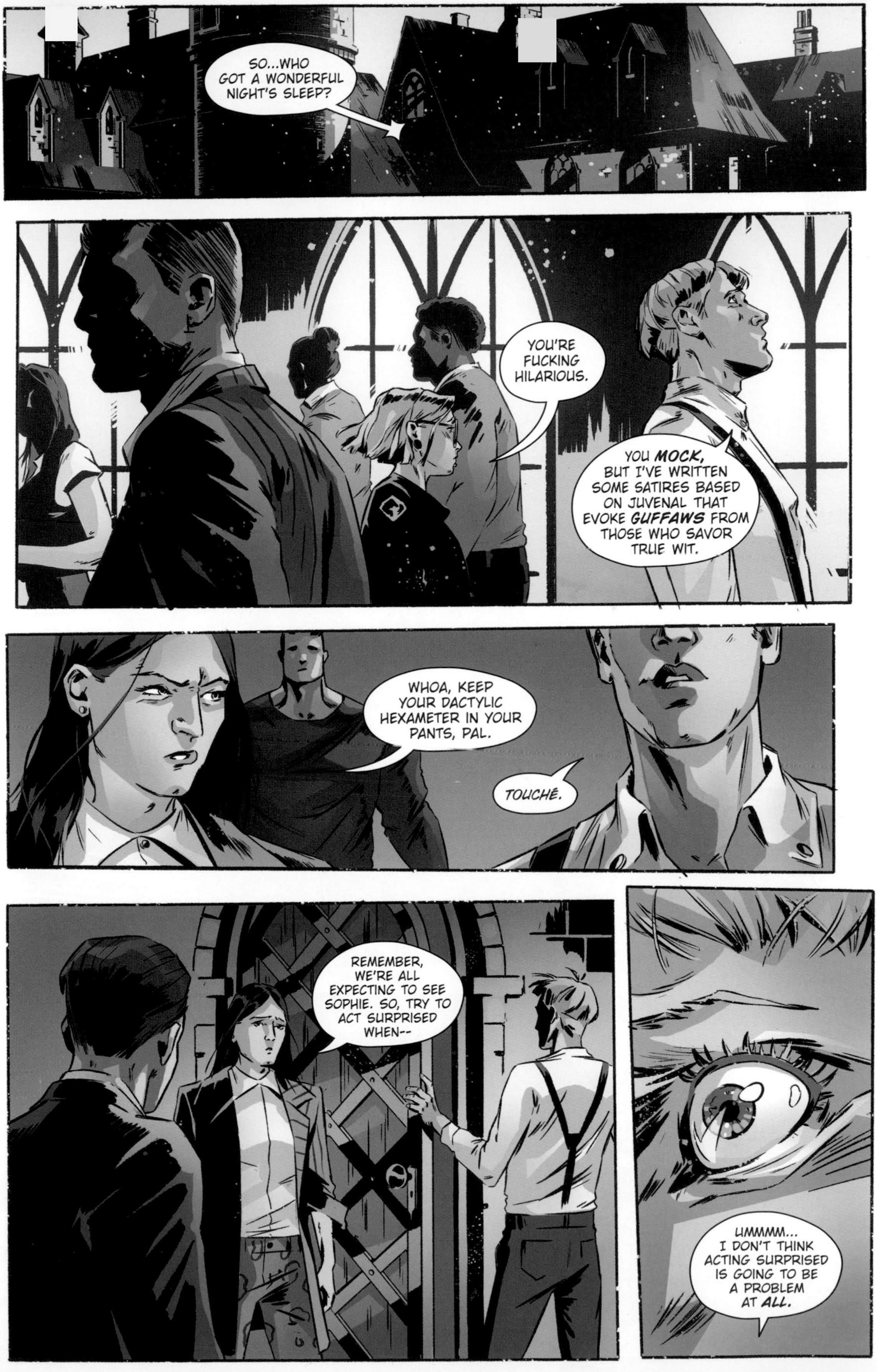
SO...WHO GOT A WONDERFUL NIGHT'S SLEEP?
YOU'RE FUCKING HILARIOUS.
YOU **MOCK,** BUT I'VE WRITTEN SOME SATIRES BASED ON JUVENAL THAT EVOKE **GUFFAWS** FROM THOSE WHO SAVOR TRUE WIT.
WHOA, KEEP YOUR DACTYLIC HEXAMETER IN YOUR PANTS, PAL.
TOUCHÉ.
REMEMBER, WE'RE ALL EXPECTING TO SEE SOPHIE. SO, TRY TO ACT SURPRISED WHEN--
UMMMM... I DON'T THINK ACTING SURPRISED IS GOING TO BE A PROBLEM AT **ALL.**

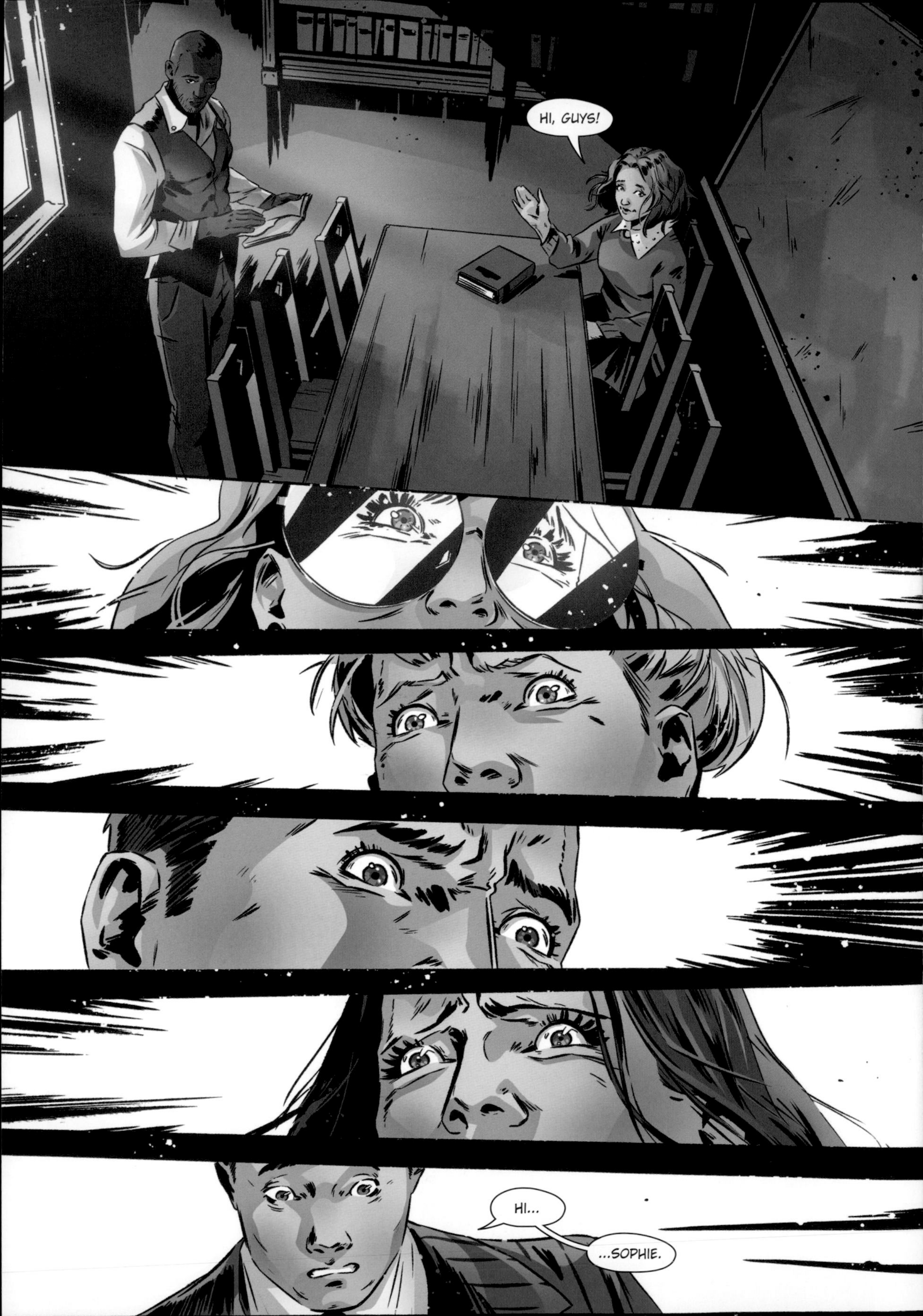
HI, GUYS!
HI...
...SOPHIE.

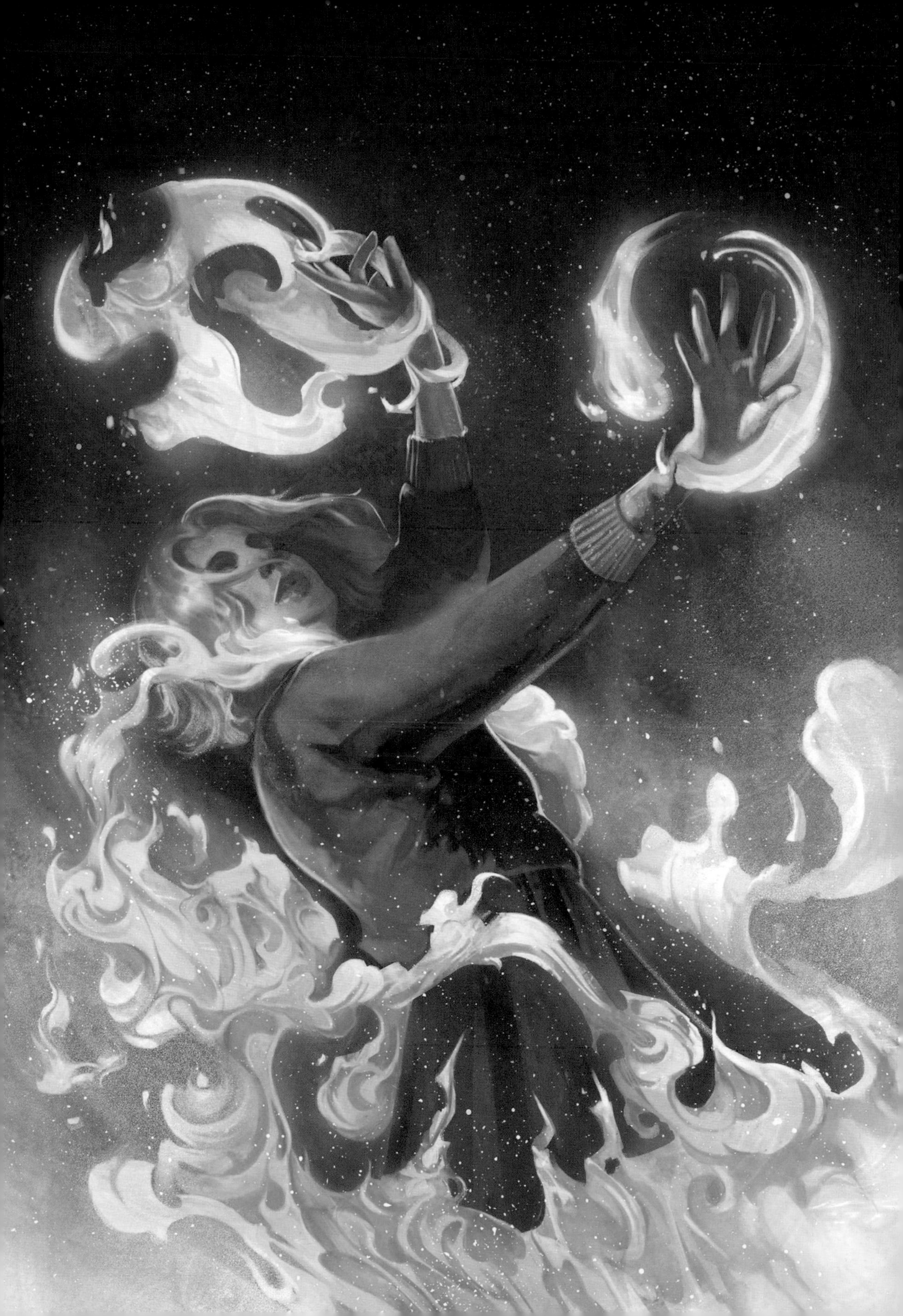

CHAPTER
THREE

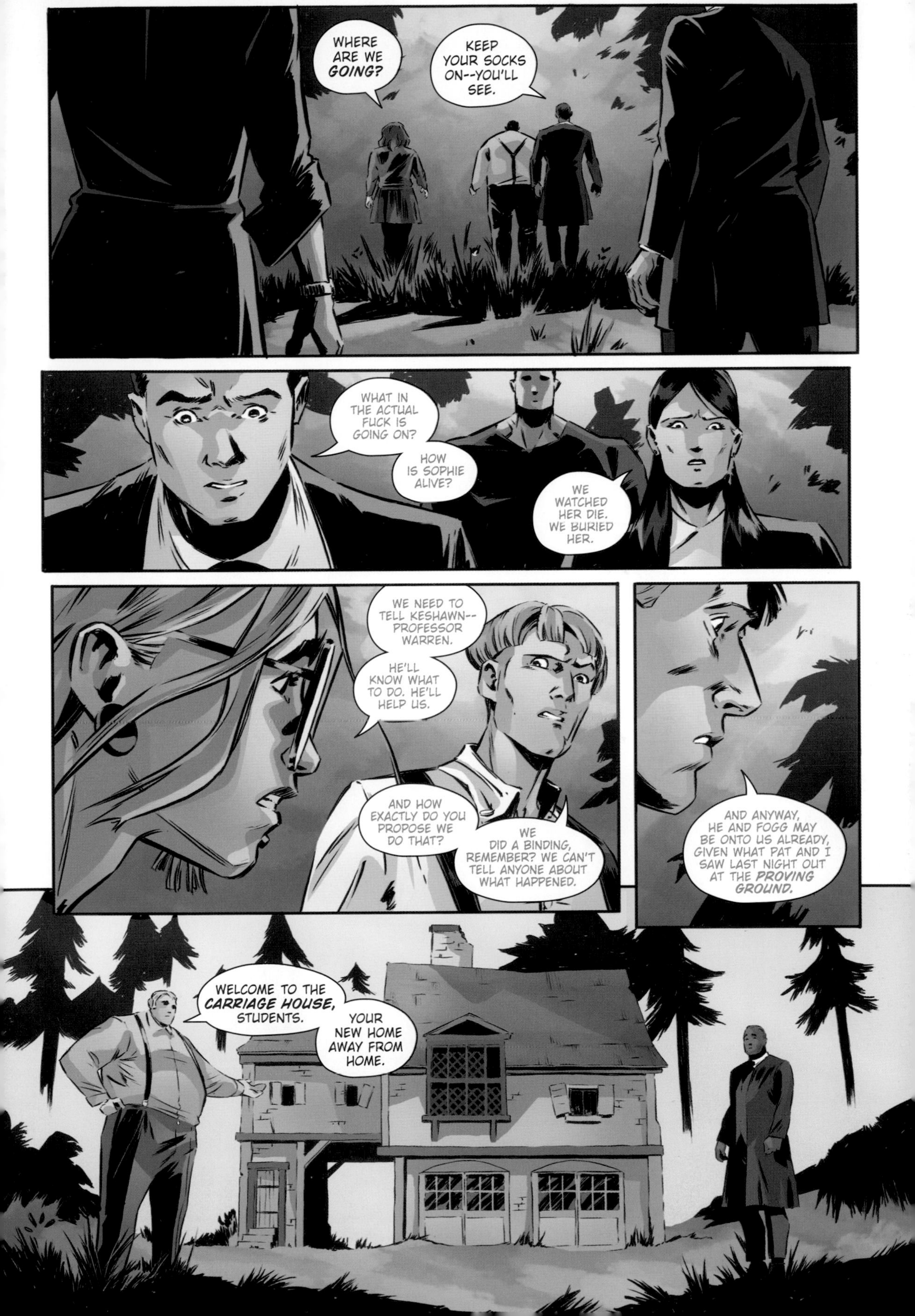
WHERE ARE WE GOING?
KEEP YOUR SOCKS ON--YOU'LL SEE.
WHAT IN THE ACTUAL FUCK IS GOING ON?
HOW IS SOPHIE ALIVE?
WE WATCHED HER DIE. WE BURIED HER.
WE NEED TO TELL KESHAWN-- PROFESSOR WARREN.
HE'LL KNOW WHAT TO DO. HE'LL HELP US.
AND HOW EXACTLY DO YOU PROPOSE WE DO THAT?
WE DID A BINDING, REMEMBER? WE CAN'T TELL ANYONE ABOUT WHAT HAPPENED.
AND ANYWAY, HE AND FOGG MAY BE ONTO US ALREADY, GIVEN WHAT PAT AND I SAW LAST NIGHT OUT AT THE PROVING GROUND.
WELCOME TO THE CARRIAGE HOUSE, STUDENTS.
YOUR NEW HOME AWAY FROM HOME.

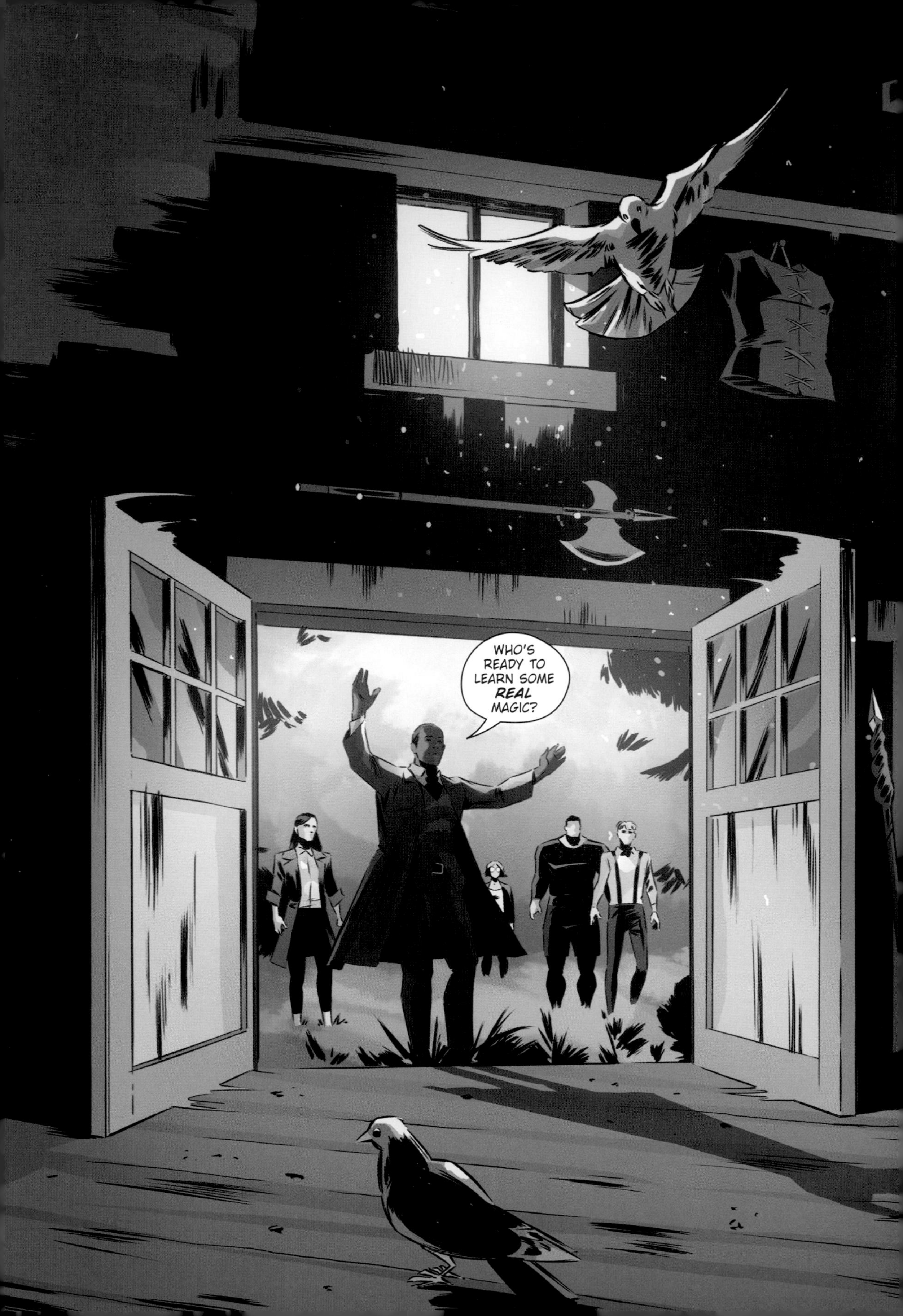
WHO'S READY TO LEARN SOME REAL MAGIC?

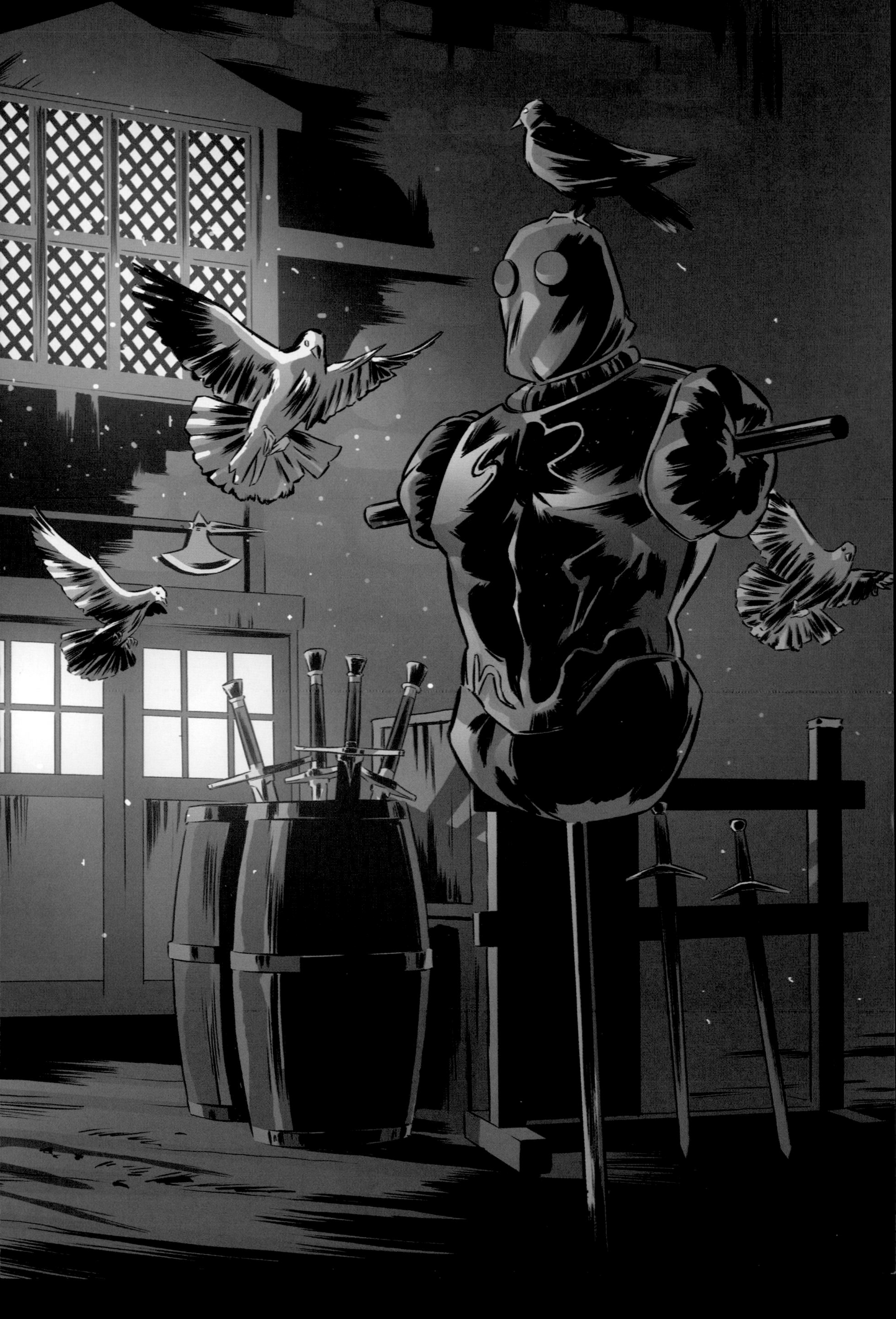

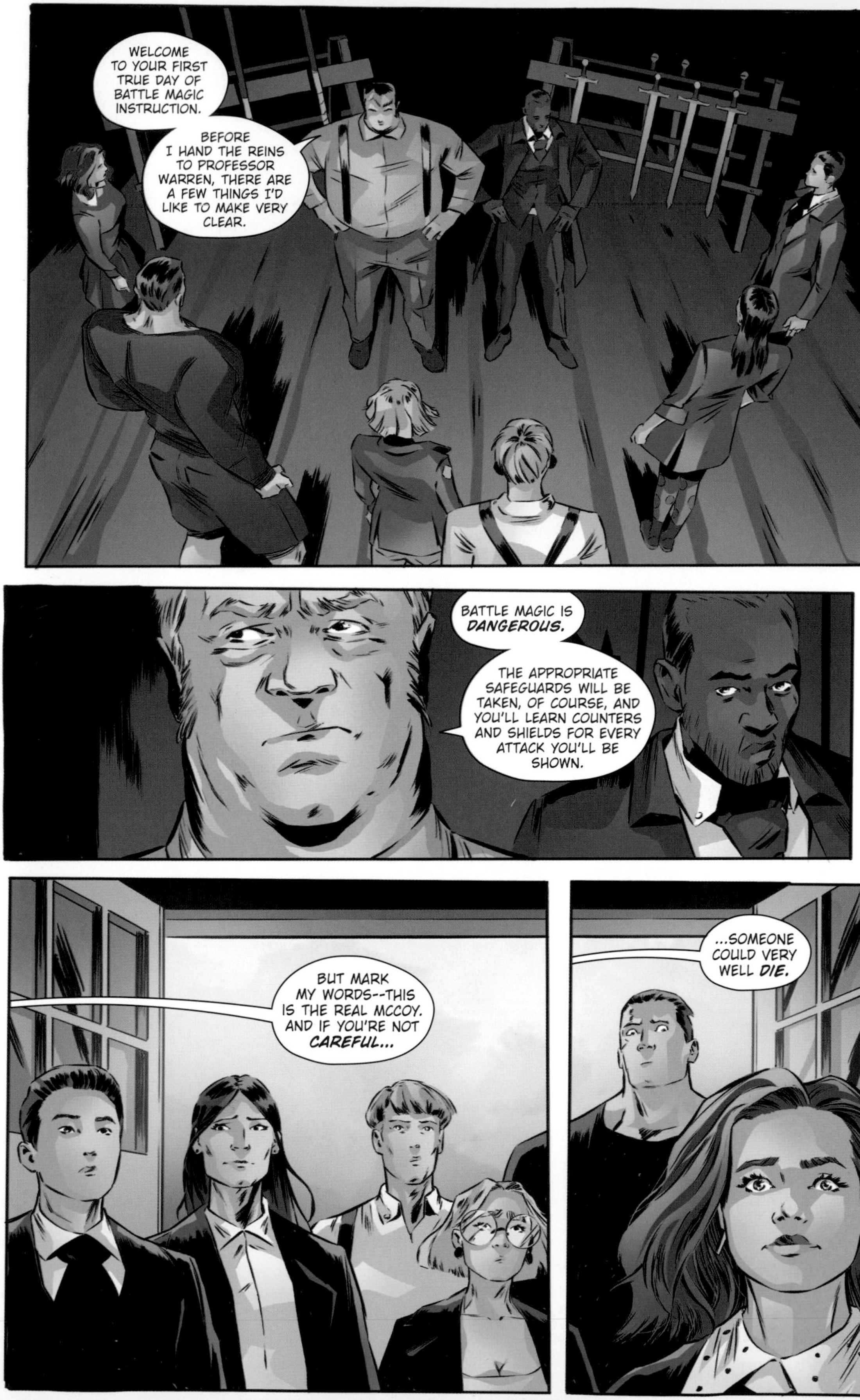
WELCOME TO YOUR FIRST TRUE DAY OF BATTLE MAGIC INSTRUCTION.
BEFORE I HAND THE REINS TO PROFESSOR WARREN, THERE ARE A FEW THINGS I'D LIKE TO MAKE VERY CLEAR.
BATTLE MAGIC IS ***DANGEROUS.***
THE APPROPRIATE SAFEGUARDS WILL BE TAKEN, OF COURSE, AND YOU'LL LEARN COUNTERS AND SHIELDS FOR EVERY ATTACK YOU'LL BE SHOWN.
BUT MARK MY WORDS--THIS IS THE REAL MCCOY. AND IF YOU'RE NOT ***CAREFUL...***
...SOMEONE COULD VERY WELL ***DIE.***

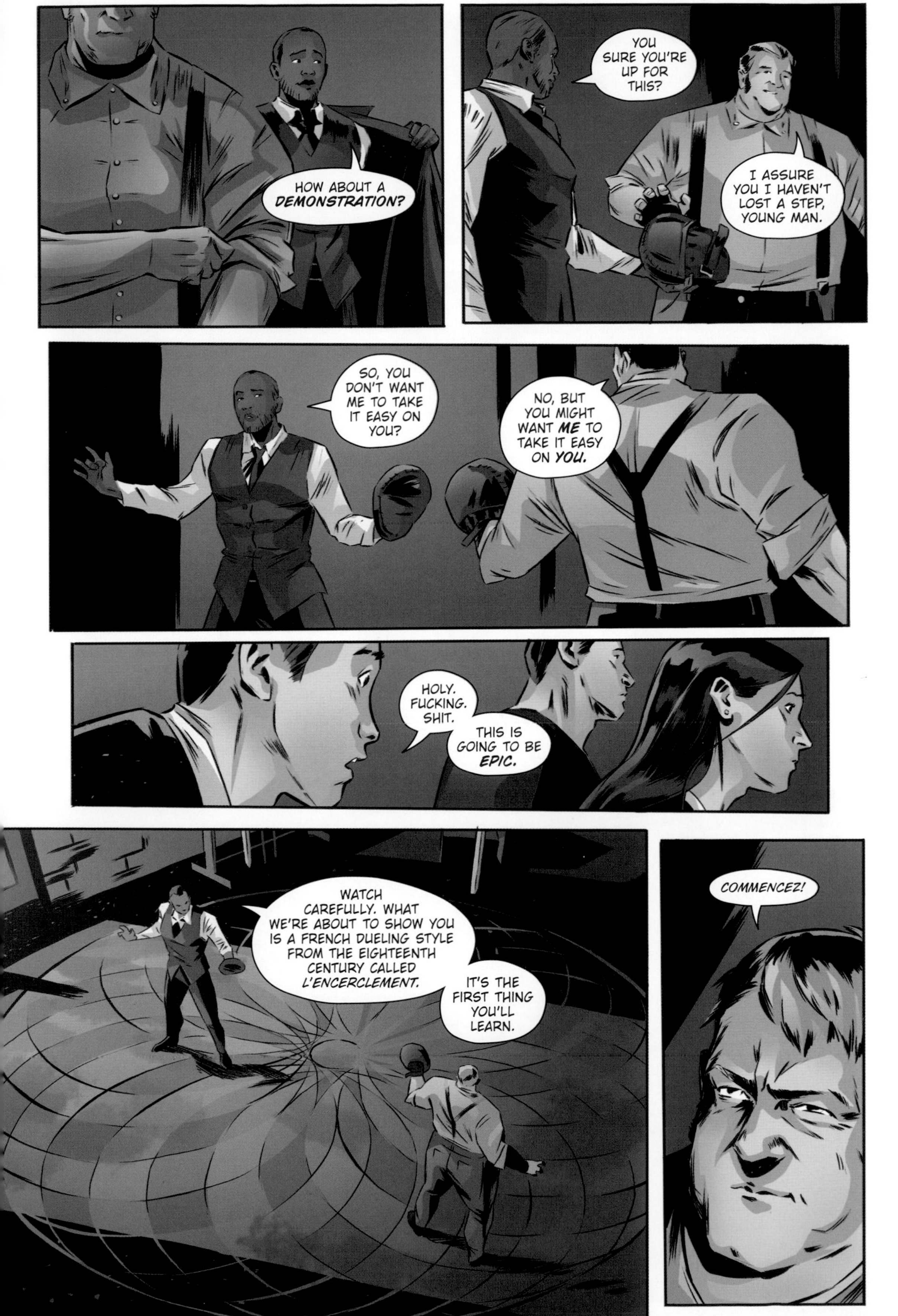
HOW ABOUT A DEMONSTRATION?
YOU SURE YOU'RE UP FOR THIS?
I ASSURE YOU I HAVEN'T LOST A STEP, YOUNG MAN.
SO, YOU DON'T WANT ME TO TAKE IT EASY ON YOU?
NO, BUT YOU MIGHT WANT ME TO TAKE IT EASY ON YOU.
HOLY. FUCKING. SHIT.
THIS IS GOING TO BE EPIC.
WATCH CAREFULLY. WHAT WE'RE ABOUT TO SHOW YOU IS A FRENCH DUELING STYLE FROM THE EIGHTEENTH CENTURY CALLED L'ENCERCLEMENT.
IT'S THE FIRST THING YOU'LL LEARN.
COMMENCEZ!

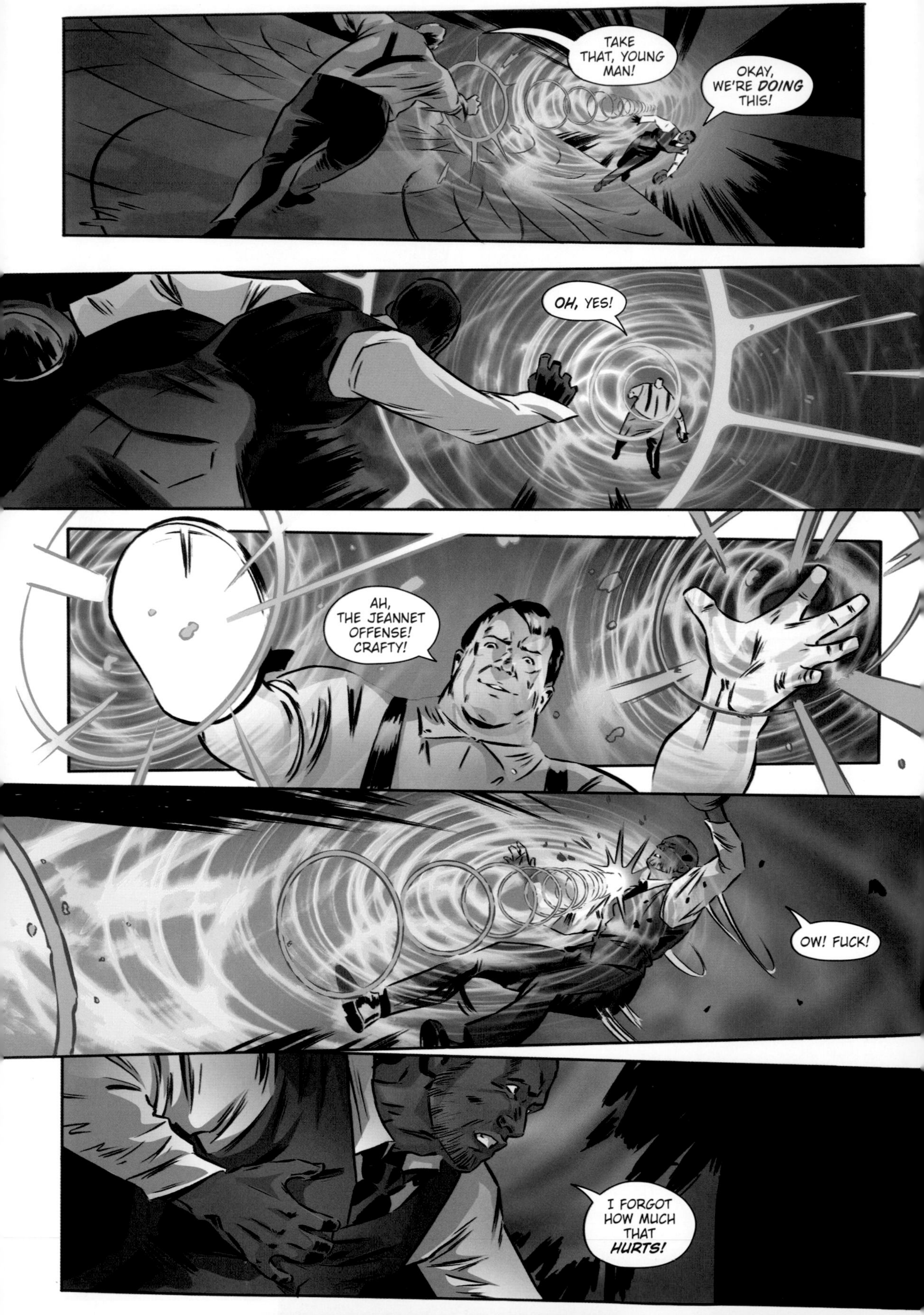
TAKE THAT, YOUNG MAN!
OKAY, WE'RE DOING THIS!
OH, YES!
AH, THE JEANNET OFFENSE! CRAFTY!
OW! FUCK!
I FORGOT HOW MUCH THAT HURTS!

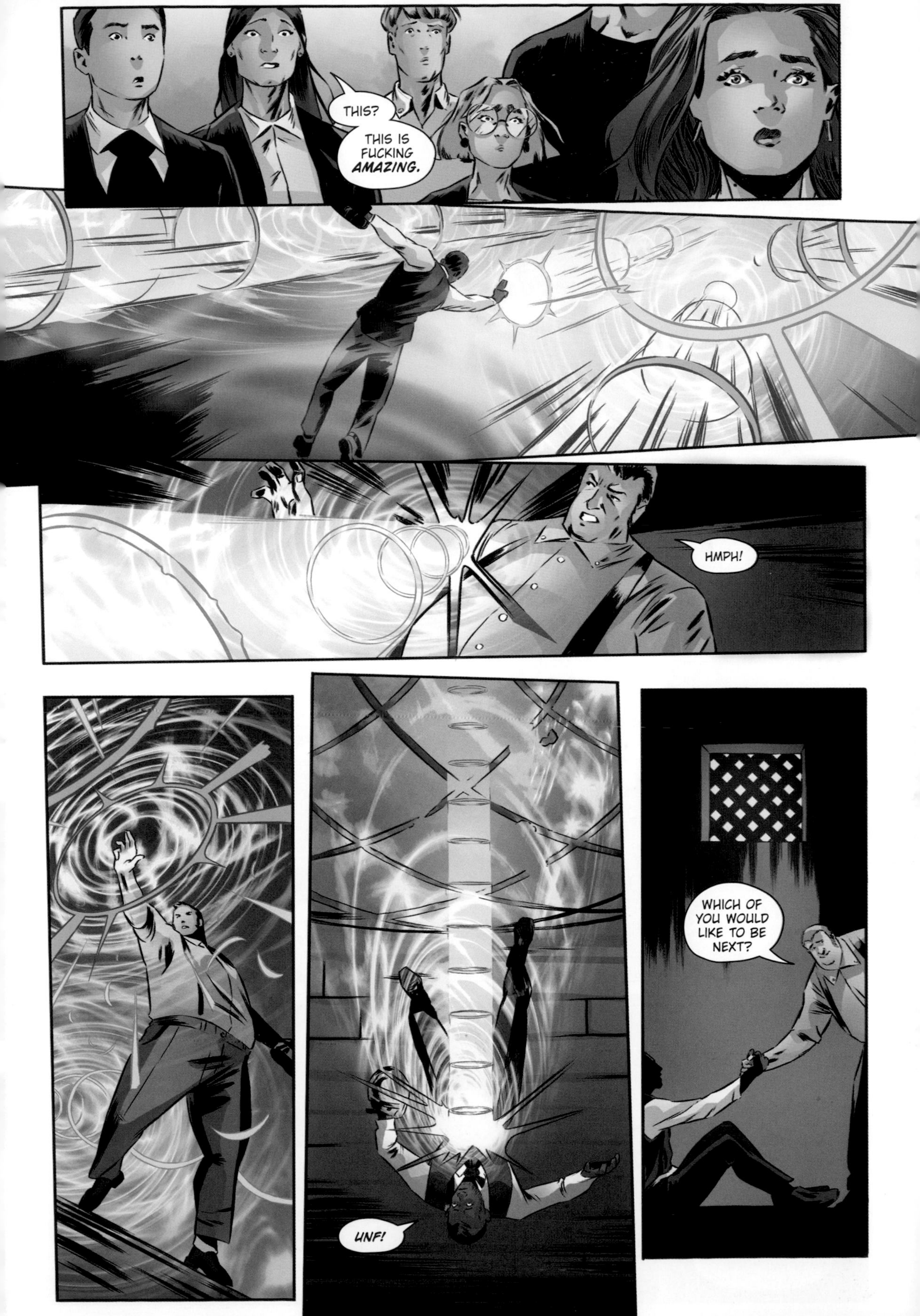
THIS?
THIS IS FUCKING AMAZING.
HMPH!
UNF!
WHICH OF YOU WOULD LIKE TO BE NEXT?

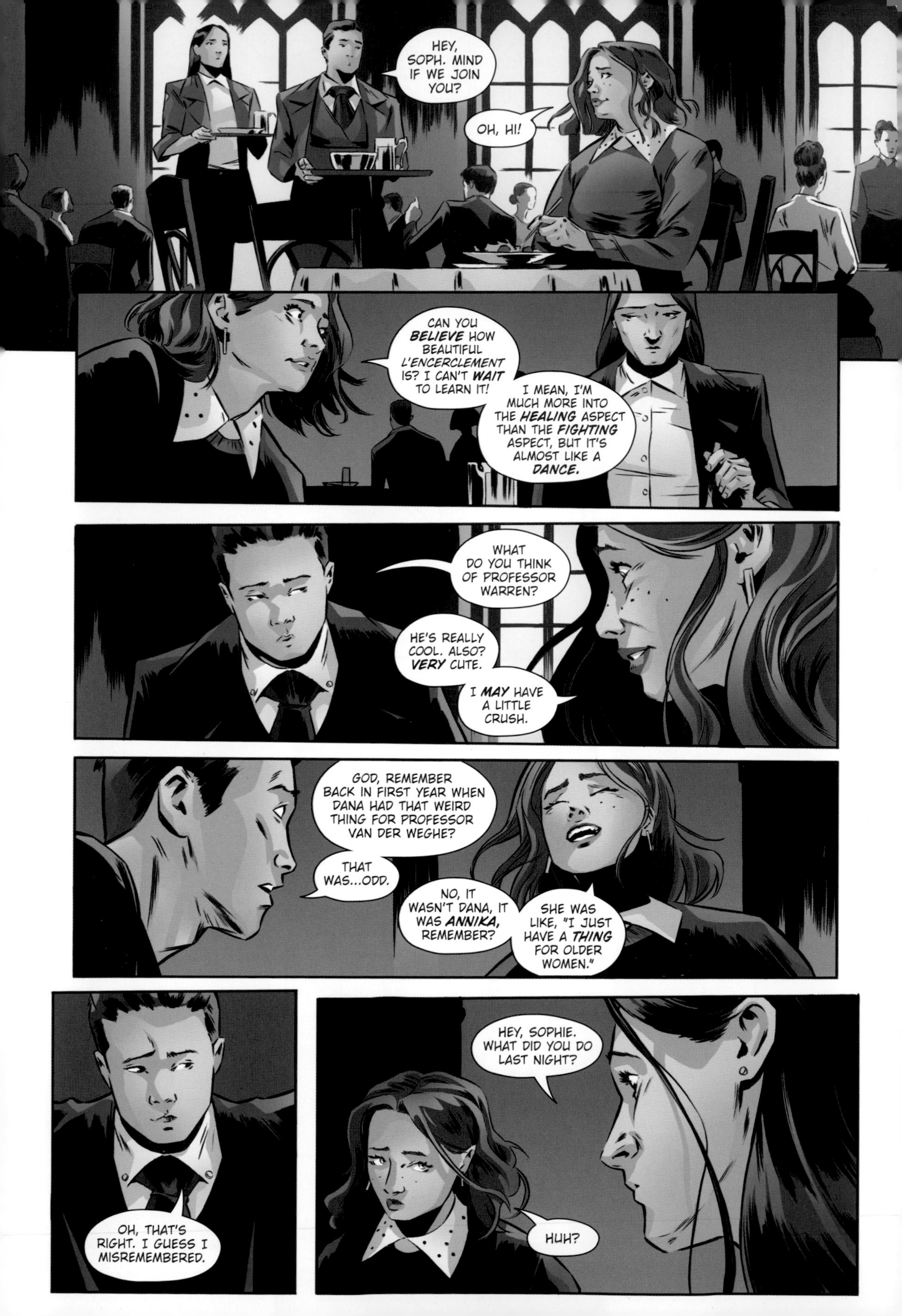

HEY, SOPH. MIND IF WE JOIN YOU?
OH, HI!
CAN YOU BELIEVE HOW BEAUTIFUL L'ENCERCLEMENT IS? I CAN'T WAIT TO LEARN IT!
I MEAN, I'M MUCH MORE INTO THE HEALING ASPECT THAN THE FIGHTING ASPECT, BUT IT'S ALMOST LIKE A DANCE.
WHAT DO YOU THINK OF PROFESSOR WARREN?
HE'S REALLY COOL. ALSO? VERY CUTE.
I MAY HAVE A LITTLE CRUSH.
GOD, REMEMBER BACK IN FIRST YEAR WHEN DANA HAD THAT WEIRD THING FOR PROFESSOR VAN DER WEGHE?
THAT WAS...ODD.
NO, IT WASN'T DANA, IT WAS ANNIKA, REMEMBER?
SHE WAS LIKE, "I JUST HAVE A THING FOR OLDER WOMEN."
OH, THAT'S RIGHT. I GUESS I MISREMEMBERED.
HEY, SOPHIE. WHAT DID YOU DO LAST NIGHT?
HUH?

WHAT, YOU MEAN AFTER WE DID THE BIG MAGIC SHOWDOWN IN THE WOODS?

I DON'T REALLY REMEMBER. I GUESS I JUST CAME BACK AND WENT TO BED. I WAS PRETTY TIRED, I SUPPOSE.

THAT FIRE SPELL YOU DID WAS PRETTY COOL.

THE *PRAYER TO XIUHTECUHTLI?* YEAH, I LOVE THAT ONE.

IT KINDA GOT AWAY FROM ME, THOUGH, HUH!

I'M GONNA GO STUDY FOR A BIT IN THE LIBRARY. I *REALLY* WANT TO DO WELL IN BIOMAGIC THIS SEMESTER. DO YOU GUYS WANT TO JOIN ME AFTER DINNER?

SURE, MAYBE!

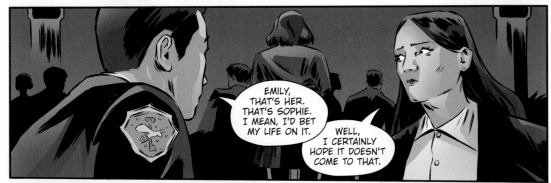

EMILY, THAT'S HER. THAT'S SOPHIE. I MEAN, I'D BET MY LIFE ON IT.

WELL, I CERTAINLY HOPE IT DOESN'T COME TO THAT.

SO, WHAT? WAS SHE *RESURRECTED?* WAS LAST NIGHT JUST A BAD *DREAM?*

I DON'T KNOW. BUT ONE THING *IS* FOR SURE.

SOPHIE'S ALIVE.

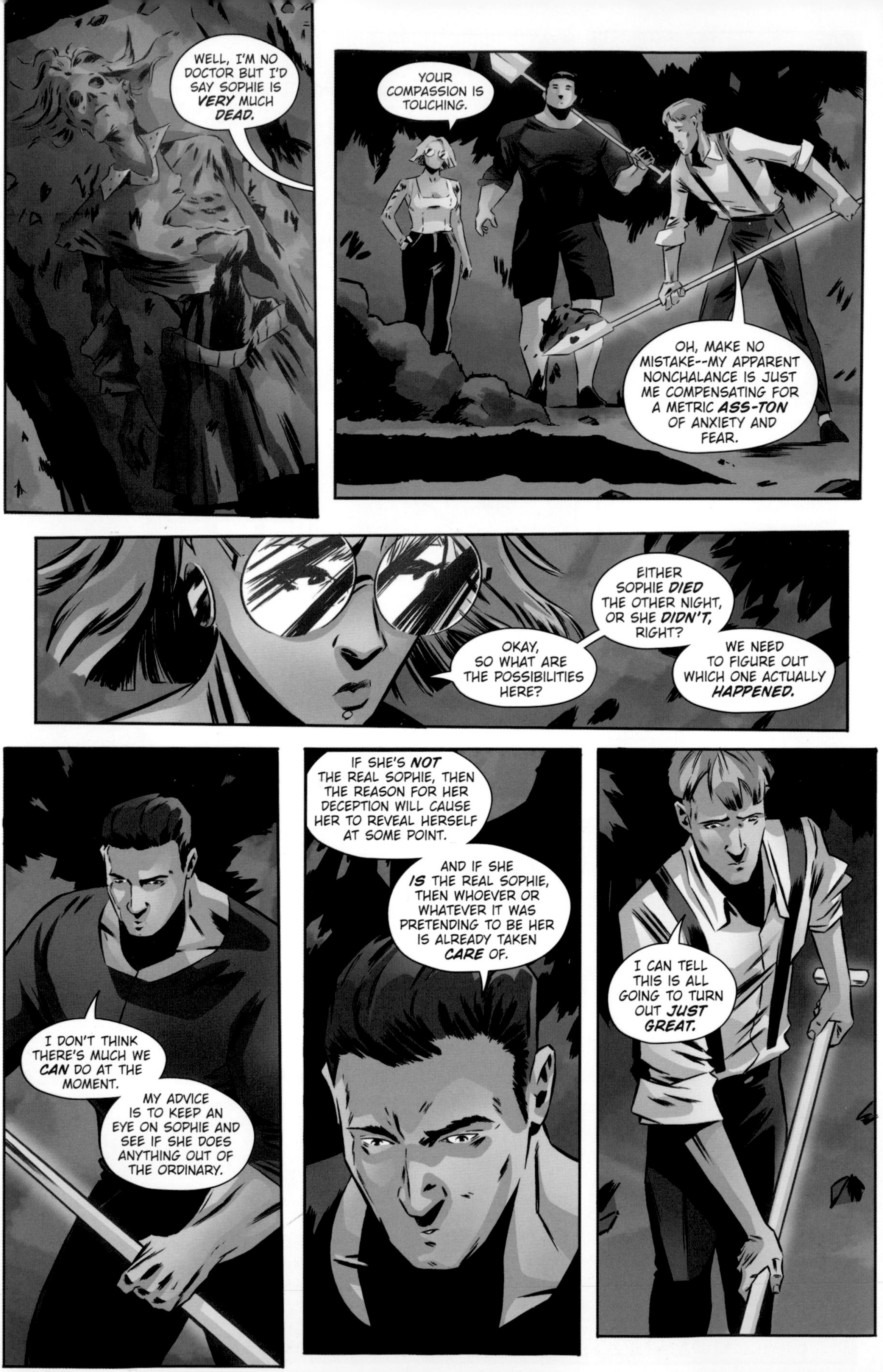
WELL, I'M NO DOCTOR BUT I'D SAY SOPHIE IS **VERY** MUCH **DEAD.**
YOUR COMPASSION IS TOUCHING.
OH, MAKE NO MISTAKE--MY APPARENT NONCHALANCE IS JUST ME COMPENSATING FOR A METRIC **ASS-TON** OF ANXIETY AND FEAR.
OKAY, SO WHAT ARE THE POSSIBILITIES HERE?
EITHER SOPHIE **DIED** THE OTHER NIGHT, OR SHE **DIDN'T,** RIGHT?
WE NEED TO FIGURE OUT WHICH ONE ACTUALLY **HAPPENED.**
I DON'T THINK THERE'S MUCH WE **CAN** DO AT THE MOMENT.
MY ADVICE IS TO KEEP AN EYE ON SOPHIE AND SEE IF SHE DOES ANYTHING OUT OF THE ORDINARY.
IF SHE'S **NOT** THE REAL SOPHIE, THEN THE REASON FOR HER DECEPTION WILL CAUSE HER TO REVEAL HERSELF AT SOME POINT.
AND IF SHE **IS** THE REAL SOPHIE, THEN WHOEVER OR WHATEVER IT WAS PRETENDING TO BE HER IS ALREADY TAKEN **CARE** OF.
I CAN TELL THIS IS ALL GOING TO TURN OUT **JUST GREAT.**

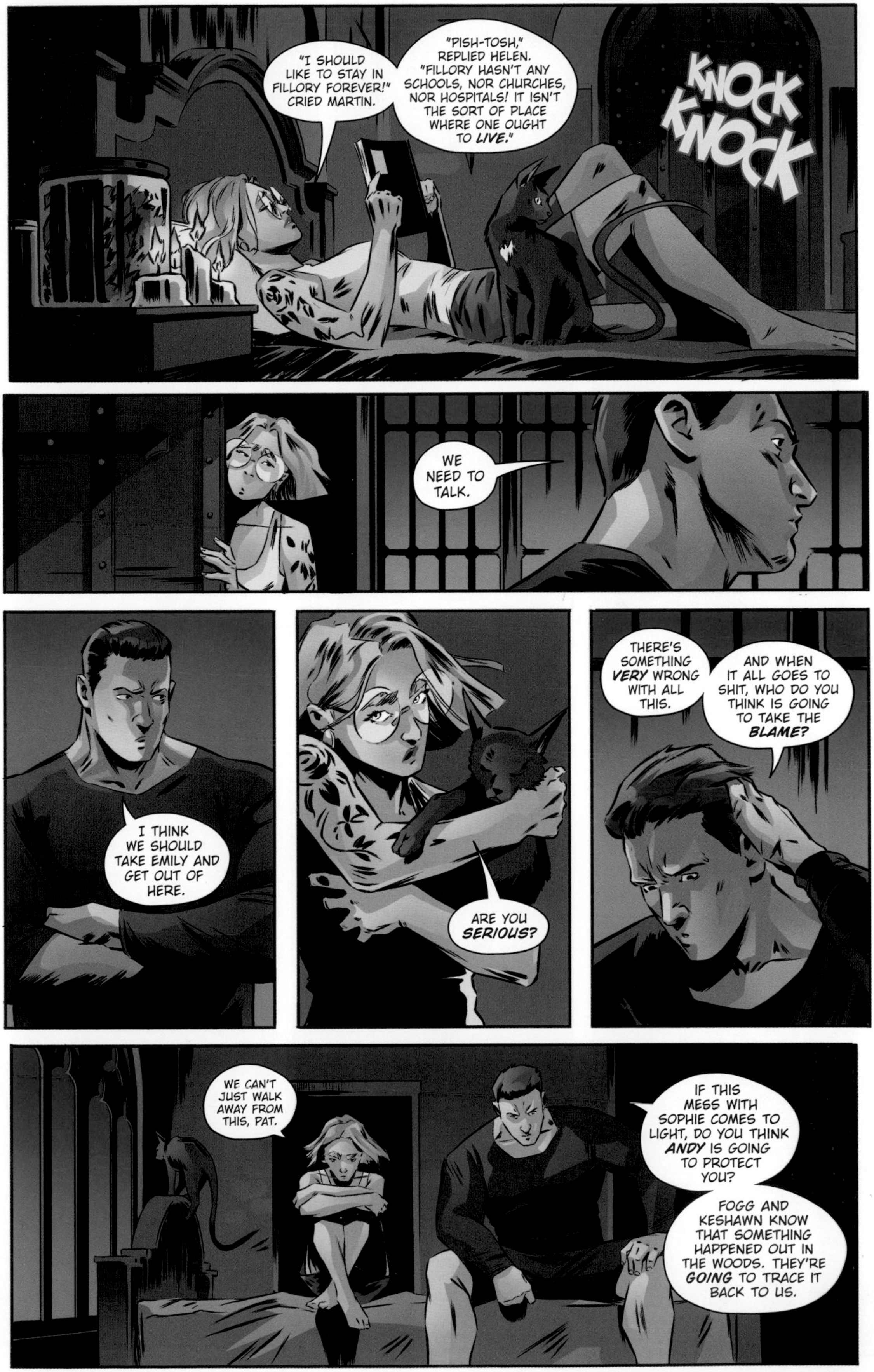
"I SHOULD LIKE TO STAY IN FILLORY FOREVER!" CRIED MARTIN.
"PISH-TOSH," REPLIED HELEN. "FILLORY HASN'T ANY SCHOOLS, NOR CHURCHES, NOR HOSPITALS! IT ISN'T THE SORT OF PLACE WHERE ONE OUGHT TO *LIVE*."
KNOCK KNOCK
WE NEED TO TALK.
I THINK WE SHOULD TAKE EMILY AND GET OUT OF HERE.
ARE YOU *SERIOUS?*
THERE'S SOMETHING *VERY* WRONG WITH ALL THIS.
AND WHEN IT ALL GOES TO SHIT, WHO DO YOU THINK IS GOING TO TAKE THE *BLAME?*
WE CAN'T JUST WALK AWAY FROM THIS, PAT.
IF THIS MESS WITH SOPHIE COMES TO LIGHT, DO YOU THINK *ANDY* IS GOING TO PROTECT YOU?
FOGG AND KESHAWN KNOW THAT SOMETHING HAPPENED OUT IN THE WOODS. THEY'RE *GOING* TO TRACE IT BACK TO US.

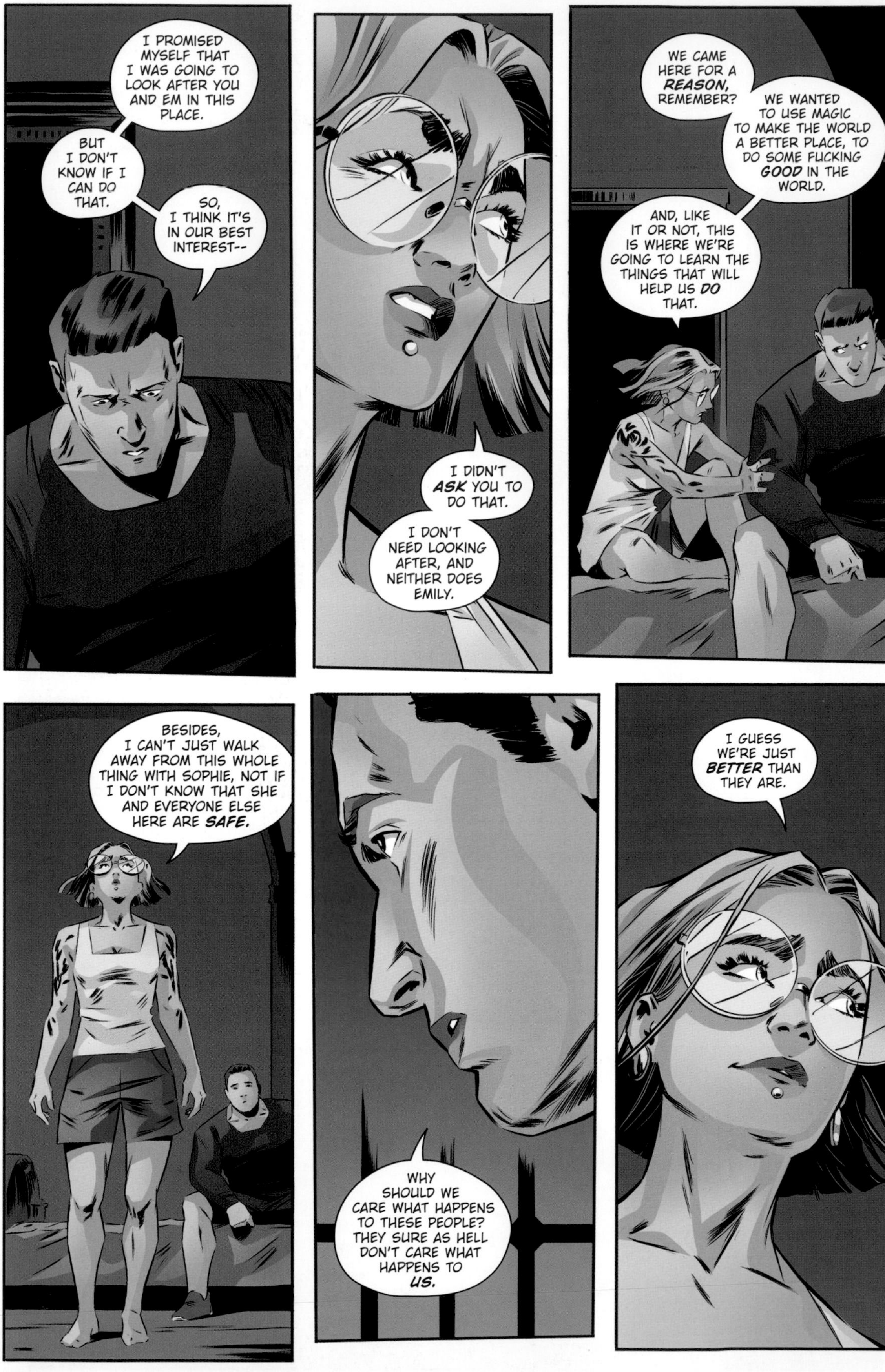
I PROMISED MYSELF THAT I WAS GOING TO LOOK AFTER YOU AND EM IN THIS PLACE.
BUT I DON'T KNOW IF I CAN DO THAT.
SO, I THINK IT'S IN OUR BEST INTEREST--
I DIDN'T ***ASK*** YOU TO DO THAT.
I DON'T NEED LOOKING AFTER, AND NEITHER DOES EMILY.
WE CAME HERE FOR A ***REASON,*** REMEMBER?
WE WANTED TO USE MAGIC TO MAKE THE WORLD A BETTER PLACE, TO DO SOME FUCKING ***GOOD*** IN THE WORLD.
AND, LIKE IT OR NOT, THIS IS WHERE WE'RE GOING TO LEARN THE THINGS THAT WILL HELP US ***DO*** THAT.
BESIDES, I CAN'T JUST WALK AWAY FROM THIS WHOLE THING WITH SOPHIE, NOT IF I DON'T KNOW THAT SHE AND EVERYONE ELSE HERE ARE ***SAFE.***
WHY SHOULD WE CARE WHAT HAPPENS TO THESE PEOPLE? THEY SURE AS HELL DON'T CARE WHAT HAPPENS TO ***US.***
I GUESS WE'RE JUST ***BETTER*** THAN THEY ARE.

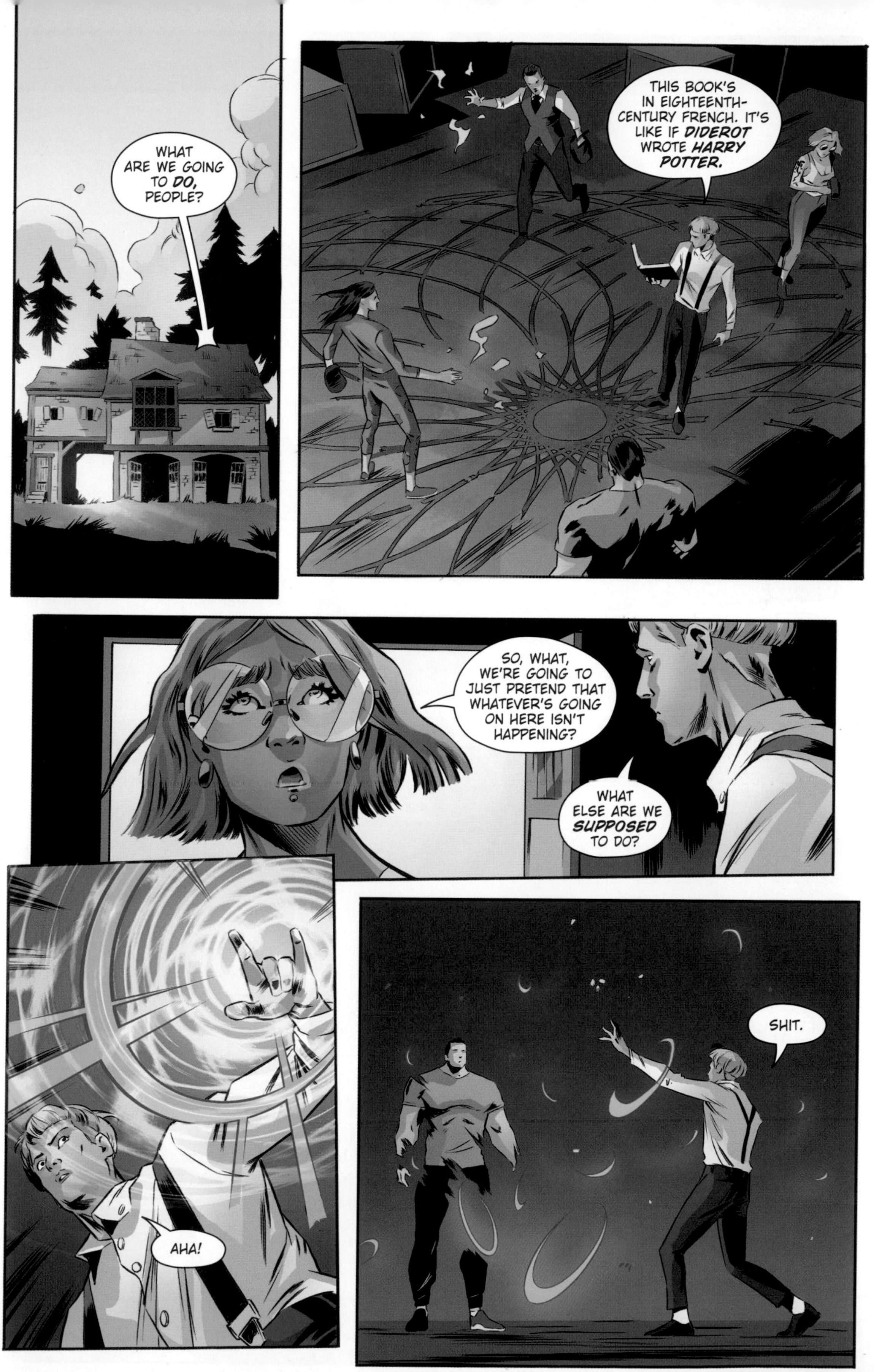
WHAT ARE WE GOING TO DO, PEOPLE?
THIS BOOK'S IN EIGHTEENTH-CENTURY FRENCH. IT'S LIKE IF DIDEROT WROTE HARRY POTTER.
SO, WHAT, WE'RE GOING TO JUST PRETEND THAT WHATEVER'S GOING ON HERE ISN'T HAPPENING?
WHAT ELSE ARE WE SUPPOSED TO DO?
AHA!
SHIT.

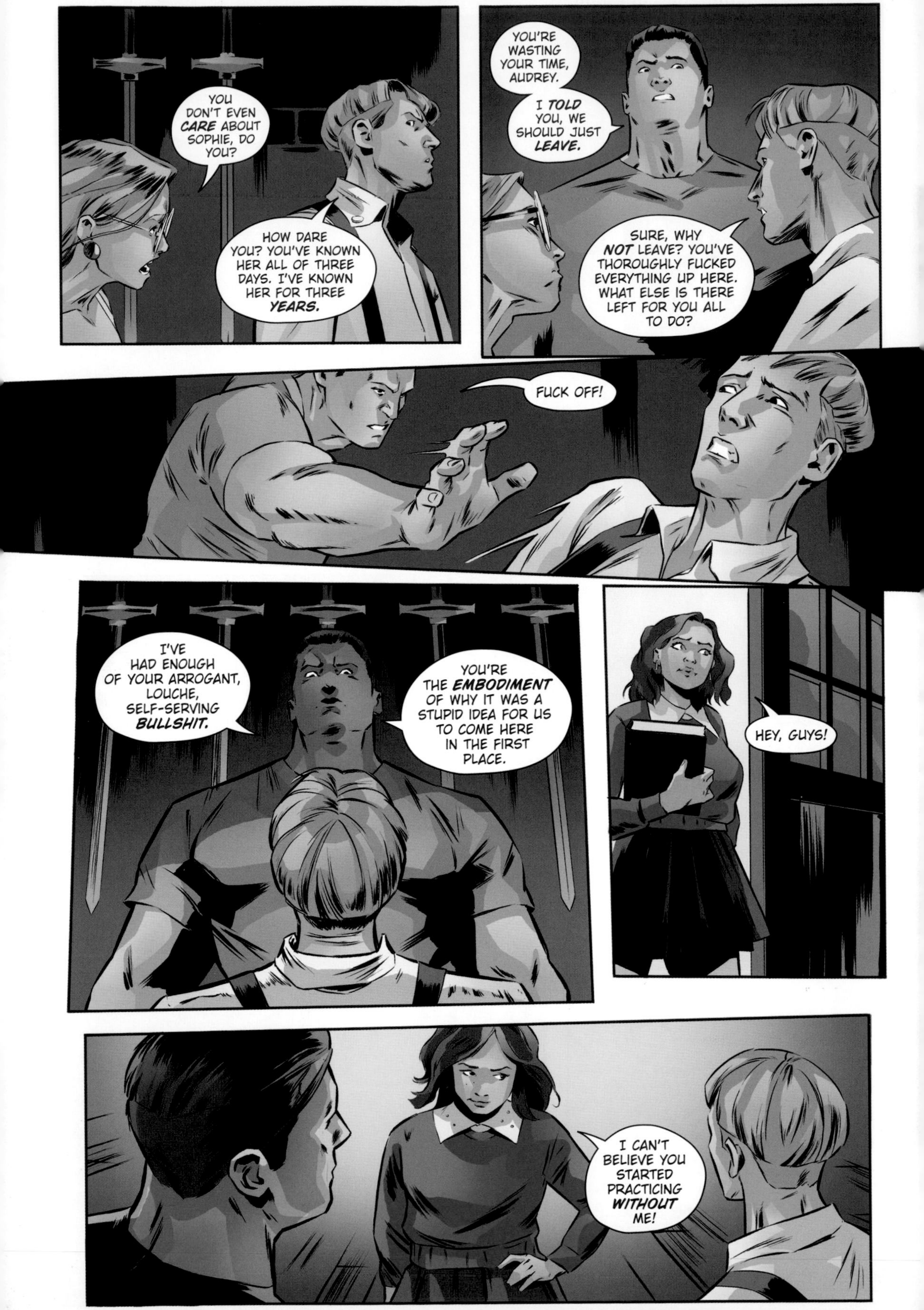
YOU DON'T EVEN CARE ABOUT SOPHIE, DO YOU?
HOW DARE YOU? YOU'VE KNOWN HER ALL OF THREE DAYS. I'VE KNOWN HER FOR THREE YEARS.
YOU'RE WASTING YOUR TIME, AUDREY.
I TOLD YOU, WE SHOULD JUST LEAVE.
SURE, WHY NOT LEAVE? YOU'VE THOROUGHLY FUCKED EVERYTHING UP HERE. WHAT ELSE IS THERE LEFT FOR YOU ALL TO DO?
FUCK OFF!
I'VE HAD ENOUGH OF YOUR ARROGANT, LOUCHE, SELF-SERVING BULLSHIT.
YOU'RE THE EMBODIMENT OF WHY IT WAS A STUPID IDEA FOR US TO COME HERE IN THE FIRST PLACE.
HEY, GUYS!
I CAN'T BELIEVE YOU STARTED PRACTICING WITHOUT ME!

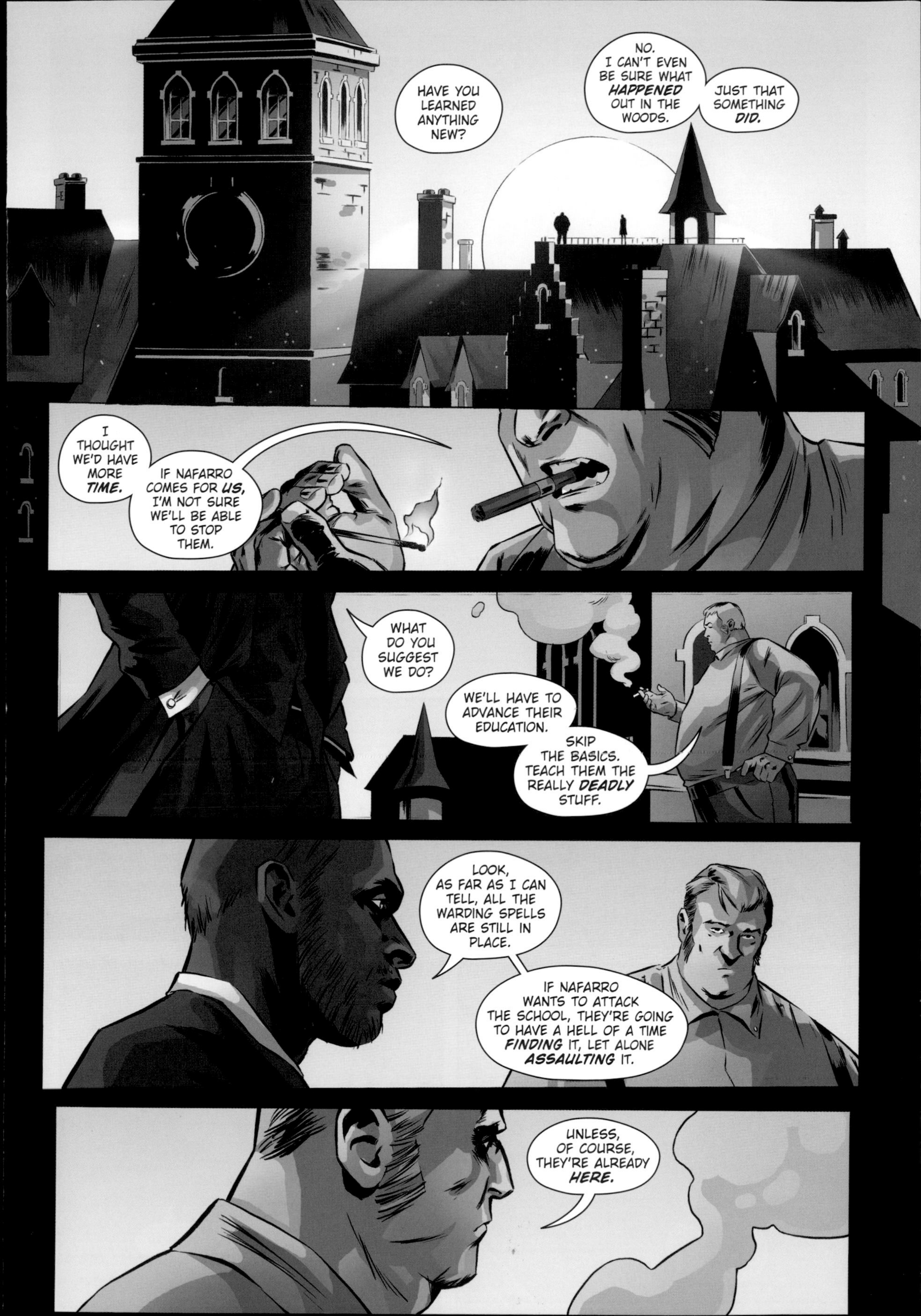
HAVE YOU LEARNED ANYTHING NEW?
NO. I CAN'T EVEN BE SURE WHAT HAPPENED OUT IN THE WOODS.
JUST THAT SOMETHING DID.
I THOUGHT WE'D HAVE MORE TIME.
IF NAFARRO COMES FOR US, I'M NOT SURE WE'LL BE ABLE TO STOP THEM.
WHAT DO YOU SUGGEST WE DO?
WE'LL HAVE TO ADVANCE THEIR EDUCATION.
SKIP THE BASICS. TEACH THEM THE REALLY DEADLY STUFF.
LOOK, AS FAR AS I CAN TELL, ALL THE WARDING SPELLS ARE STILL IN PLACE.
IF NAFARRO WANTS TO ATTACK THE SCHOOL, THEY'RE GOING TO HAVE A HELL OF A TIME FINDING IT, LET ALONE ASSAULTING IT.
UNLESS, OF COURSE, THEY'RE ALREADY HERE.

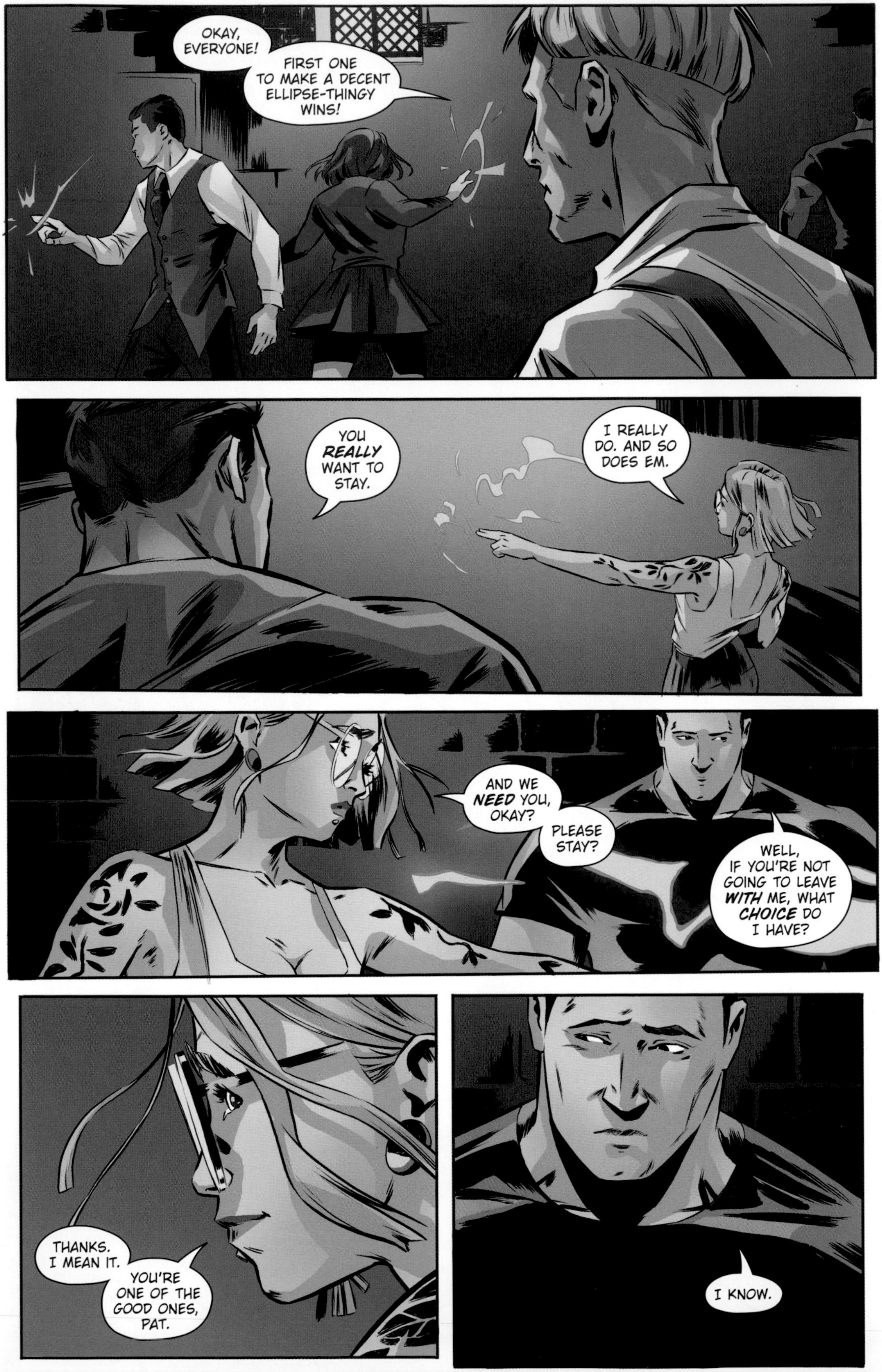
OKAY, EVERYONE!
FIRST ONE TO MAKE A DECENT ELLIPSE-THINGY WINS!
YOU **REALLY** WANT TO STAY.
I REALLY DO. AND SO DOES EM.
AND WE **NEED** YOU, OKAY?
PLEASE STAY?
WELL, IF YOU'RE NOT GOING TO LEAVE **WITH** ME, WHAT **CHOICE** DO I HAVE?
THANKS. I MEAN IT.
YOU'RE ONE OF THE GOOD ONES, PAT.
I KNOW.

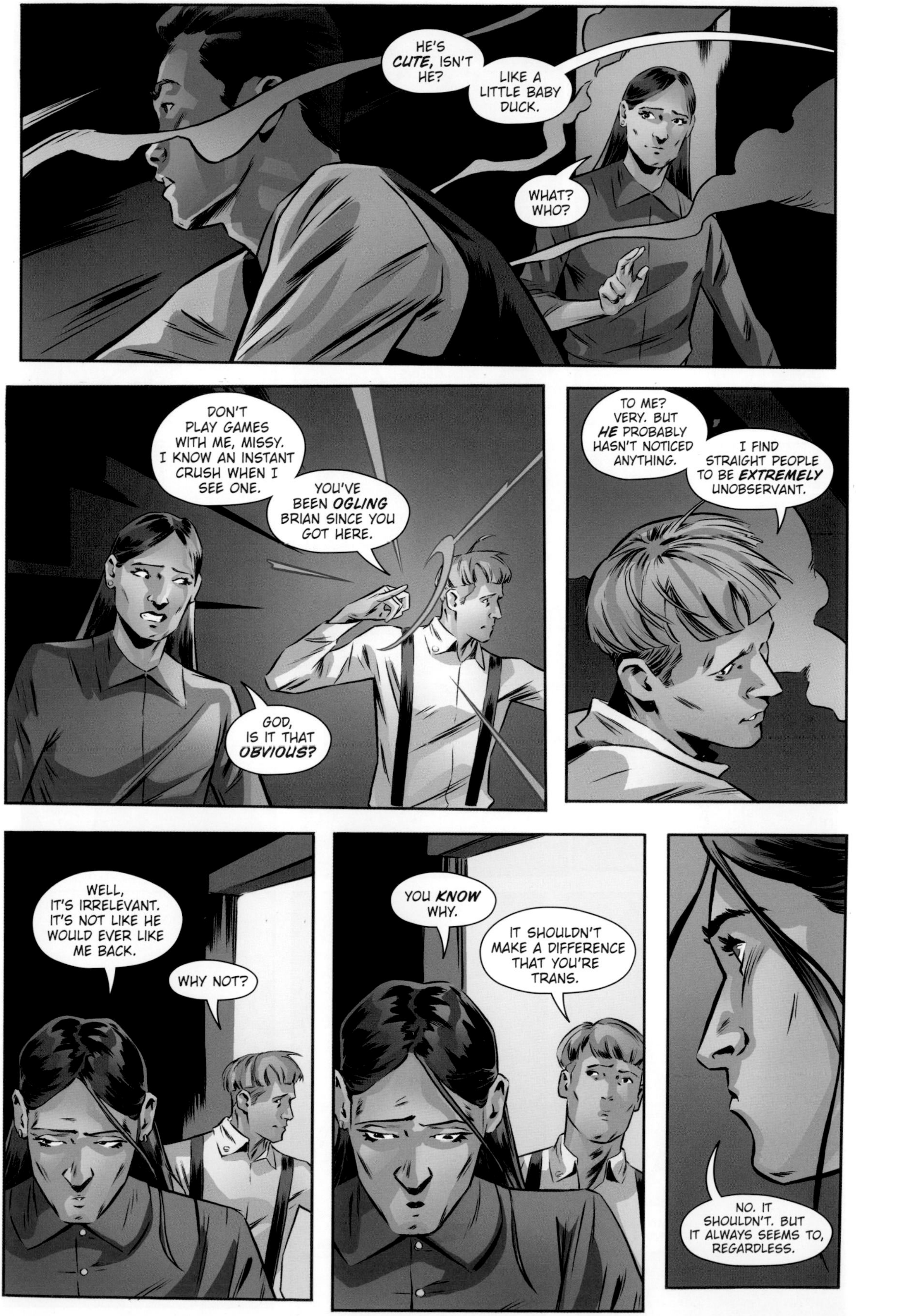
HE'S CUTE, ISN'T HE?
LIKE A LITTLE BABY DUCK.
WHAT? WHO?
DON'T PLAY GAMES WITH ME, MISSY. I KNOW AN INSTANT CRUSH WHEN I SEE ONE.
YOU'VE BEEN OGLING BRIAN SINCE YOU GOT HERE.
GOD, IS IT THAT OBVIOUS?
TO ME? VERY. BUT HE PROBABLY HASN'T NOTICED ANYTHING.
I FIND STRAIGHT PEOPLE TO BE EXTREMELY UNOBSERVANT.
WELL, IT'S IRRELEVANT. IT'S NOT LIKE HE WOULD EVER LIKE ME BACK.
WHY NOT?
YOU KNOW WHY.
IT SHOULDN'T MAKE A DIFFERENCE THAT YOU'RE TRANS.
NO. IT SHOULDN'T. BUT IT ALWAYS SEEMS TO, REGARDLESS.

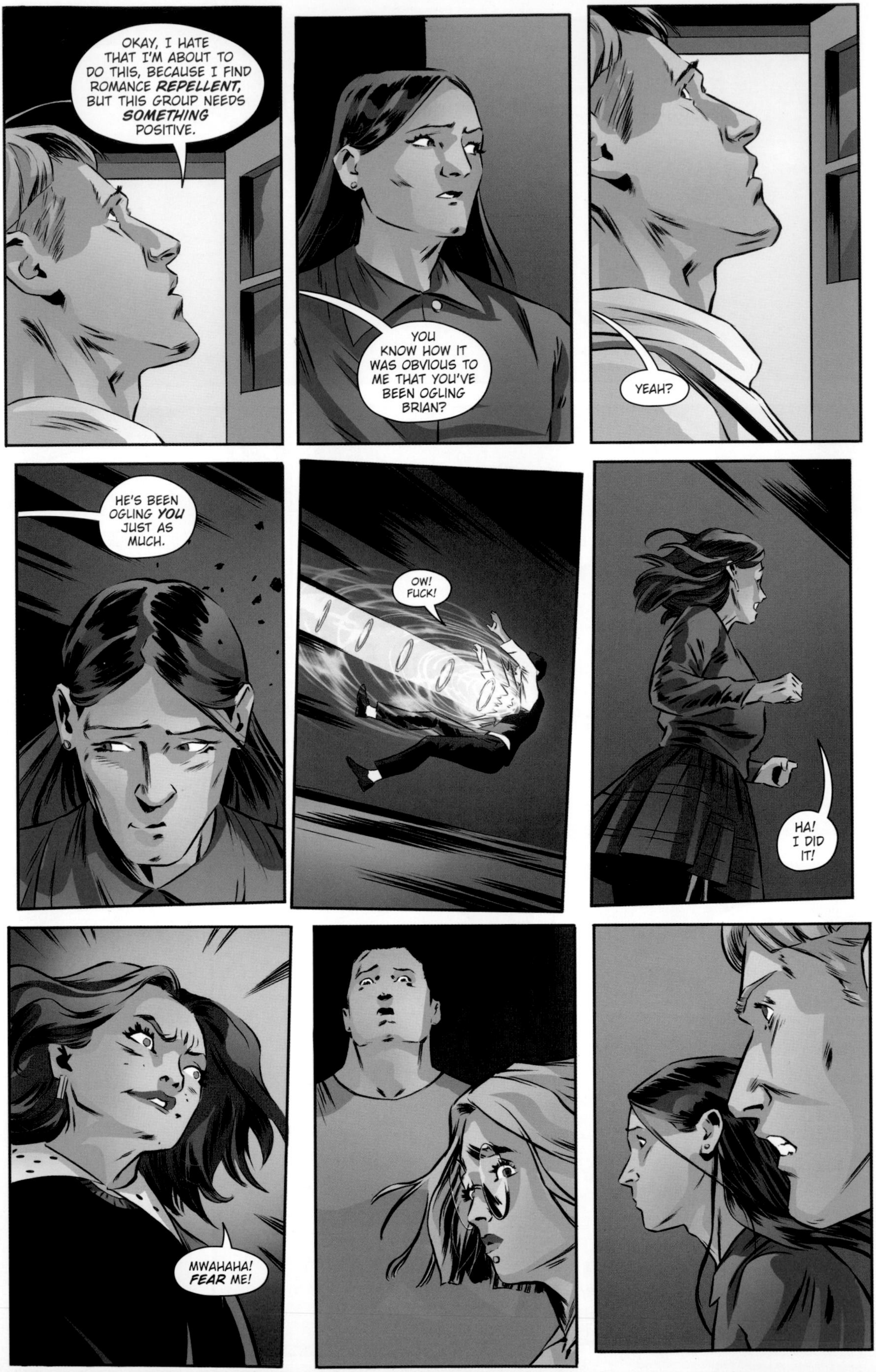
OKAY, I HATE THAT I'M ABOUT TO DO THIS, BECAUSE I FIND ROMANCE **REPELLENT,** BUT THIS GROUP NEEDS **SOMETHING** POSITIVE.
YOU KNOW HOW IT WAS OBVIOUS TO ME THAT YOU'VE BEEN OGLING BRIAN?
YEAH?
HE'S BEEN OGLING **YOU** JUST AS MUCH.
OW! FUCK!
HA! I DID IT!
MWAHAHA! **FEAR** ME!

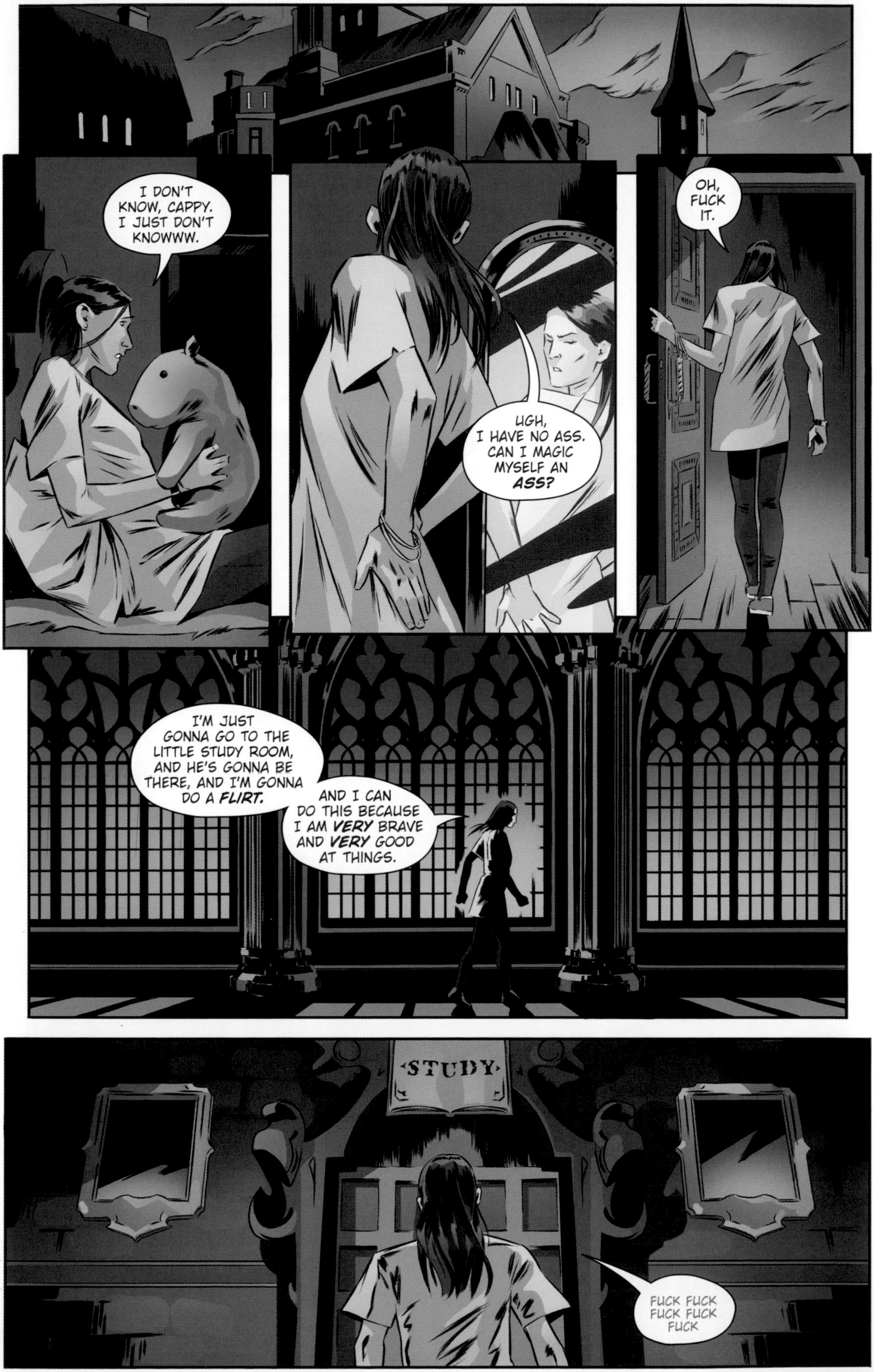
I DON'T KNOW, CAPPY. I JUST DON'T KNOWWW.
UGH, I HAVE NO ASS. CAN I MAGIC MYSELF AN **ASS?**
OH, FUCK IT.
I'M JUST GONNA GO TO THE LITTLE STUDY ROOM, AND HE'S GONNA BE THERE, AND I'M GONNA DO A **FLIRT.**
AND I CAN DO THIS BECAUSE I AM **VERY** BRAVE AND **VERY** GOOD AT THINGS.
STUDY
FUCK FUCK FUCK FUCK FUCK

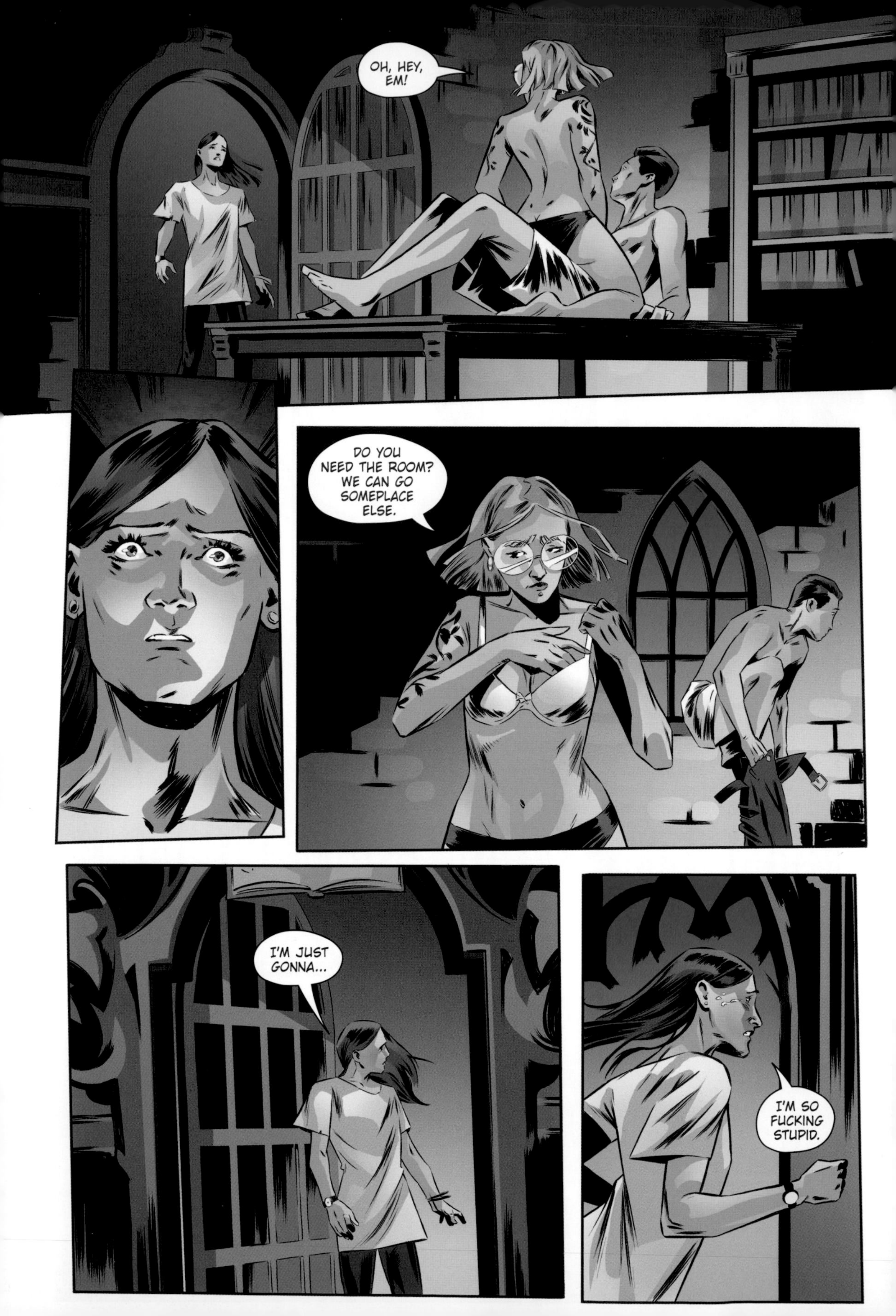
OH, HEY, EM!
DO YOU NEED THE ROOM? WE CAN GO SOMEPLACE ELSE.
I'M JUST GONNA...
I'M SO FUCKING STUPID.

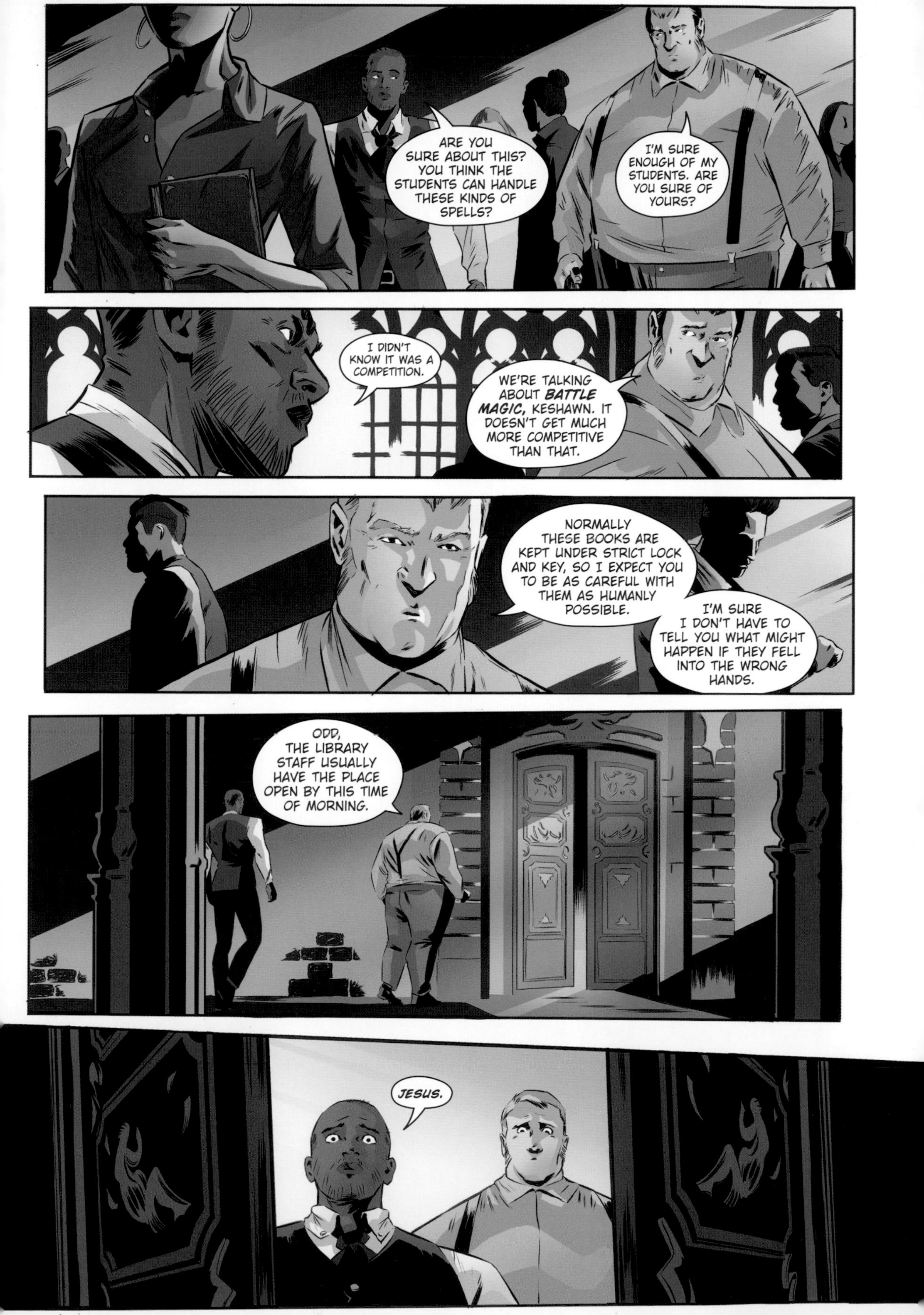
ARE YOU SURE ABOUT THIS? YOU THINK THE STUDENTS CAN HANDLE THESE KINDS OF SPELLS?
I'M SURE ENOUGH OF MY STUDENTS. ARE YOU SURE OF YOURS?
I DIDN'T KNOW IT WAS A COMPETITION.
WE'RE TALKING ABOUT **BATTLE MAGIC,** KESHAWN. IT DOESN'T GET MUCH MORE COMPETITIVE THAN THAT.
NORMALLY THESE BOOKS ARE KEPT UNDER STRICT LOCK AND KEY, SO I EXPECT YOU TO BE AS CAREFUL WITH THEM AS HUMANLY POSSIBLE.
I'M SURE I DON'T HAVE TO TELL YOU WHAT MIGHT HAPPEN IF THEY FELL INTO THE WRONG HANDS.
ODD, THE LIBRARY STAFF USUALLY HAVE THE PLACE OPEN BY THIS TIME OF MORNING.
JESUS.

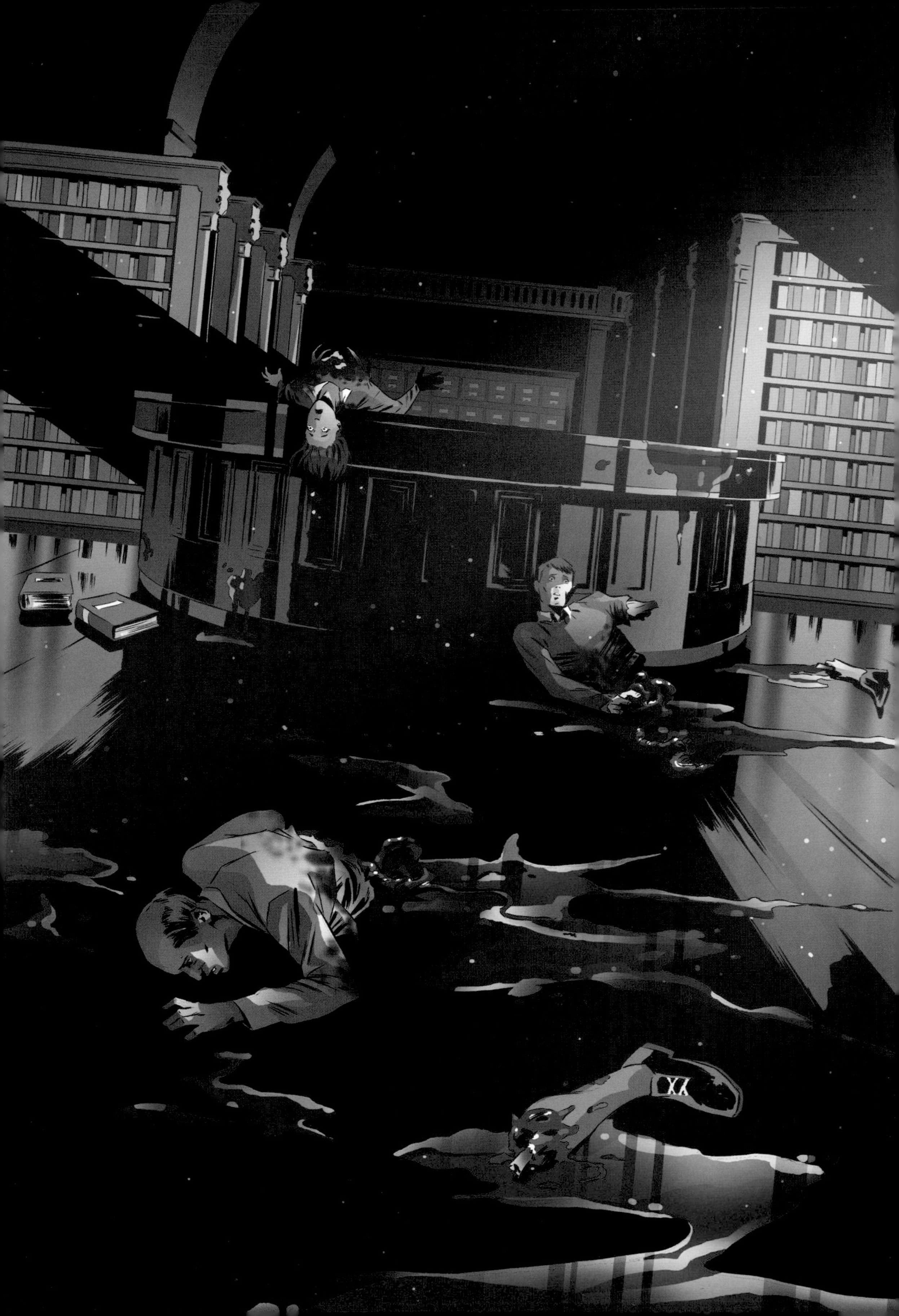

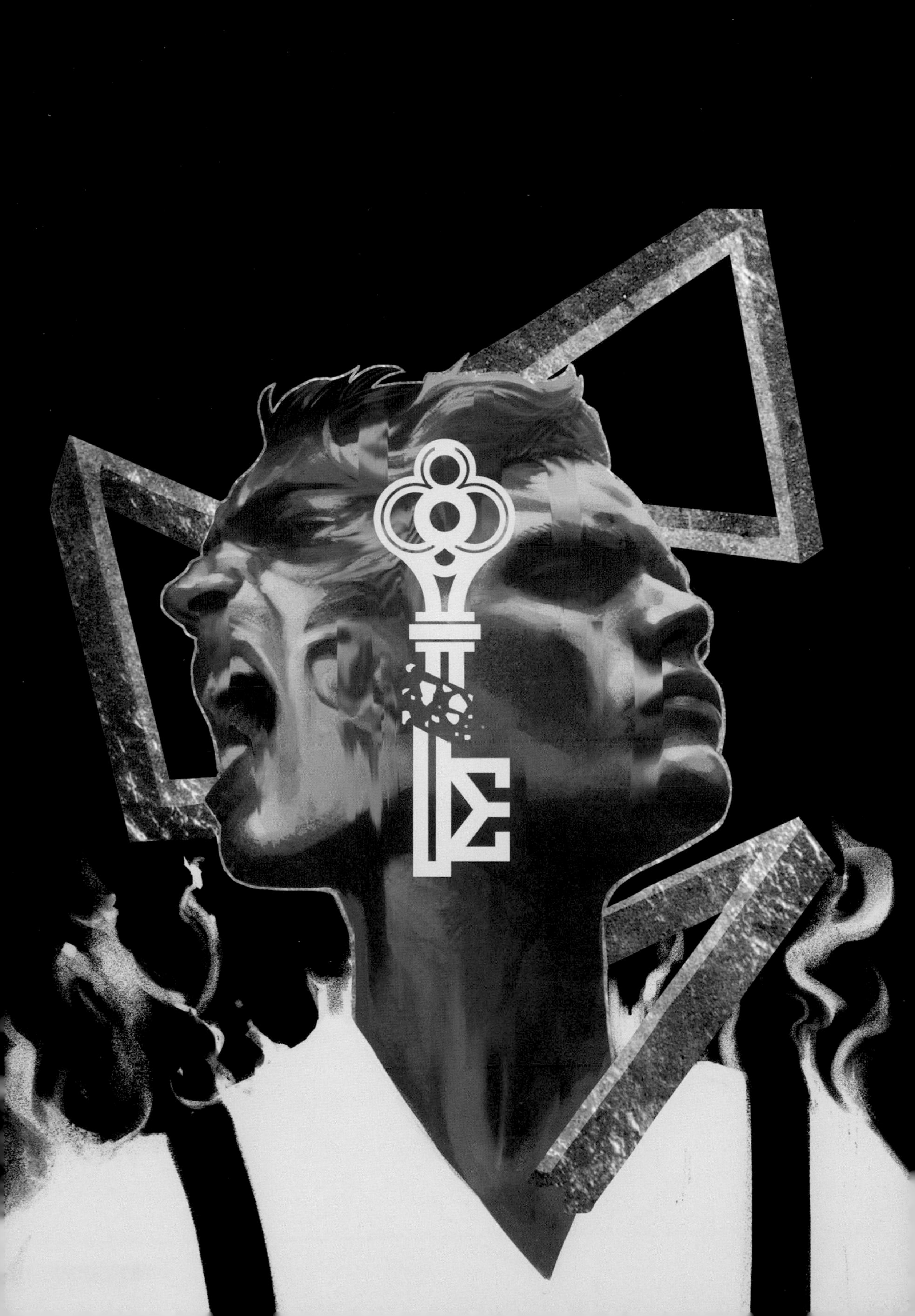

CHAPTER
FOUR

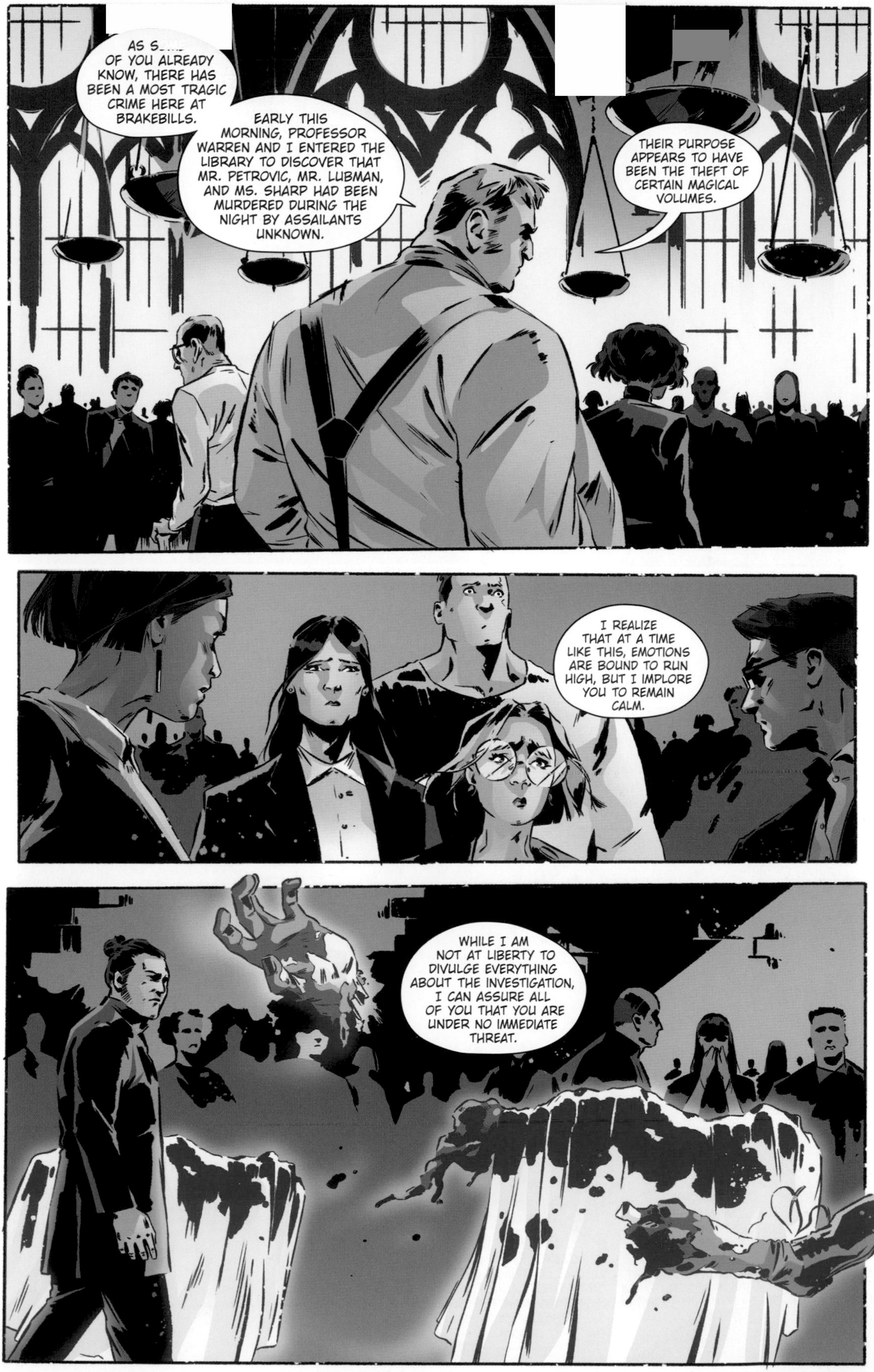
AS S
OF YOU ALREADY KNOW, THERE HAS BEEN A MOST TRAGIC CRIME HERE AT BRAKEBILLS.
EARLY THIS MORNING, PROFESSOR WARREN AND I ENTERED THE LIBRARY TO DISCOVER THAT MR. PETROVIC, MR. LUBMAN, AND MS. SHARP HAD BEEN MURDERED DURING THE NIGHT BY ASSAILANTS UNKNOWN.
THEIR PURPOSE APPEARS TO HAVE BEEN THE THEFT OF CERTAIN MAGICAL VOLUMES.
I REALIZE THAT AT A TIME LIKE THIS, EMOTIONS ARE BOUND TO RUN HIGH, BUT I IMPLORE YOU TO REMAIN CALM.
WHILE I AM NOT AT LIBERTY TO DIVULGE EVERYTHING ABOUT THE INVESTIGATION, I CAN ASSURE ALL OF YOU THAT YOU ARE UNDER NO IMMEDIATE THREAT.

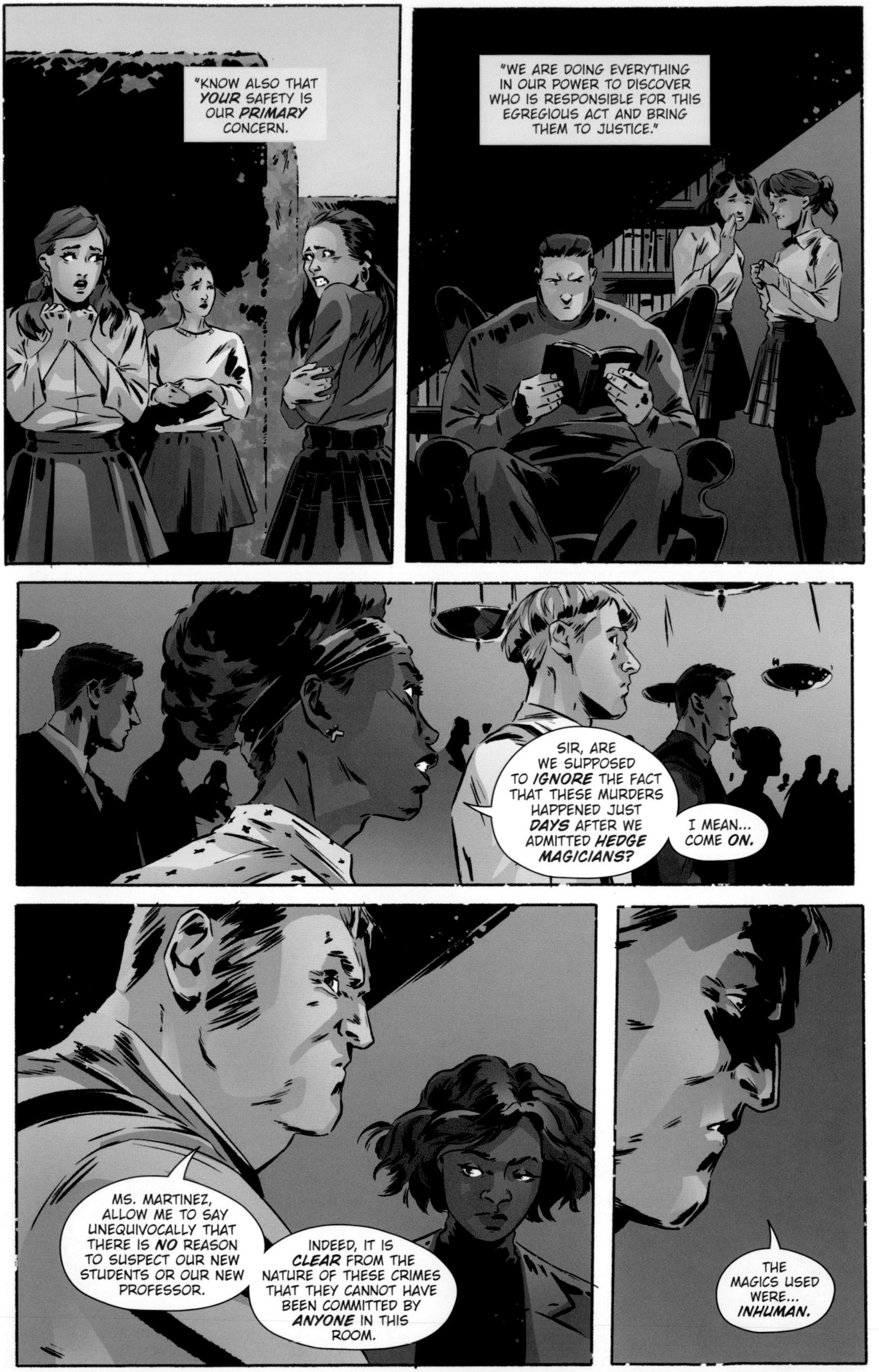
"KNOW ALSO THAT YOUR SAFETY IS OUR PRIMARY CONCERN.
"WE ARE DOING EVERYTHING IN OUR POWER TO DISCOVER WHO IS RESPONSIBLE FOR THIS EGREGIOUS ACT AND BRING THEM TO JUSTICE."
SIR, ARE WE SUPPOSED TO IGNORE THE FACT THAT THESE MURDERS HAPPENED JUST DAYS AFTER WE ADMITTED HEDGE MAGICIANS?
I MEAN... COME ON.
MS. MARTINEZ, ALLOW ME TO SAY UNEQUIVOCALLY THAT THERE IS NO REASON TO SUSPECT OUR NEW STUDENTS OR OUR NEW PROFESSOR.
INDEED, IT IS CLEAR FROM THE NATURE OF THESE CRIMES THAT THEY CANNOT HAVE BEEN COMMITTED BY ANYONE IN THIS ROOM.
THE MAGICS USED WERE... INHUMAN.

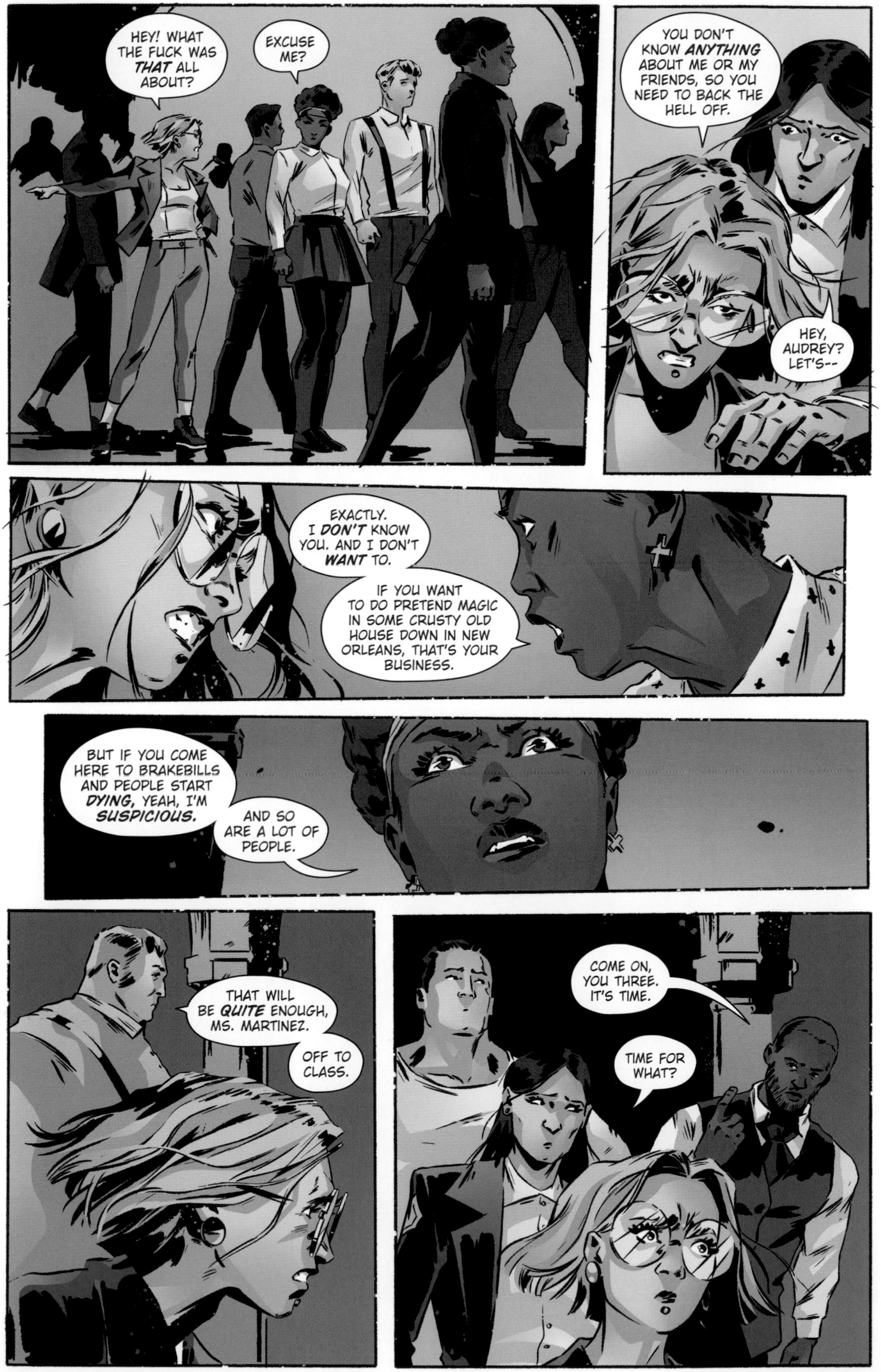

HEY! WHAT THE FUCK WAS THAT ALL ABOUT?
EXCUSE ME?
YOU DON'T KNOW ANYTHING ABOUT ME OR MY FRIENDS, SO YOU NEED TO BACK THE HELL OFF.
HEY, AUDREY? LET'S--
EXACTLY. I DON'T KNOW YOU. AND I DON'T WANT TO.
IF YOU WANT TO DO PRETEND MAGIC IN SOME CRUSTY OLD HOUSE DOWN IN NEW ORLEANS, THAT'S YOUR BUSINESS.
BUT IF YOU COME HERE TO BRAKEBILLS AND PEOPLE START DYING, YEAH, I'M SUSPICIOUS.
AND SO ARE A LOT OF PEOPLE.
THAT WILL BE QUITE ENOUGH, MS. MARTINEZ.
OFF TO CLASS.
COME ON, YOU THREE. IT'S TIME.
TIME FOR WHAT?

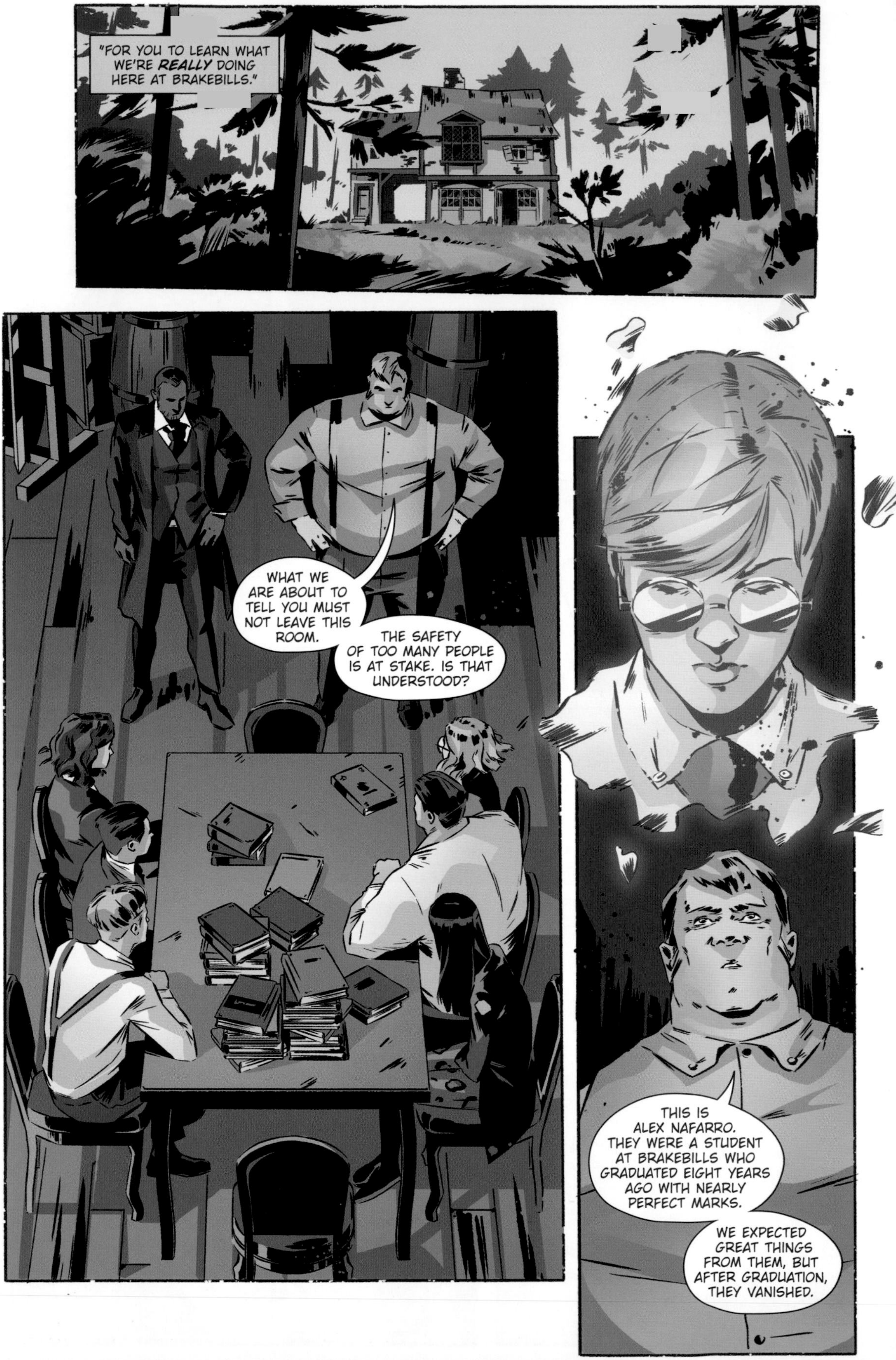
"FOR YOU TO LEARN WHAT WE'RE REALLY DOING HERE AT BRAKEBILLS."
WHAT WE ARE ABOUT TO TELL YOU MUST NOT LEAVE THIS ROOM.
THE SAFETY OF TOO MANY PEOPLE IS AT STAKE. IS THAT UNDERSTOOD?
THIS IS ALEX NAFARRO. THEY WERE A STUDENT AT BRAKEBILLS WHO GRADUATED EIGHT YEARS AGO WITH NEARLY PERFECT MARKS.
WE EXPECTED GREAT THINGS FROM THEM, BUT AFTER GRADUATION, THEY VANISHED.

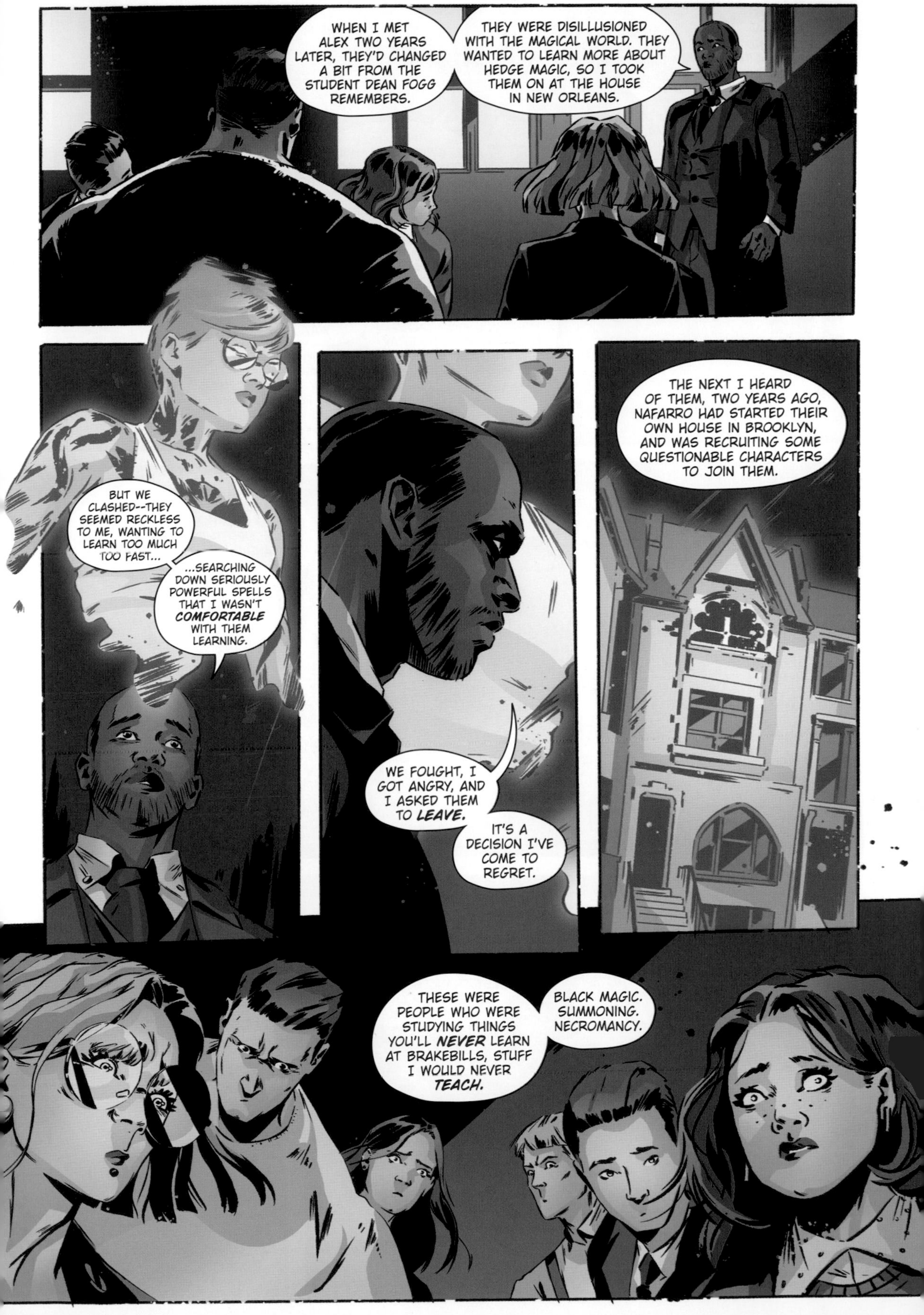
WHEN I MET ALEX TWO YEARS LATER, THEY'D CHANGED A BIT FROM THE STUDENT DEAN FOGG REMEMBERS.
THEY WERE DISILLUSIONED WITH THE MAGICAL WORLD. THEY WANTED TO LEARN MORE ABOUT HEDGE MAGIC, SO I TOOK THEM ON AT THE HOUSE IN NEW ORLEANS.
BUT WE CLASHED--THEY SEEMED RECKLESS TO ME, WANTING TO LEARN TOO MUCH TOO FAST...
...SEARCHING DOWN SERIOUSLY POWERFUL SPELLS THAT I WASN'T *COMFORTABLE* WITH THEM LEARNING.
WE FOUGHT, I GOT ANGRY, AND I ASKED THEM TO *LEAVE.*
IT'S A DECISION I'VE COME TO REGRET.
THE NEXT I HEARD OF THEM, TWO YEARS AGO, NAFARRO HAD STARTED THEIR OWN HOUSE IN BROOKLYN, AND WAS RECRUITING SOME QUESTIONABLE CHARACTERS TO JOIN THEM.
THESE WERE PEOPLE WHO WERE STUDYING THINGS YOU'LL *NEVER* LEARN AT BRAKEBILLS, STUFF I WOULD NEVER *TEACH.*
BLACK MAGIC. SUMMONING. NECROMANCY.

IT WAS NOT LONG THEREAFTER THAT THE BREAK-INS BEGAN.

FIRST, AT THE CHÂTEAU DE PEYRELADE, A MAGIC UNIVERSITY IN FRANCE.

FOLLOWED SWIFTLY BY SIMILAR OCCURRENCES AT SCHOOLS AND HEDGE MAGIC HOUSES IN BUENOS AIRES, CAIRO, AND HYDERABAD.

THEY WERE STEALING *BOOKS.* THE *SERIOUS* STUFF. THE KIND YOU KEEP UNDER LOCK AND KEY AND PRAY NEVER FALL INTO THE WRONG HANDS.

AND KILLING ANYONE WHO GOT IN THEIR WAY.

WHATEVER NAFARRO WAS UP TO, THEY WERE BECOMING MORE POWERFUL AND MORE DANGEROUS BY THE DAY.

WHY? WHAT ARE THEY DOING?

THAT'S THE SCARY THING.

WE DON'T *KNOW.* BUT WHATEVER IT IS, IT'S *BIG.*

WHEN I LEARNED ABOUT ALL THIS, I REACHED OUT TO PROFESSOR WARREN, AND WE DECIDED THE THREAT NAFARRO AND THEIR COMPATRIOTS POSED WAS TOO SERIOUS TO IGNORE.

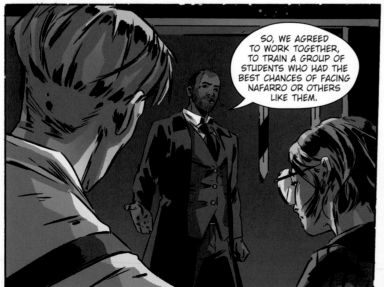

SO, WE AGREED TO WORK TOGETHER, TO TRAIN A GROUP OF STUDENTS WHO HAD THE BEST CHANCES OF FACING NAFARRO OR OTHERS LIKE THEM.

WE THOUGHT WE'D HAVE A *LOT* MORE TIME BEFORE ANY KIND OF CONFRONTATION WOULD EVER TAKE PLACE, BUT IT SEEMS LIKE WE NO LONGER HAVE THAT *LUXURY.*

THEY'VE COME TO *BRAKEBILLS.*

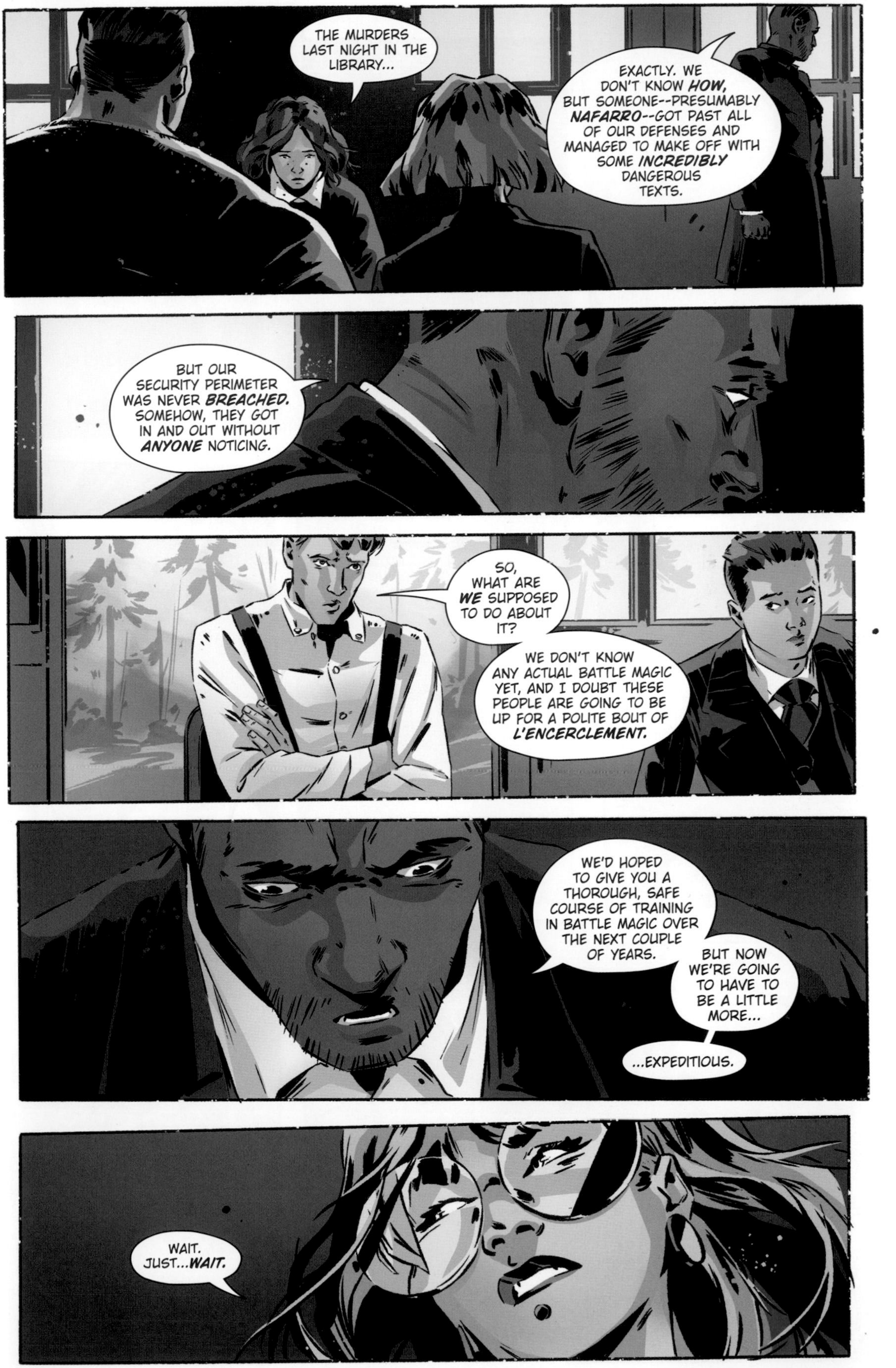
THE MURDERS LAST NIGHT IN THE LIBRARY...
EXACTLY. WE DON'T KNOW HOW, BUT SOMEONE--PRESUMABLY NAFARRO--GOT PAST ALL OF OUR DEFENSES AND MANAGED TO MAKE OFF WITH SOME INCREDIBLY DANGEROUS TEXTS.
BUT OUR SECURITY PERIMETER WAS NEVER BREACHED. SOMEHOW, THEY GOT IN AND OUT WITHOUT ANYONE NOTICING.
SO, WHAT ARE WE SUPPOSED TO DO ABOUT IT?
WE DON'T KNOW ANY ACTUAL BATTLE MAGIC YET, AND I DOUBT THESE PEOPLE ARE GOING TO BE UP FOR A POLITE BOUT OF L'ENCERCLEMENT.
WE'D HOPED TO GIVE YOU A THOROUGH, SAFE COURSE OF TRAINING IN BATTLE MAGIC OVER THE NEXT COUPLE OF YEARS.
BUT NOW WE'RE GOING TO HAVE TO BE A LITTLE MORE...
...EXPEDITIOUS.
WAIT. JUST...WAIT.

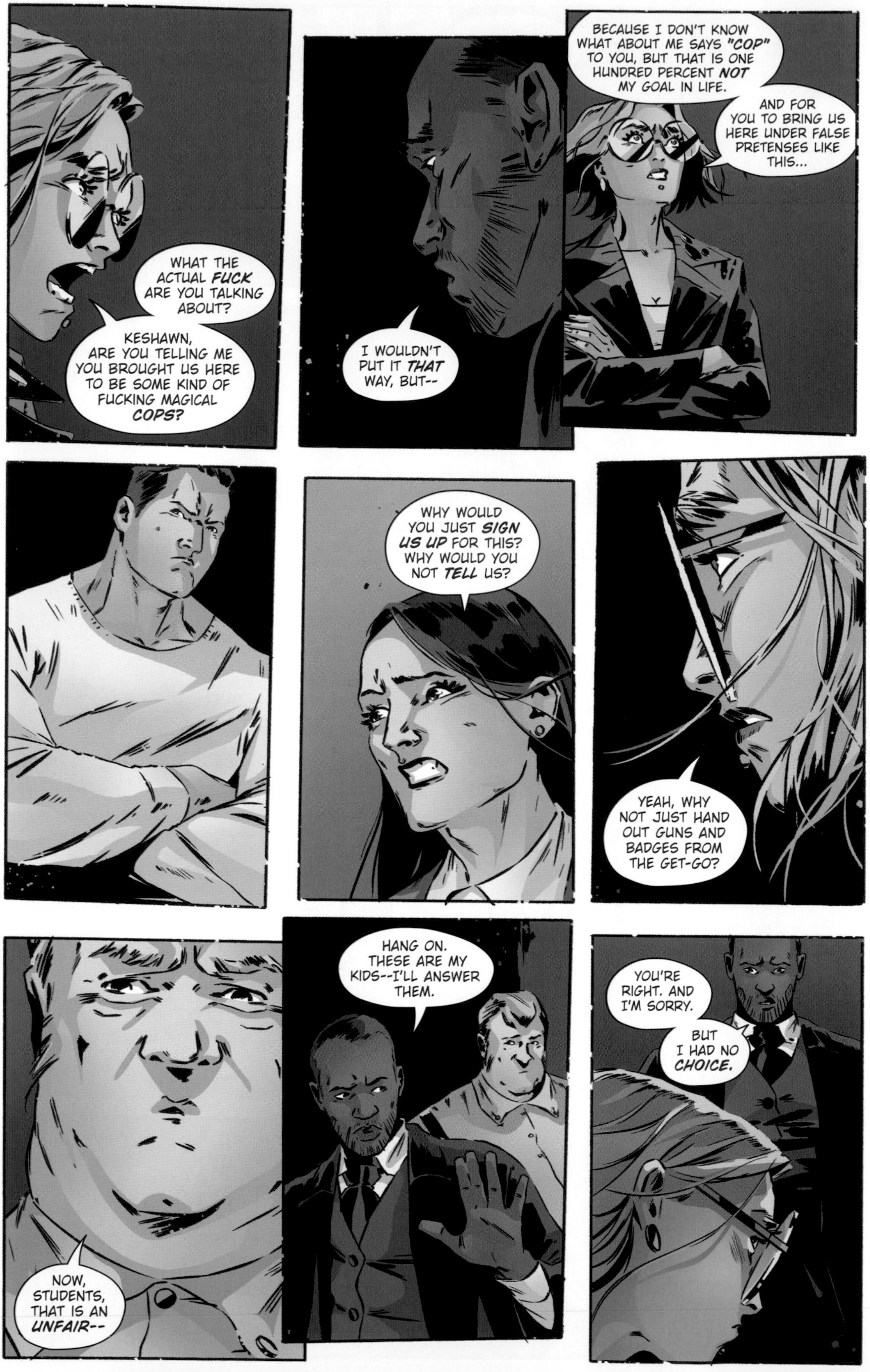
WHAT THE ACTUAL FUCK ARE YOU TALKING ABOUT?
KESHAWN, ARE YOU TELLING ME YOU BROUGHT US HERE TO BE SOME KIND OF FUCKING MAGICAL COPS?
I WOULDN'T PUT IT THAT WAY, BUT--
BECAUSE I DON'T KNOW WHAT ABOUT ME SAYS "COP" TO YOU, BUT THAT IS ONE HUNDRED PERCENT NOT MY GOAL IN LIFE.
AND FOR YOU TO BRING US HERE UNDER FALSE PRETENSES LIKE THIS...
WHY WOULD YOU JUST SIGN US UP FOR THIS? WHY WOULD YOU NOT TELL US?
YEAH, WHY NOT JUST HAND OUT GUNS AND BADGES FROM THE GET-GO?
NOW, STUDENTS, THAT IS AN UNFAIR--
HANG ON. THESE ARE MY KIDS--I'LL ANSWER THEM.
YOU'RE RIGHT. AND I'M SORRY.
BUT I HAD NO CHOICE.

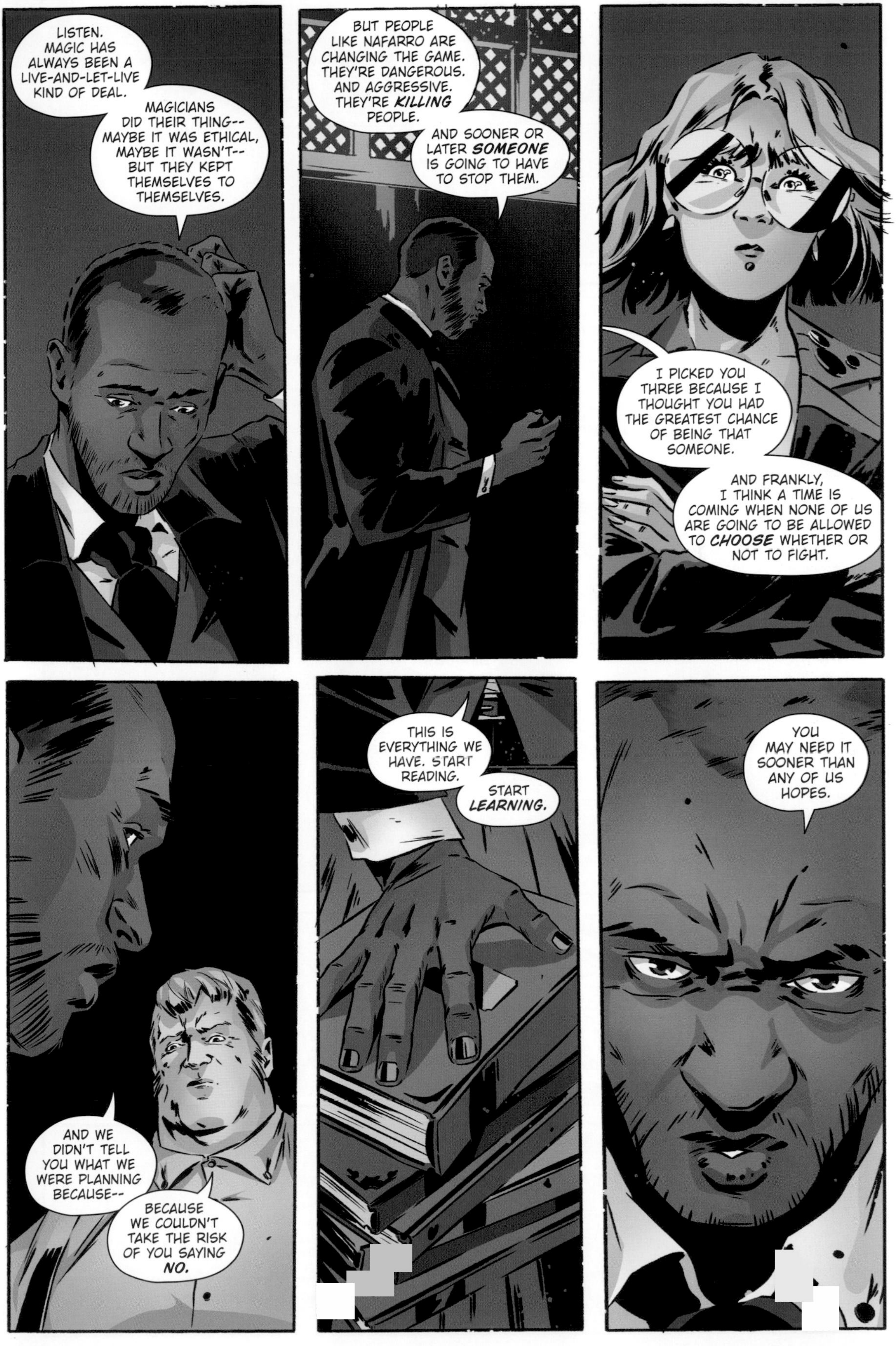
LISTEN. MAGIC HAS ALWAYS BEEN A LIVE-AND-LET-LIVE KIND OF DEAL.
MAGICIANS DID THEIR THING-- MAYBE IT WAS ETHICAL, MAYBE IT WASN'T-- BUT THEY KEPT THEMSELVES TO THEMSELVES.
BUT PEOPLE LIKE NAFARRO ARE CHANGING THE GAME. THEY'RE DANGEROUS. AND AGGRESSIVE. THEY'RE *KILLING* PEOPLE.
AND SOONER OR LATER *SOMEONE* IS GOING TO HAVE TO STOP THEM.
I PICKED YOU THREE BECAUSE I THOUGHT YOU HAD THE GREATEST CHANCE OF BEING THAT SOMEONE.
AND FRANKLY, I THINK A TIME IS COMING WHEN NONE OF US ARE GOING TO BE ALLOWED TO *CHOOSE* WHETHER OR NOT TO FIGHT.
AND WE DIDN'T TELL YOU WHAT WE WERE PLANNING BECAUSE--
BECAUSE WE COULDN'T TAKE THE RISK OF YOU SAYING *NO.*
THIS IS EVERYTHING WE HAVE. START READING.
START *LEARNING.*
YOU MAY NEED IT SOONER THAN ANY OF US HOPES.

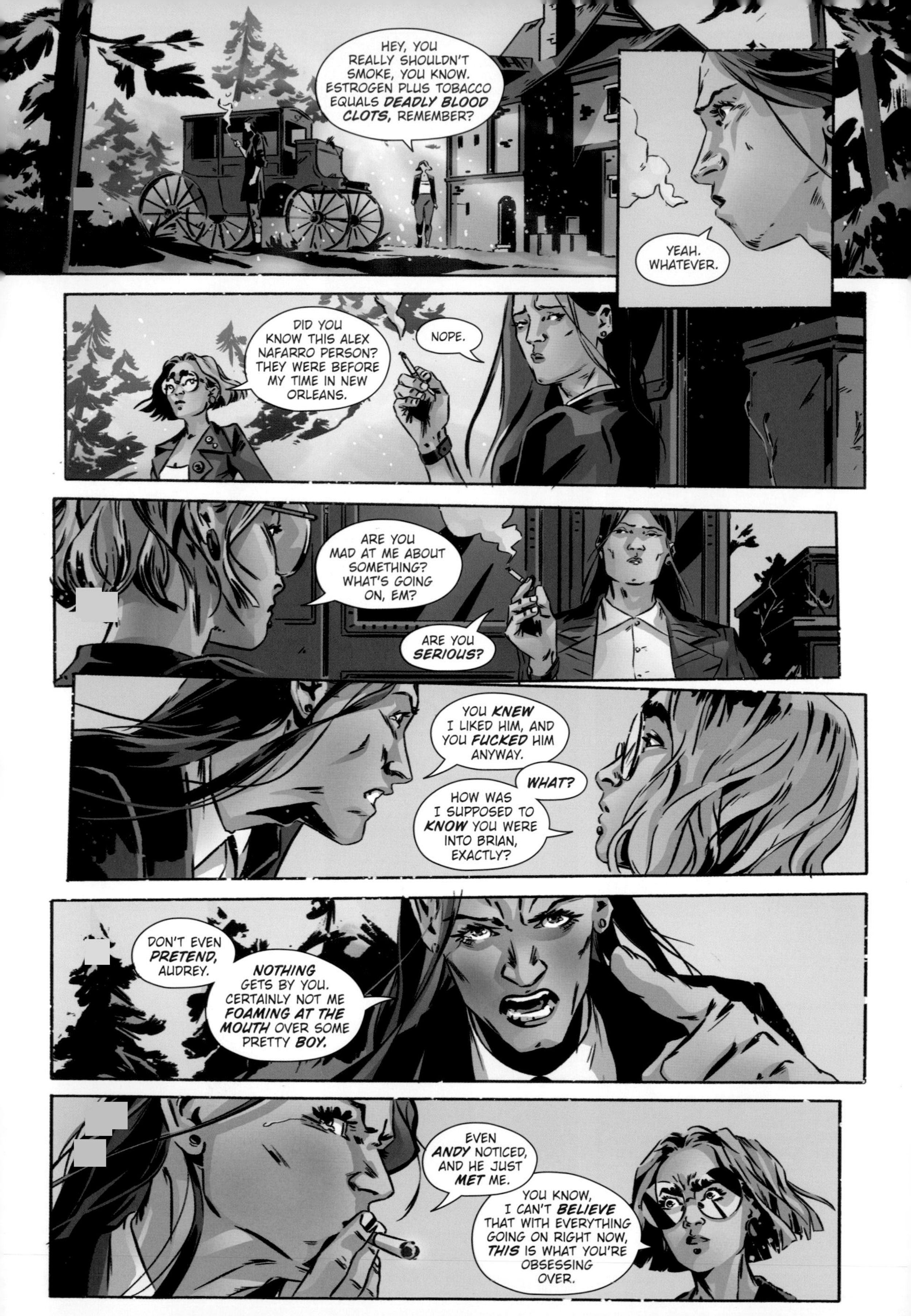
HEY, YOU REALLY SHOULDN'T SMOKE, YOU KNOW. ESTROGEN PLUS TOBACCO EQUALS DEADLY BLOOD CLOTS, REMEMBER?
YEAH. WHATEVER.
DID YOU KNOW THIS ALEX NAFARRO PERSON? THEY WERE BEFORE MY TIME IN NEW ORLEANS.
NOPE.
ARE YOU MAD AT ME ABOUT SOMETHING? WHAT'S GOING ON, EM?
ARE YOU SERIOUS?
YOU KNEW I LIKED HIM, AND YOU FUCKED HIM ANYWAY.
WHAT?
HOW WAS I SUPPOSED TO KNOW YOU WERE INTO BRIAN, EXACTLY?
DON'T EVEN PRETEND, AUDREY.
NOTHING GETS BY YOU. CERTAINLY NOT ME FOAMING AT THE MOUTH OVER SOME PRETTY BOY.
EVEN ANDY NOTICED, AND HE JUST MET ME.
YOU KNOW, I CAN'T BELIEVE THAT WITH EVERYTHING GOING ON RIGHT NOW, THIS IS WHAT YOU'RE OBSESSING OVER.

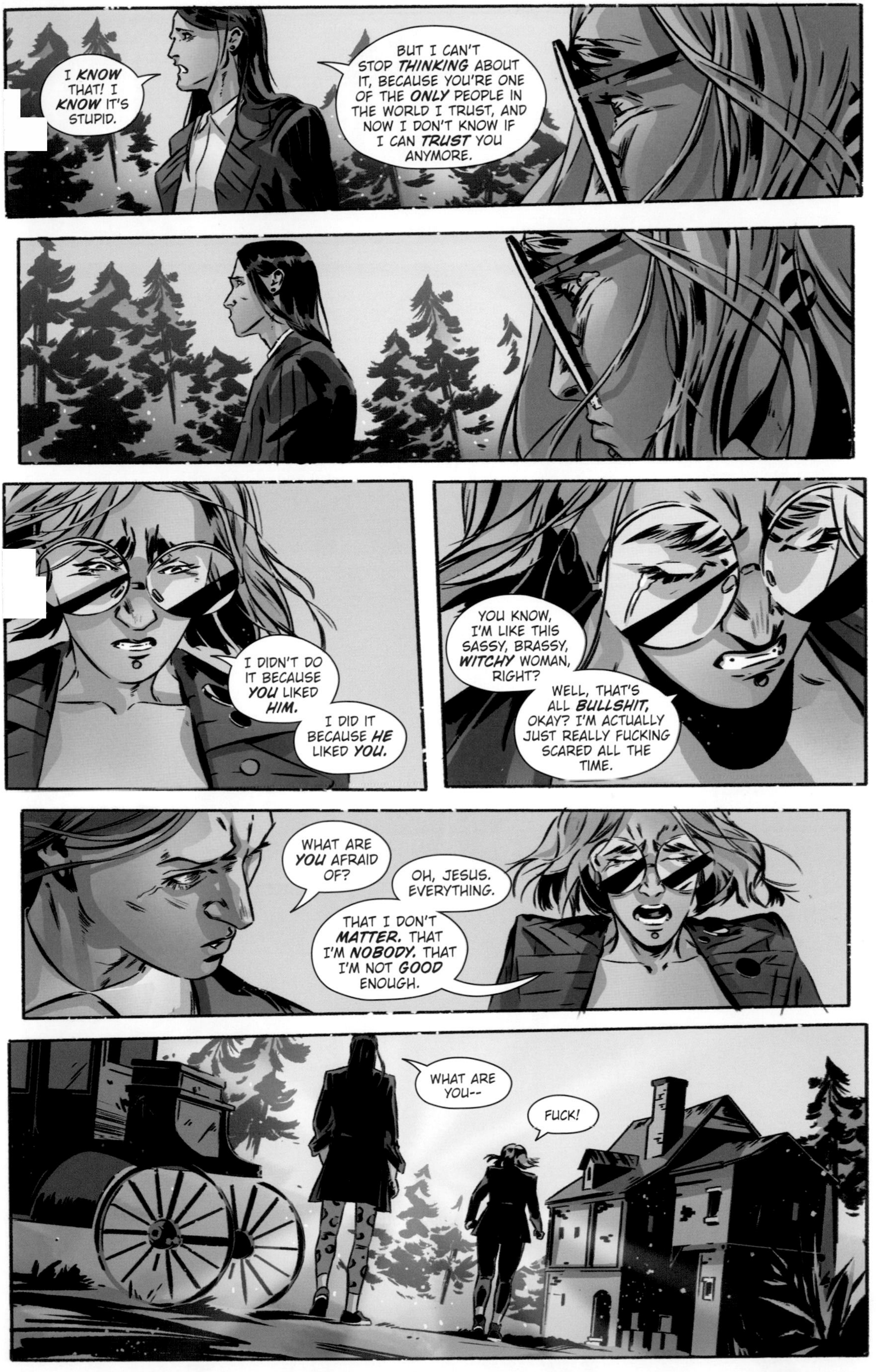

I KNOW THAT! I KNOW IT'S STUPID.
BUT I CAN'T STOP THINKING ABOUT IT, BECAUSE YOU'RE ONE OF THE ONLY PEOPLE IN THE WORLD I TRUST, AND NOW I DON'T KNOW IF I CAN TRUST YOU ANYMORE.
I DIDN'T DO IT BECAUSE YOU LIKED HIM.
I DID IT BECAUSE HE LIKED YOU.
YOU KNOW, I'M LIKE THIS SASSY, BRASSY, WITCHY WOMAN, RIGHT?
WELL, THAT'S ALL BULLSHIT, OKAY? I'M ACTUALLY JUST REALLY FUCKING SCARED ALL THE TIME.
WHAT ARE YOU AFRAID OF?
OH, JESUS. EVERYTHING.
THAT I DON'T MATTER. THAT I'M NOBODY. THAT I'M NOT GOOD ENOUGH.
WHAT ARE YOU--
FUCK!

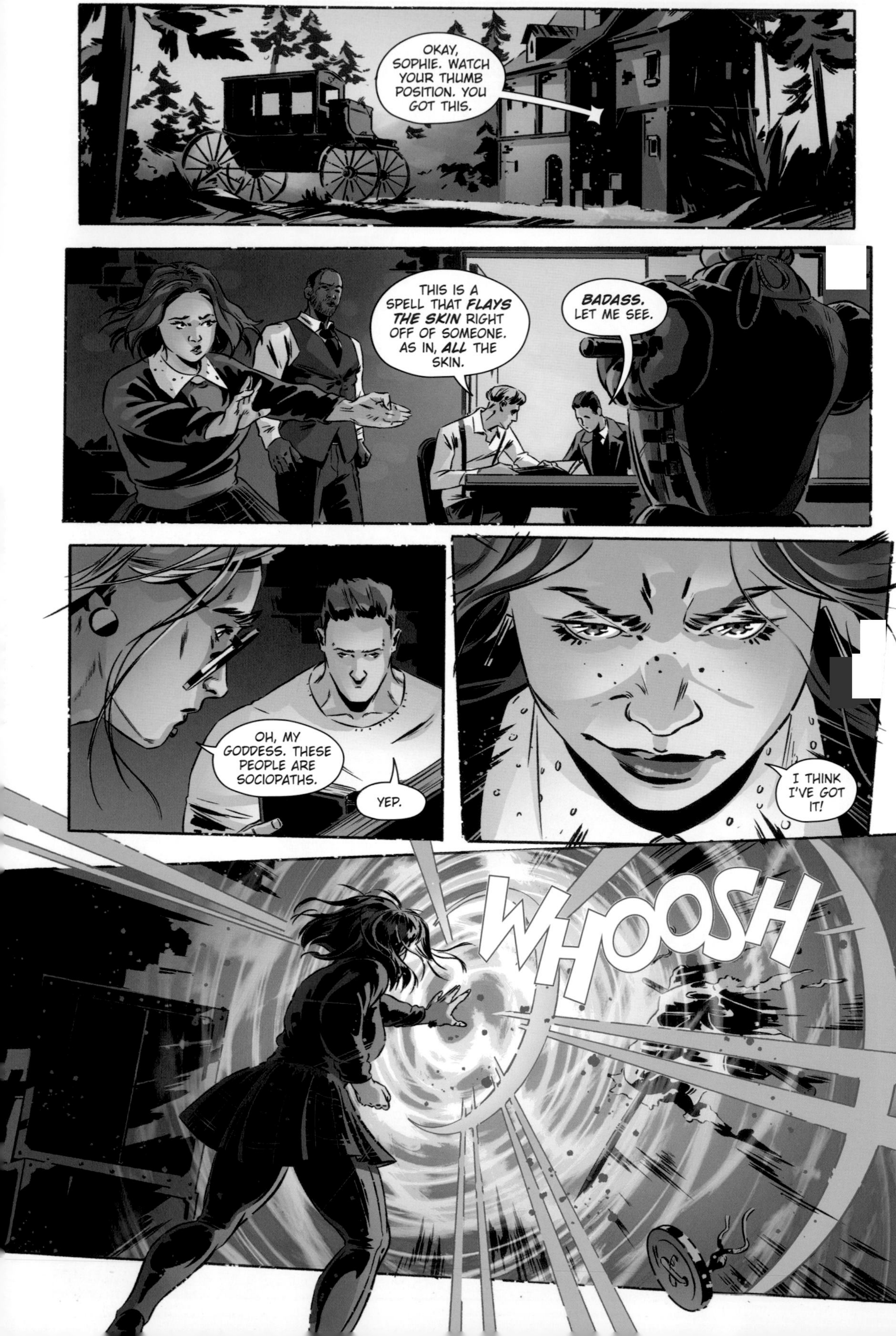

OKAY, SOPHIE. WATCH YOUR THUMB POSITION. YOU GOT THIS.
THIS IS A SPELL THAT FLAYS THE SKIN RIGHT OFF OF SOMEONE. AS IN, ALL THE SKIN.
BADASS. LET ME SEE.
OH, MY GODDESS. THESE PEOPLE ARE SOCIOPATHS.
YEP.
I THINK I'VE GOT IT!
WHOOSH

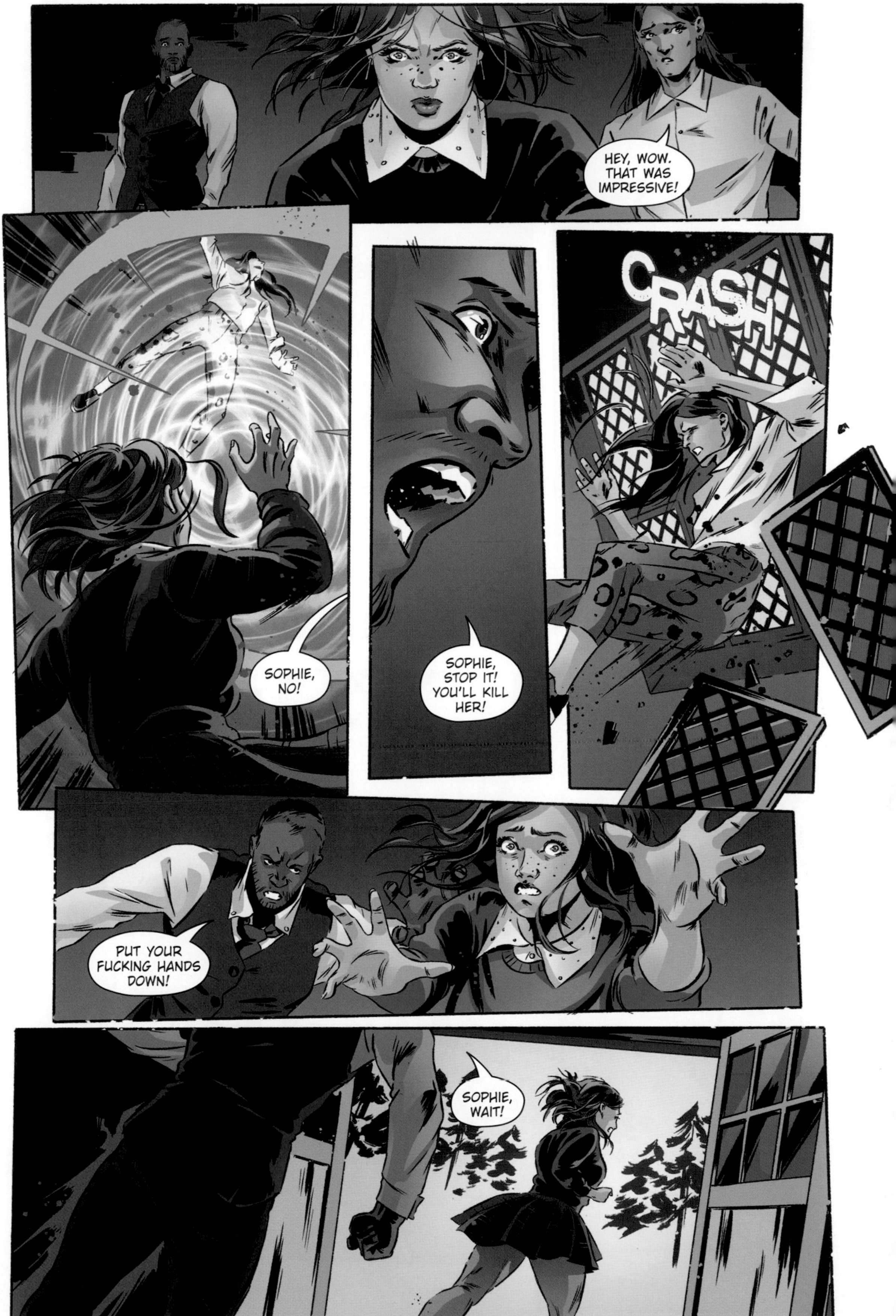
HEY, WOW. THAT WAS IMPRESSIVE!
SOPHIE, NO!
SOPHIE, STOP IT! YOU'LL KILL HER!
CRASH!
PUT YOUR FUCKING HANDS DOWN!
SOPHIE, WAIT!

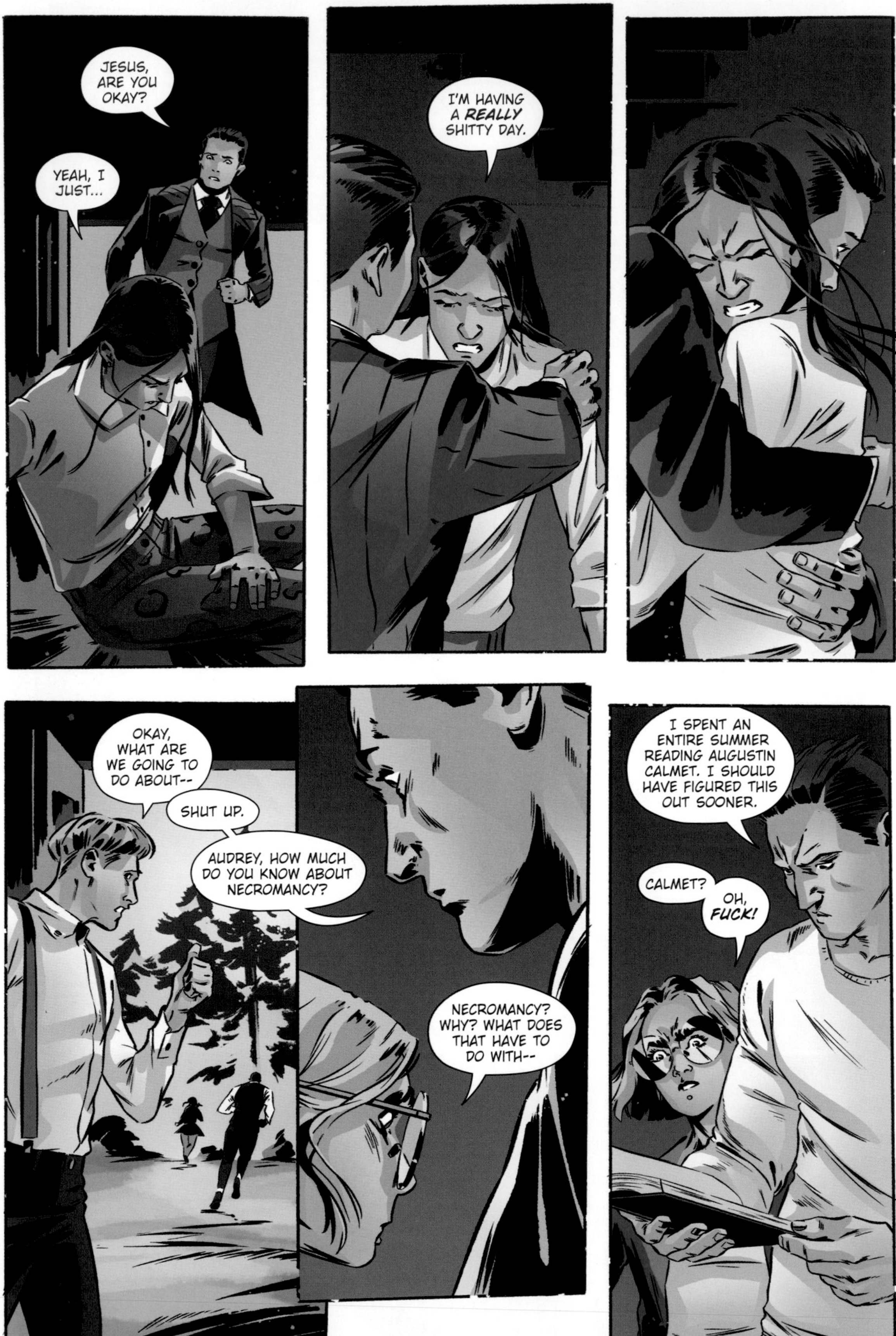
JESUS, ARE YOU OKAY?
YEAH, I JUST...
I'M HAVING A *REALLY* SHITTY DAY.
OKAY, WHAT ARE WE GOING TO DO ABOUT--
SHUT UP.
AUDREY, HOW MUCH DO YOU KNOW ABOUT NECROMANCY?
NECROMANCY? WHY? WHAT DOES THAT HAVE TO DO WITH--
I SPENT AN ENTIRE SUMMER READING AUGUSTIN CALMET. I SHOULD HAVE FIGURED THIS OUT SOONER.
CALMET?
OH, *FUCK!*

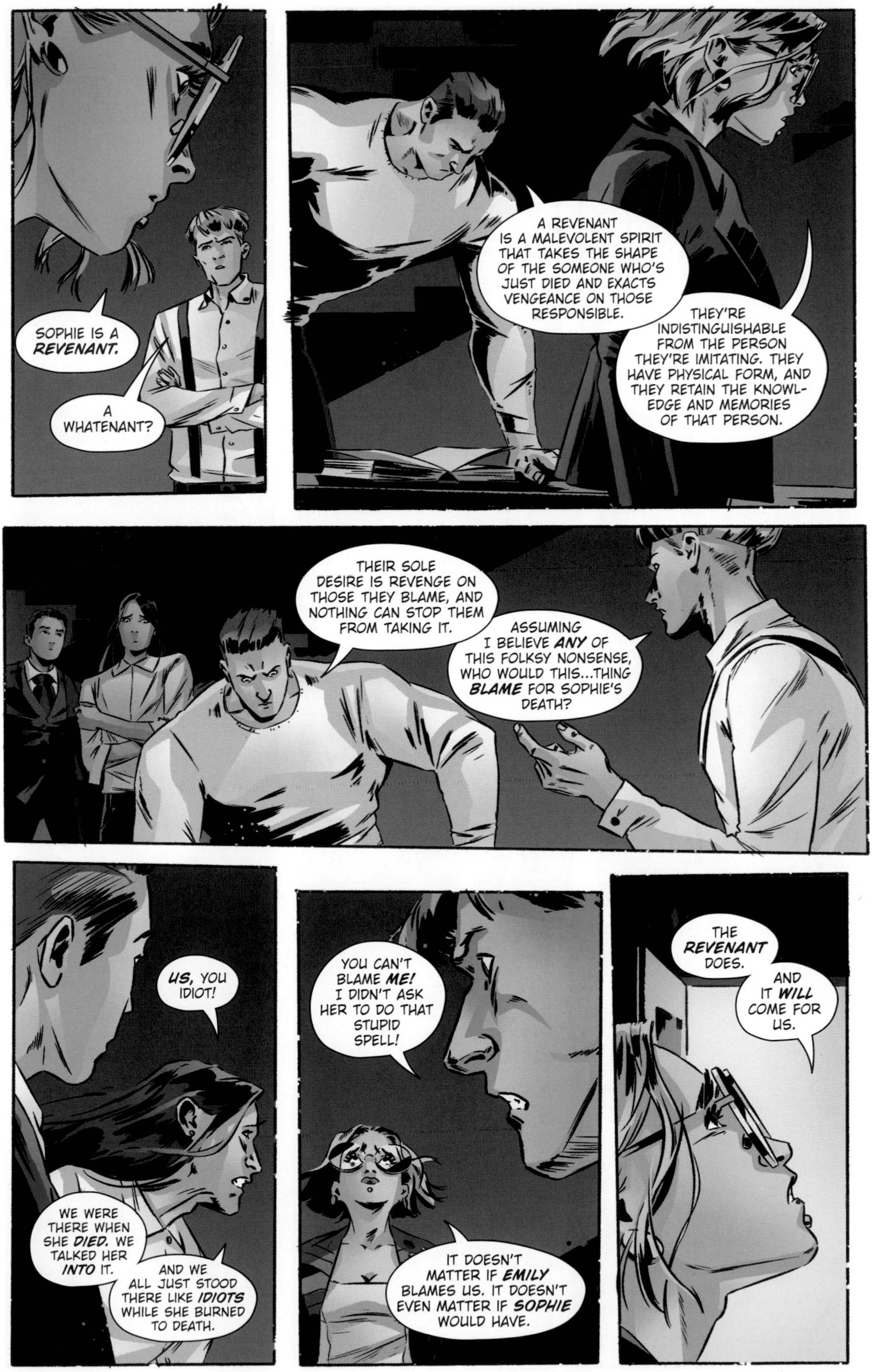

SOPHIE IS A *REVENANT.*
A WHATENANT?
A REVENANT IS A MALEVOLENT SPIRIT THAT TAKES THE SHAPE OF THE SOMEONE WHO'S JUST DIED AND EXACTS VENGEANCE ON THOSE RESPONSIBLE.
THEY'RE INDISTINGUISHABLE FROM THE PERSON THEY'RE IMITATING. THEY HAVE PHYSICAL FORM, AND THEY RETAIN THE KNOWL-EDGE AND MEMORIES OF THAT PERSON.
THEIR SOLE DESIRE IS REVENGE ON THOSE THEY BLAME, AND NOTHING CAN STOP THEM FROM TAKING IT.
ASSUMING I BELIEVE *ANY* OF THIS FOLKSY NONSENSE, WHO WOULD THIS...THING *BLAME* FOR SOPHIE'S DEATH?
US, YOU IDIOT!
WE WERE THERE WHEN SHE *DIED.* WE TALKED HER *INTO* IT.
AND WE ALL JUST STOOD THERE LIKE *IDIOTS* WHILE SHE BURNED TO DEATH.
YOU CAN'T BLAME *ME!* I DIDN'T ASK HER TO DO THAT STUPID SPELL!
IT DOESN'T MATTER IF *EMILY* BLAMES US. IT DOESN'T EVEN MATTER IF *SOPHIE* WOULD HAVE.
THE *REVENANT* DOES.
AND IT *WILL* COME FOR US.

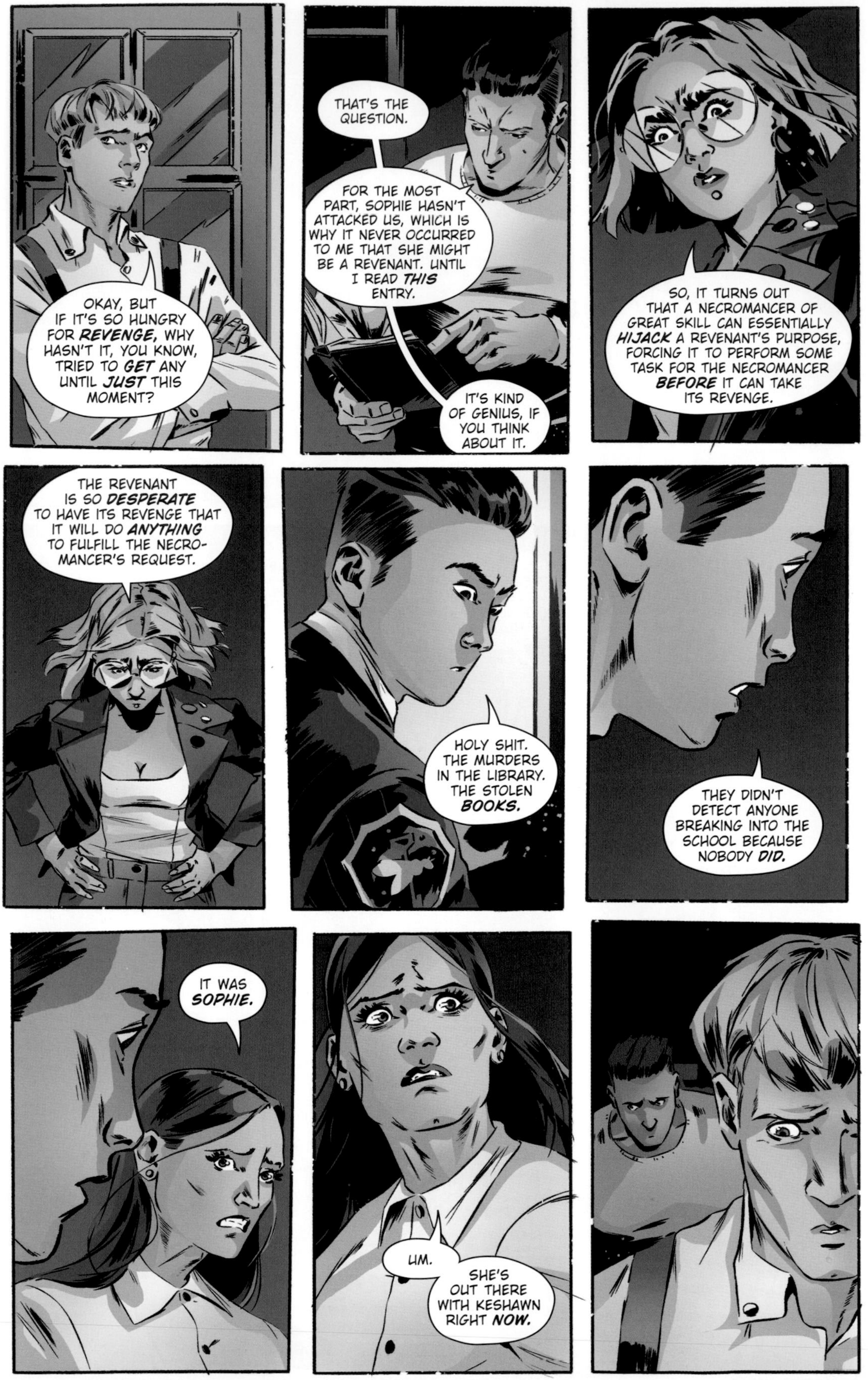
OKAY, BUT IF IT'S SO HUNGRY FOR REVENGE, WHY HASN'T IT, YOU KNOW, TRIED TO GET ANY UNTIL JUST THIS MOMENT?
THAT'S THE QUESTION.
FOR THE MOST PART, SOPHIE HASN'T ATTACKED US, WHICH IS WHY IT NEVER OCCURRED TO ME THAT SHE MIGHT BE A REVENANT. UNTIL I READ THIS ENTRY.
IT'S KIND OF GENIUS, IF YOU THINK ABOUT IT.
SO, IT TURNS OUT THAT A NECROMANCER OF GREAT SKILL CAN ESSENTIALLY HIJACK A REVENANT'S PURPOSE, FORCING IT TO PERFORM SOME TASK FOR THE NECROMANCER BEFORE IT CAN TAKE ITS REVENGE.
THE REVENANT IS SO DESPERATE TO HAVE ITS REVENGE THAT IT WILL DO ANYTHING TO FULFILL THE NECROMANCER'S REQUEST.
HOLY SHIT. THE MURDERS IN THE LIBRARY. THE STOLEN BOOKS.
THEY DIDN'T DETECT ANYONE BREAKING INTO THE SCHOOL BECAUSE NOBODY DID.
IT WAS SOPHIE.
UM.
SHE'S OUT THERE WITH KESHAWN RIGHT NOW.

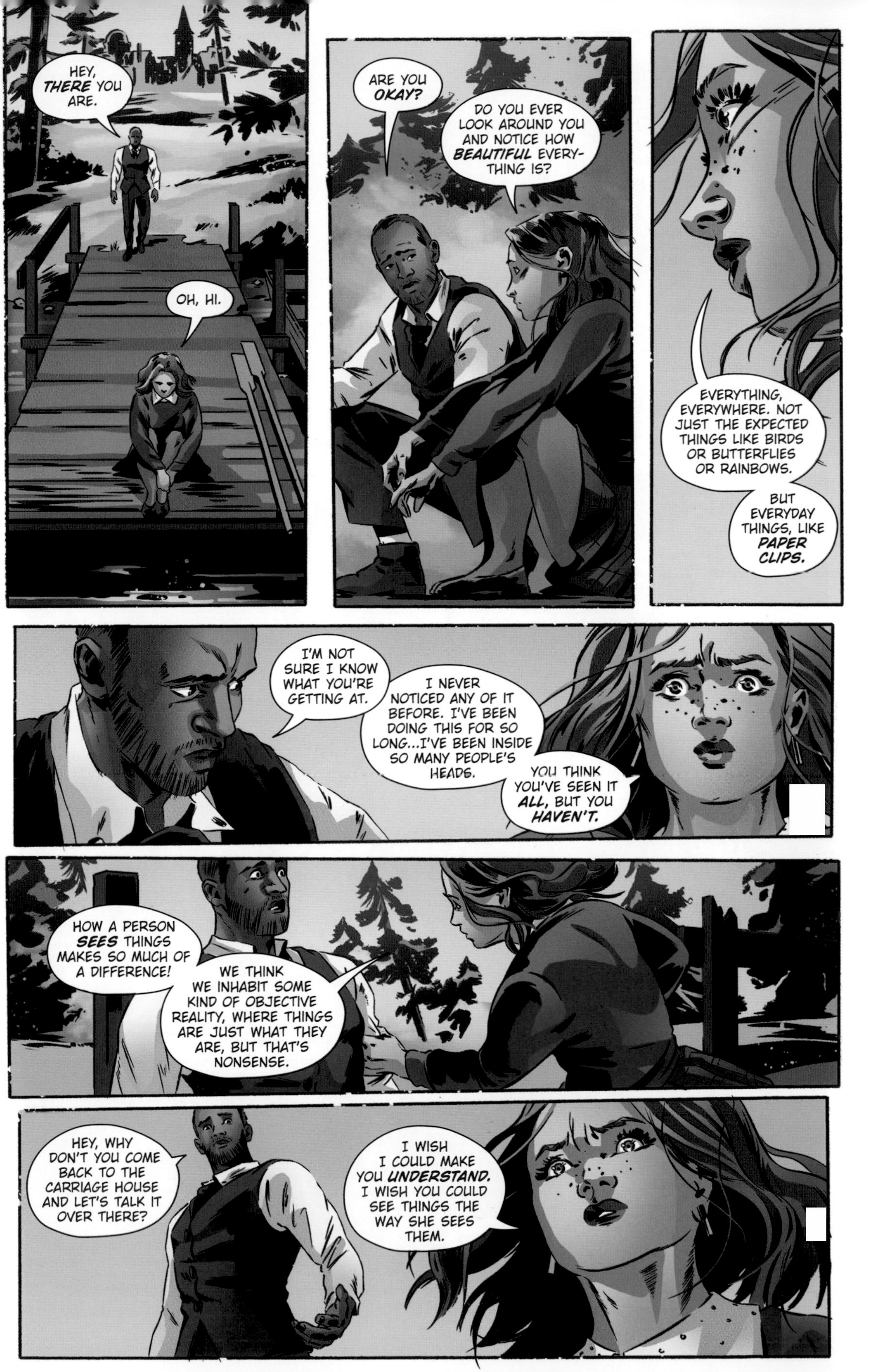

HEY, THERE YOU ARE.
OH, HI.
ARE YOU OKAY?
DO YOU EVER LOOK AROUND YOU AND NOTICE HOW BEAUTIFUL EVERY-THING IS?
EVERYTHING, EVERYWHERE. NOT JUST THE EXPECTED THINGS LIKE BIRDS OR BUTTERFLIES OR RAINBOWS.
BUT EVERYDAY THINGS, LIKE PAPER CLIPS.
I'M NOT SURE I KNOW WHAT YOU'RE GETTING AT.
I NEVER NOTICED ANY OF IT BEFORE. I'VE BEEN DOING THIS FOR SO LONG...I'VE BEEN INSIDE SO MANY PEOPLE'S HEADS.
YOU THINK YOU'VE SEEN IT ALL, BUT YOU HAVEN'T.
HOW A PERSON SEES THINGS MAKES SO MUCH OF A DIFFERENCE!
WE THINK WE INHABIT SOME KIND OF OBJECTIVE REALITY, WHERE THINGS ARE JUST WHAT THEY ARE, BUT THAT'S NONSENSE.
HEY, WHY DON'T YOU COME BACK TO THE CARRIAGE HOUSE AND LET'S TALK IT OVER THERE?
I WISH I COULD MAKE YOU UNDERSTAND. I WISH YOU COULD SEE THINGS THE WAY SHE SEES THEM.

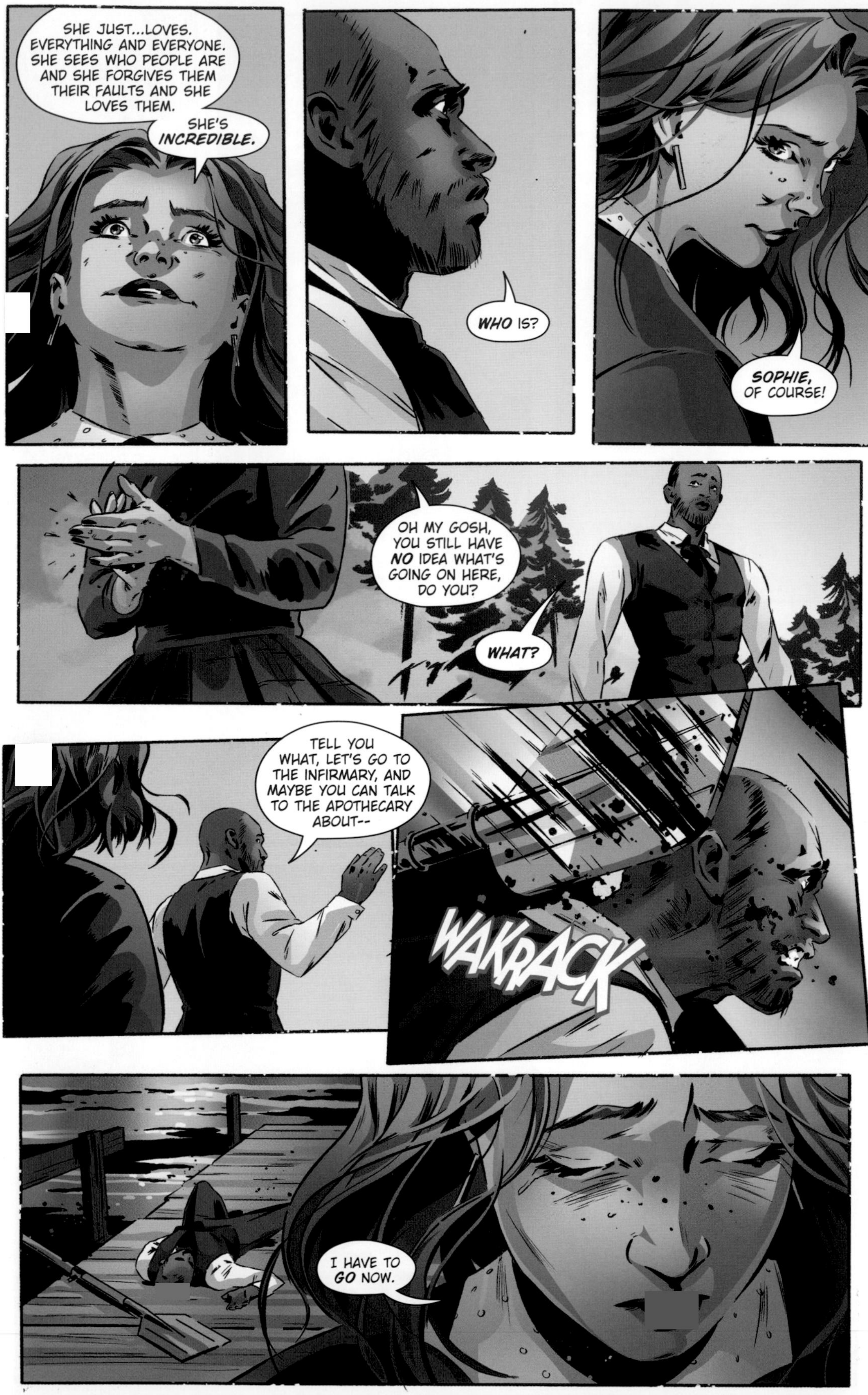
SHE JUST...LOVES. EVERYTHING AND EVERYONE. SHE SEES WHO PEOPLE ARE AND SHE FORGIVES THEM THEIR FAULTS AND SHE LOVES THEM.
SHE'S INCREDIBLE.
WHO IS?
SOPHIE, OF COURSE!
OH MY GOSH, YOU STILL HAVE NO IDEA WHAT'S GOING ON HERE, DO YOU?
WHAT?
TELL YOU WHAT, LET'S GO TO THE INFIRMARY, AND MAYBE YOU CAN TALK TO THE APOTHECARY ABOUT--
WAKRACK
I HAVE TO GO NOW.

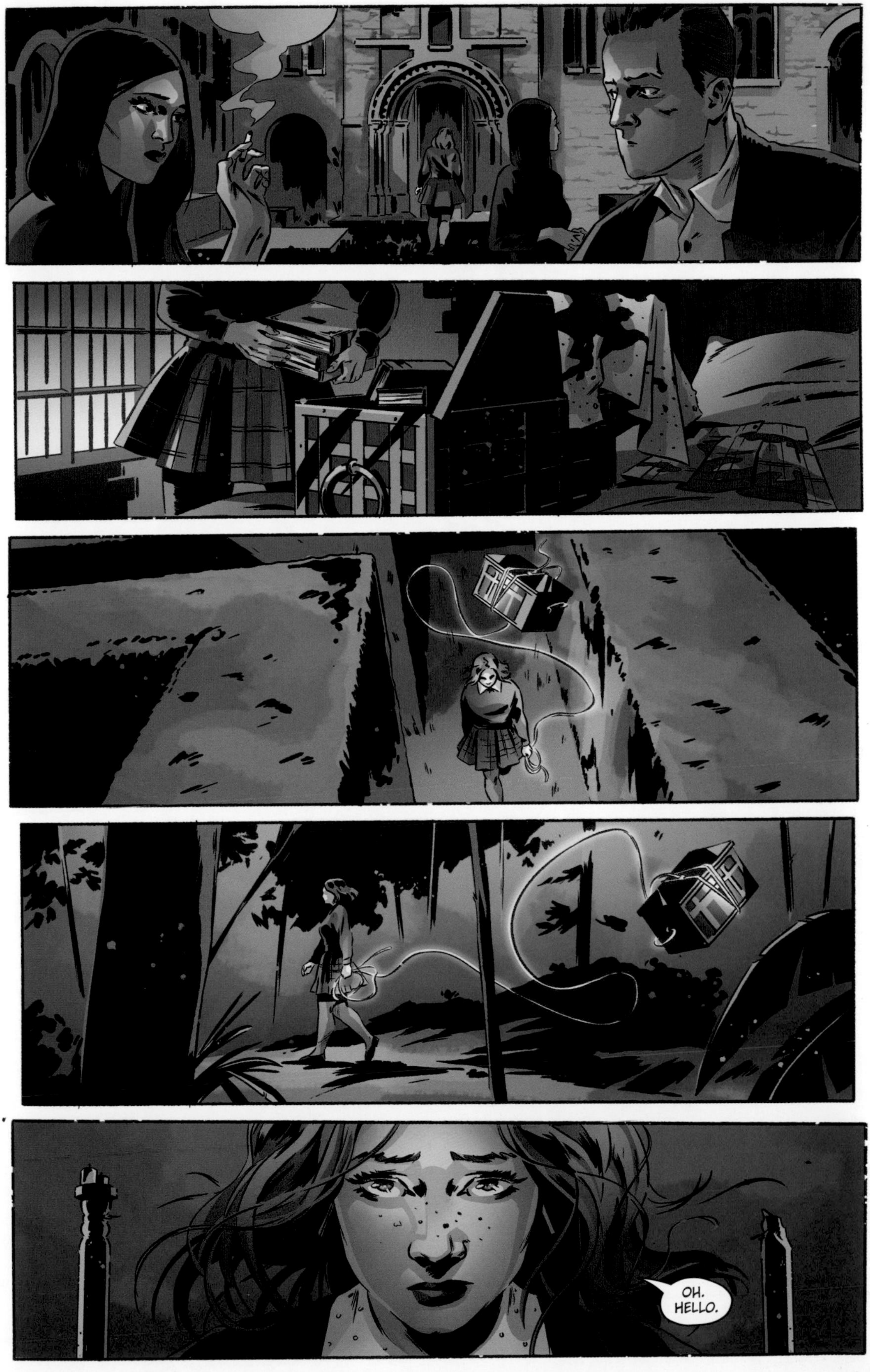
OH. HELLO.

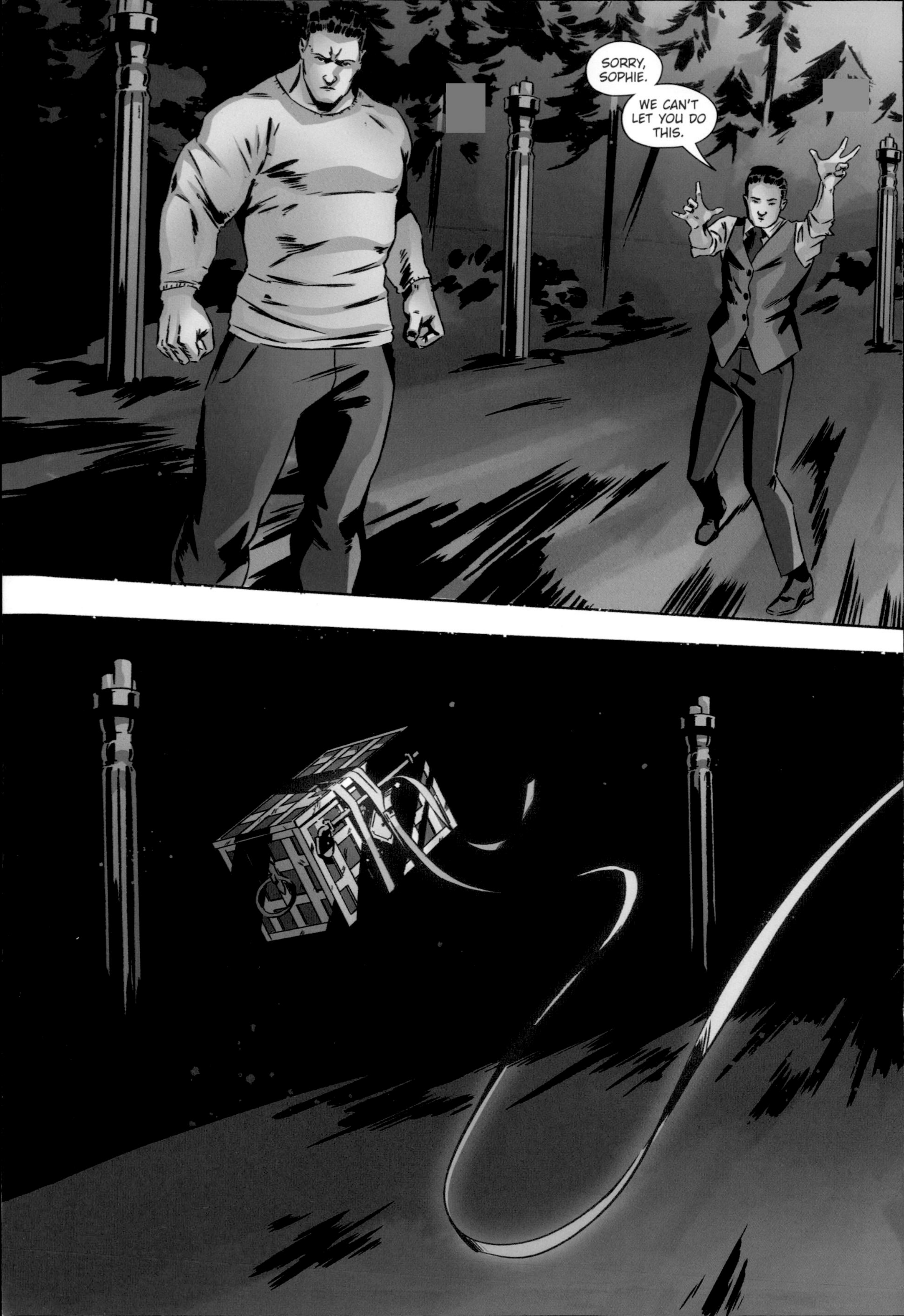
SORRY, SOPHIE.
WE CAN'T LET YOU DO THIS.

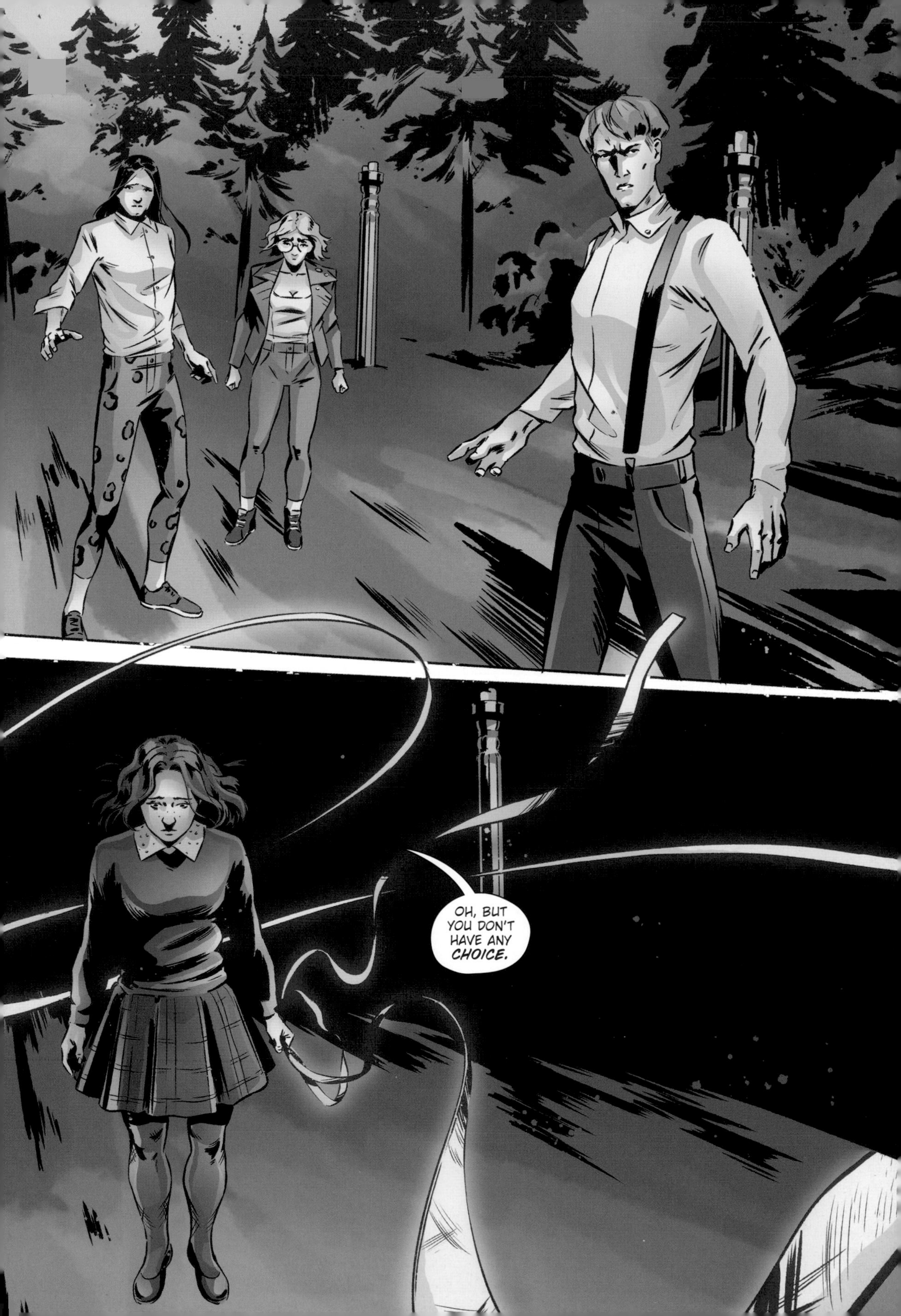
OH, BUT YOU DON'T HAVE ANY CHOICE.

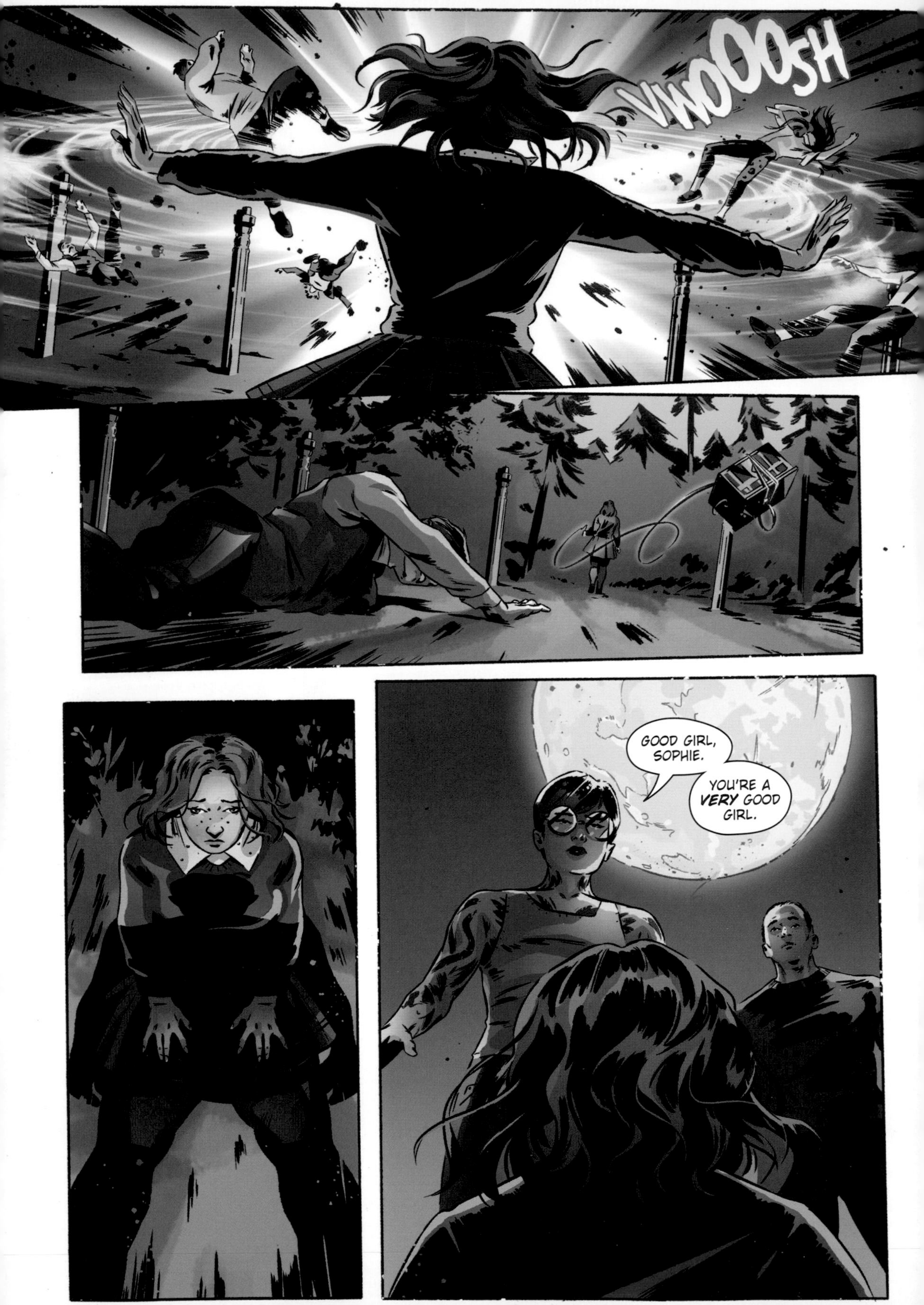
VWOOOSH
GOOD GIRL, SOPHIE.
YOU'RE A VERY GOOD GIRL.

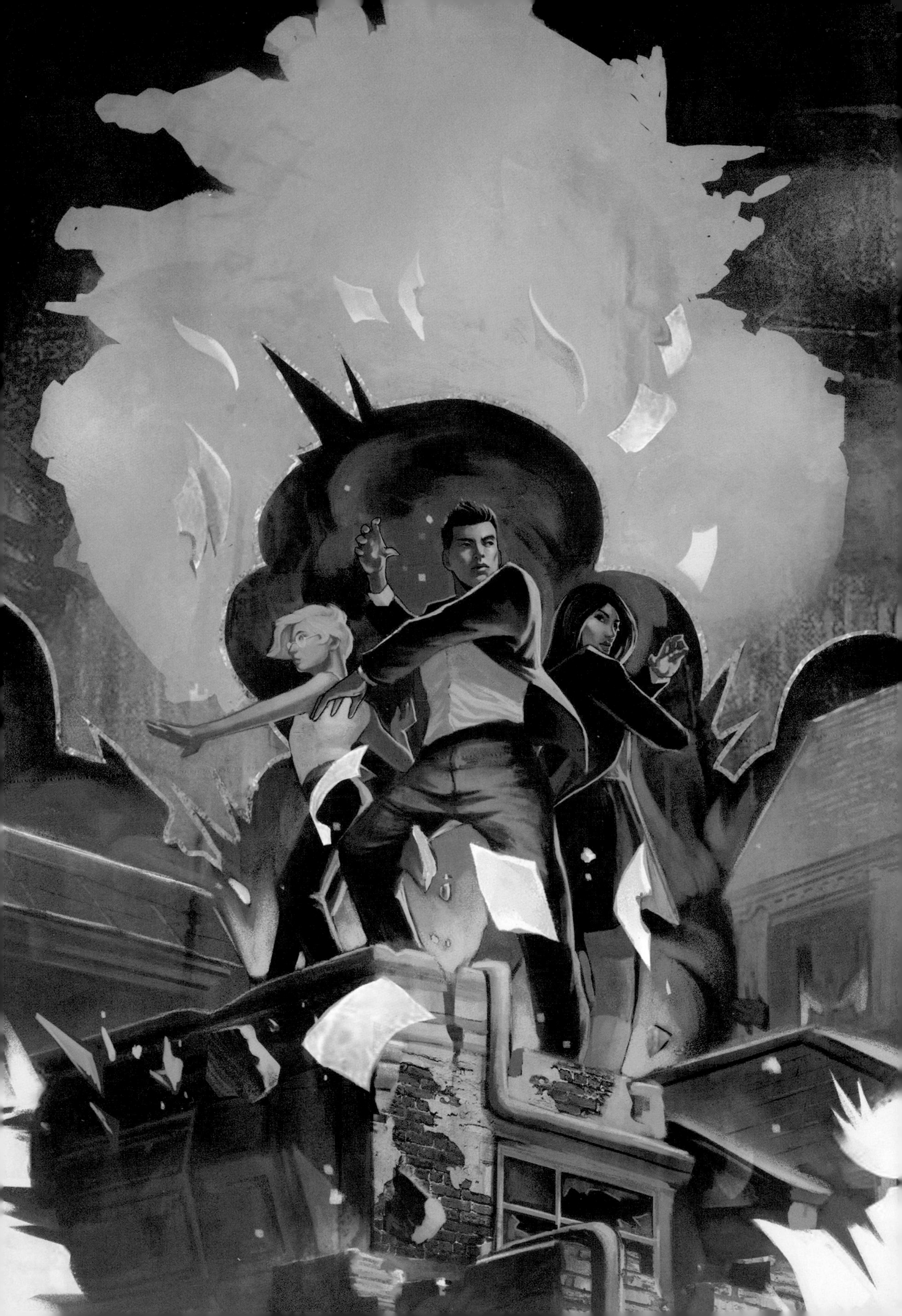

CHAPTER
FIVE

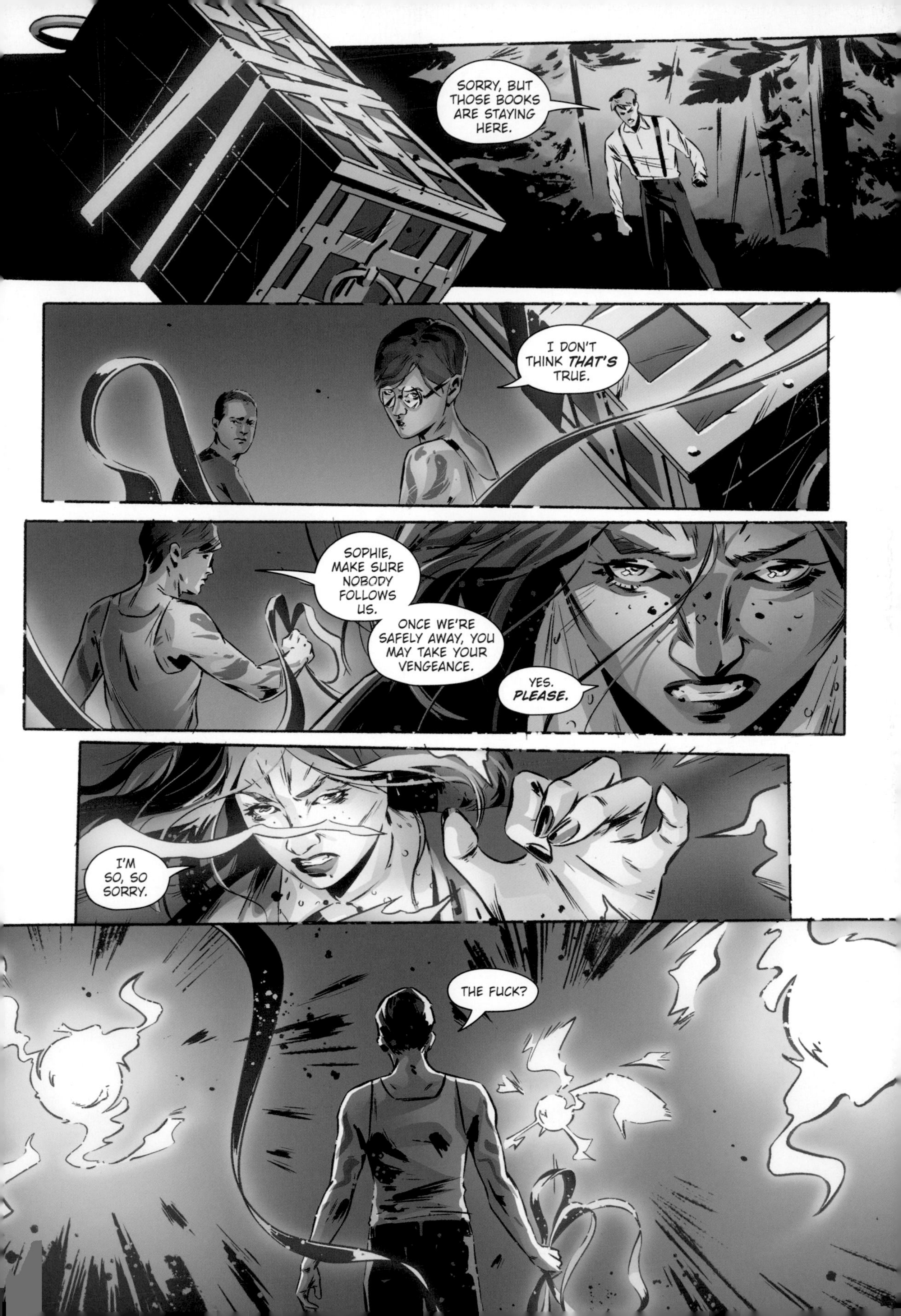
SORRY, BUT THOSE BOOKS ARE STAYING HERE.
I DON'T THINK *THAT'S* TRUE.
SOPHIE, MAKE SURE NOBODY FOLLOWS US.
ONCE WE'RE SAFELY AWAY, YOU MAY TAKE YOUR VENGEANCE.
YES. ***PLEASE.***
I'M SO, SO SORRY.
THE FUCK?

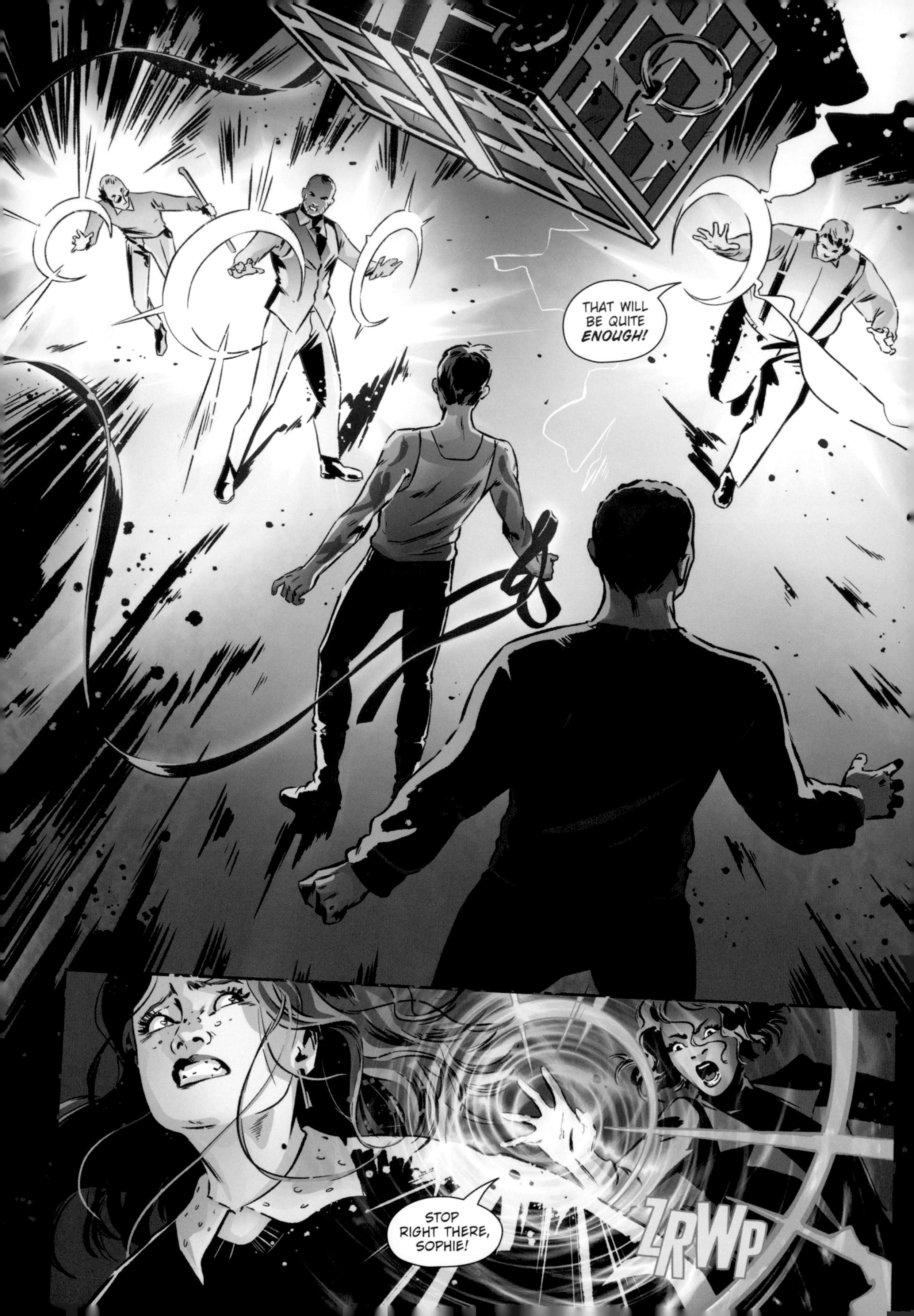
THAT WILL BE QUITE ENOUGH!
STOP RIGHT THERE, SOPHIE!
ZRWP

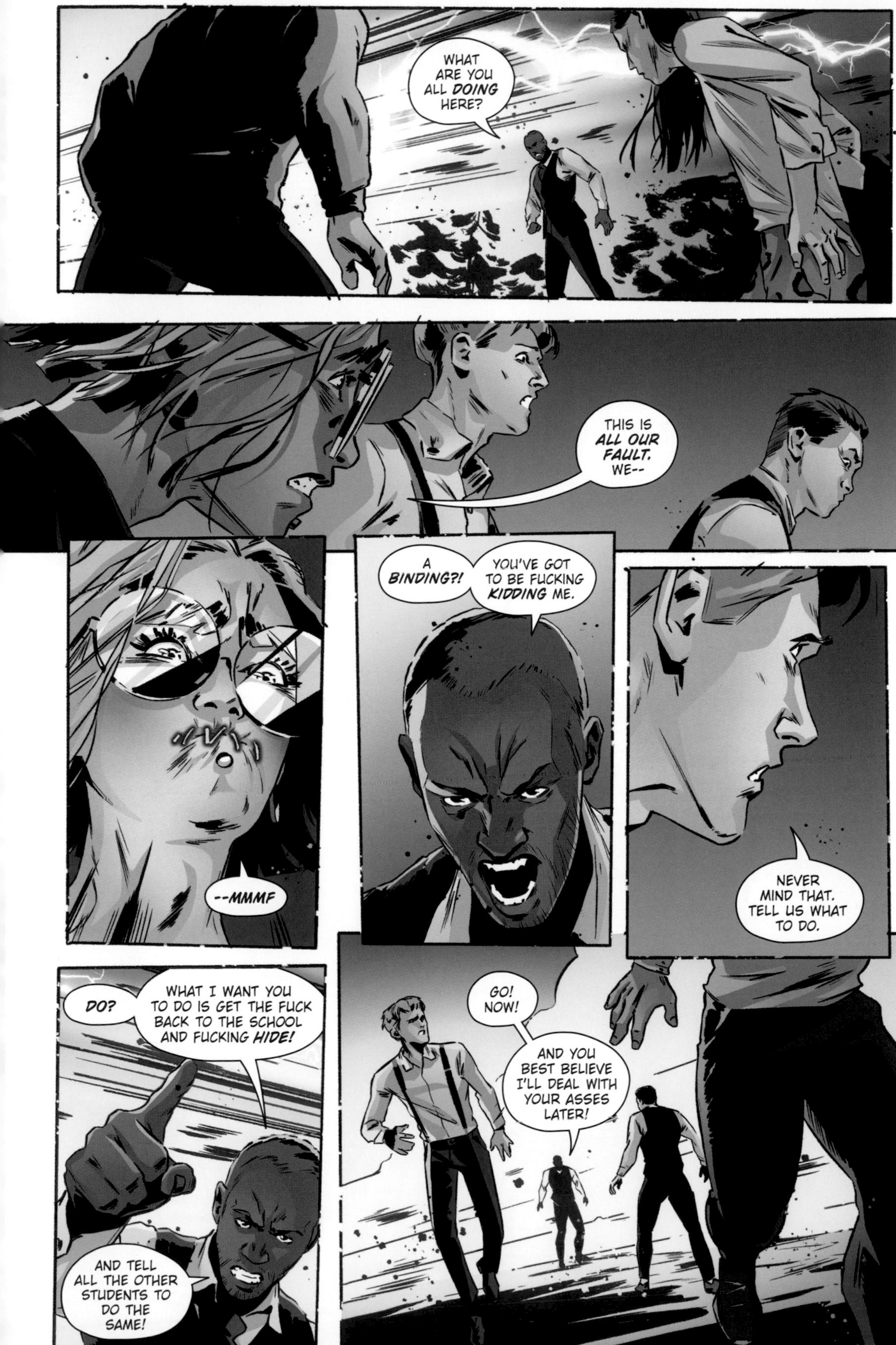
WHAT ARE YOU ALL DOING HERE?
THIS IS ALL OUR FAULT. WE--
--MMMF
A BINDING?!
YOU'VE GOT TO BE FUCKING KIDDING ME.
NEVER MIND THAT. TELL US WHAT TO DO.
DO?
WHAT I WANT YOU TO DO IS GET THE FUCK BACK TO THE SCHOOL AND FUCKING HIDE!
AND TELL ALL THE OTHER STUDENTS TO DO THE SAME!
GO! NOW!
AND YOU BEST BELIEVE I'LL DEAL WITH YOUR ASSES LATER!

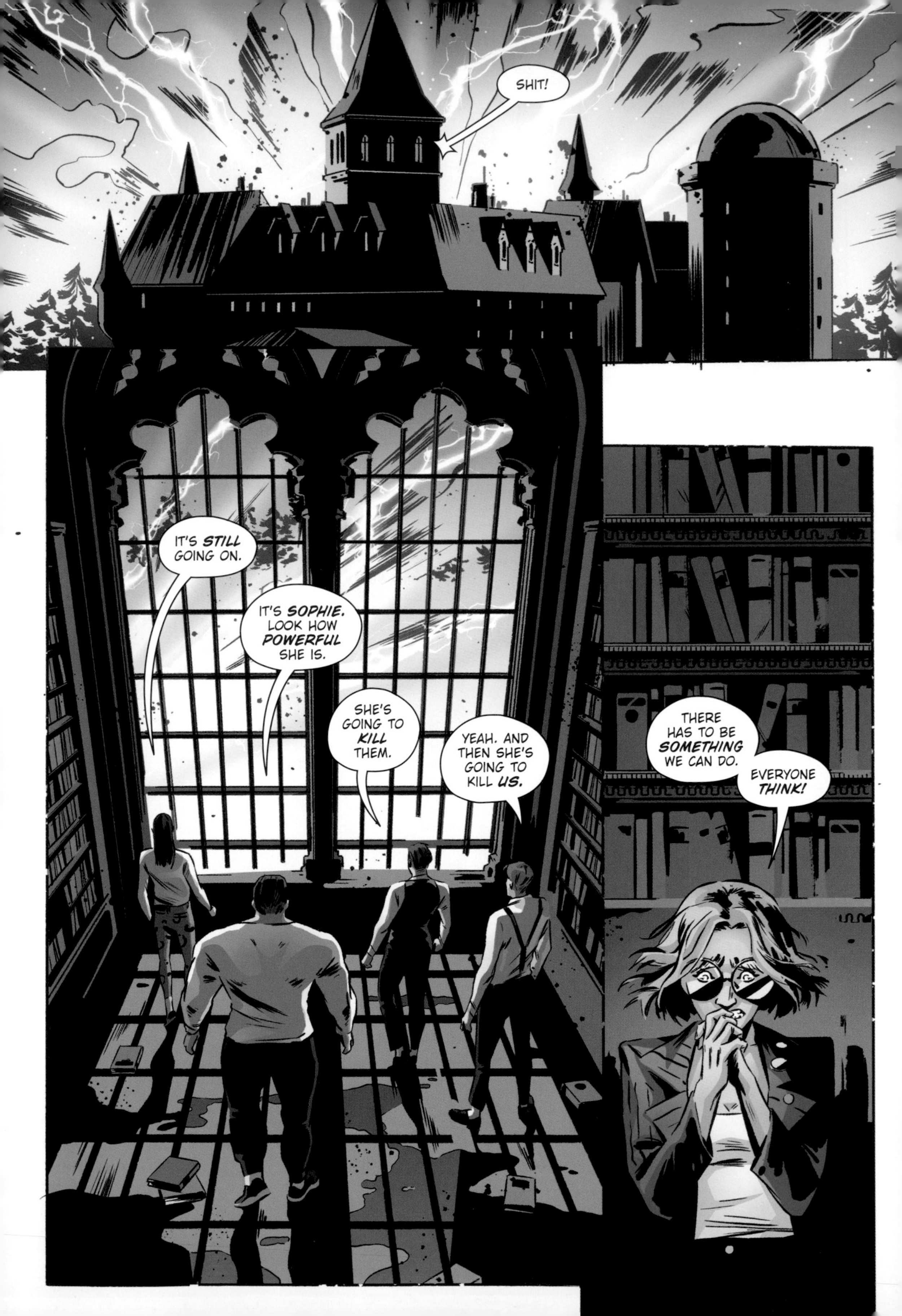
SHIT!
IT'S STILL GOING ON.
IT'S SOPHIE. LOOK HOW POWERFUL SHE IS.
SHE'S GOING TO KILL THEM.
YEAH. AND THEN SHE'S GOING TO KILL US.
THERE HAS TO BE SOMETHING WE CAN DO.
EVERYONE THINK!

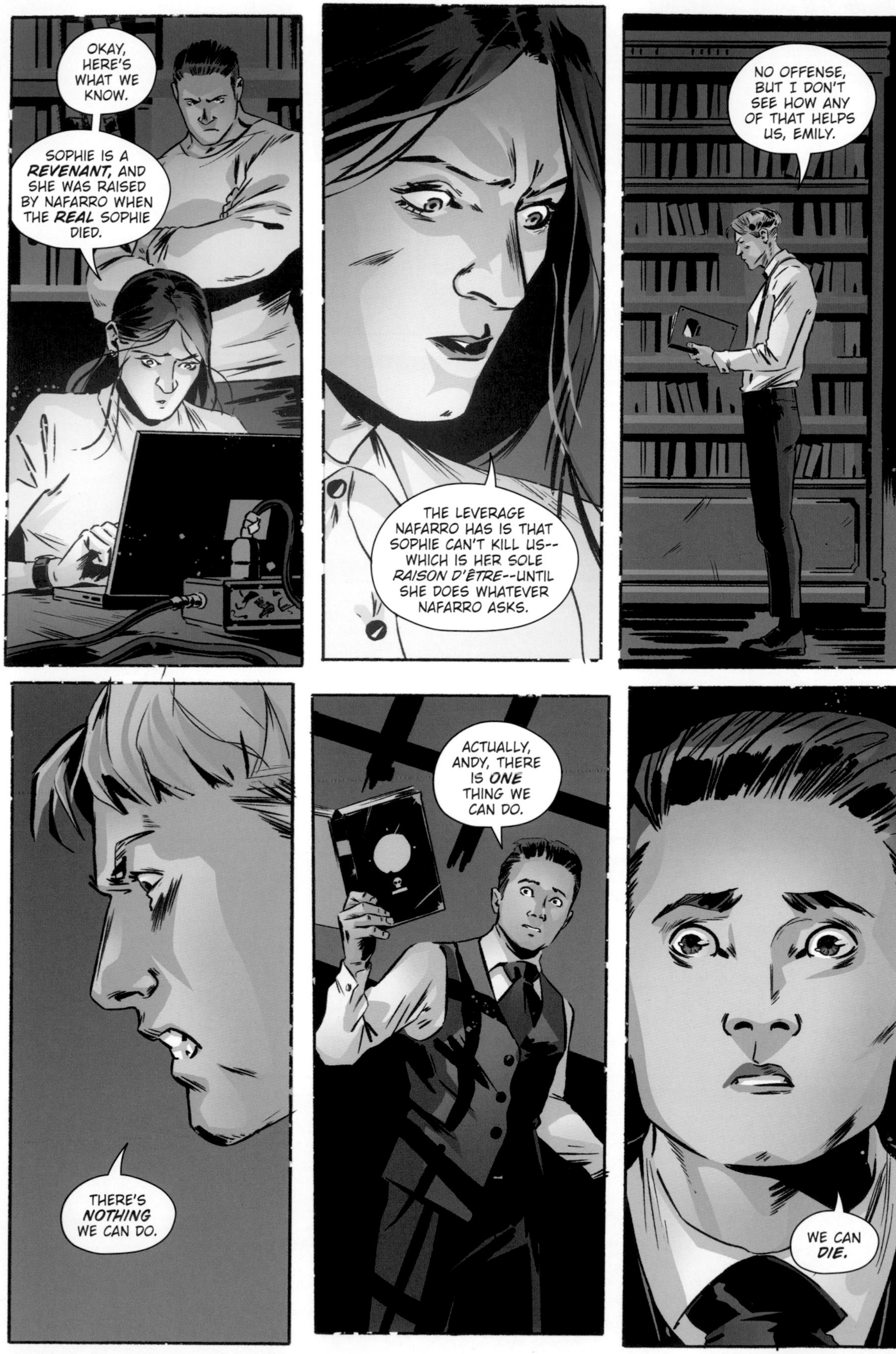
OKAY, HERE'S WHAT WE KNOW.
SOPHIE IS A ***REVENANT,*** AND SHE WAS RAISED BY NAFARRO WHEN THE ***REAL*** SOPHIE DIED.
THE LEVERAGE NAFARRO HAS IS THAT SOPHIE CAN'T KILL US--WHICH IS HER SOLE *RAISON D'ÊTRE*--UNTIL SHE DOES WHATEVER NAFARRO ASKS.
NO OFFENSE, BUT I DON'T SEE HOW ANY OF THAT HELPS US, EMILY.
THERE'S ***NOTHING*** WE CAN DO.
ACTUALLY, ANDY, THERE IS ***ONE*** THING WE CAN DO.
WE CAN ***DIE.***

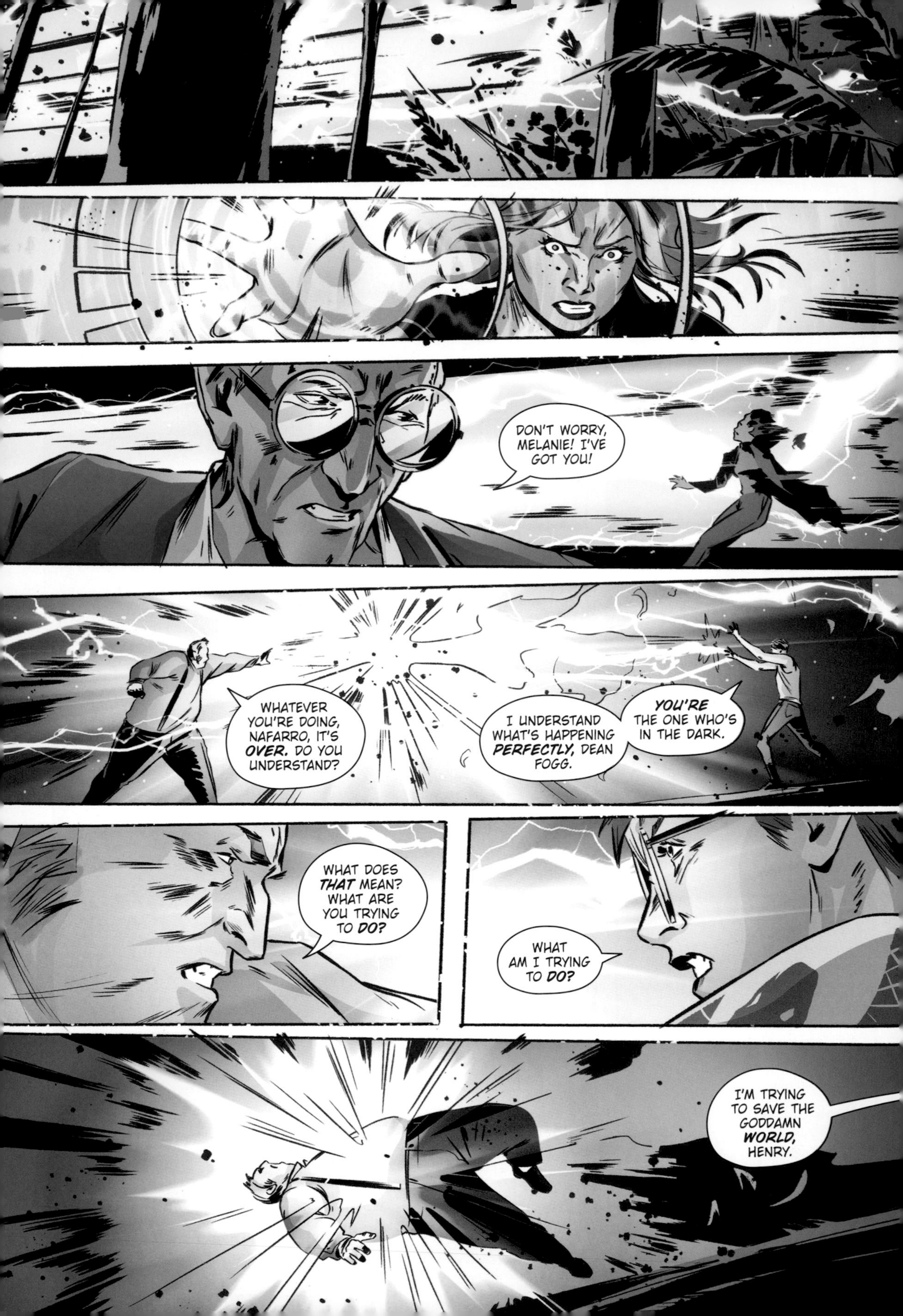
DON'T WORRY, MELANIE! I'VE GOT YOU!
WHATEVER YOU'RE DOING, NAFARRO, IT'S OVER. DO YOU UNDERSTAND?
I UNDERSTAND WHAT'S HAPPENING PERFECTLY, DEAN FOGG.
YOU'RE THE ONE WHO'S IN THE DARK.
WHAT DOES THAT MEAN? WHAT ARE YOU TRYING TO DO?
WHAT AM I TRYING TO DO?
I'M TRYING TO SAVE THE GODDAMN WORLD, HENRY.

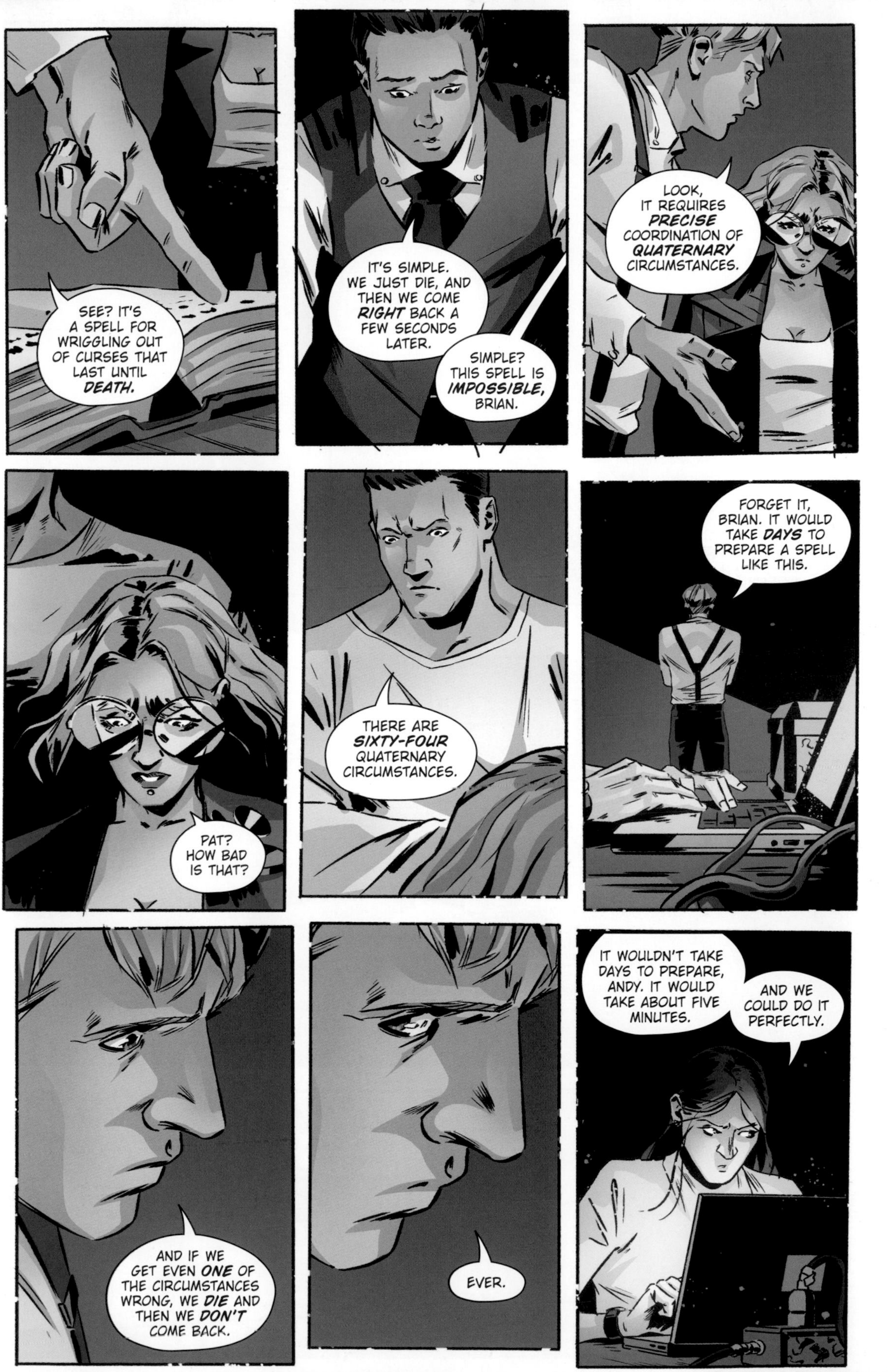
SEE? IT'S A SPELL FOR WRIGGLING OUT OF CURSES THAT LAST UNTIL ***DEATH.***
IT'S SIMPLE. WE JUST DIE, AND THEN WE COME ***RIGHT*** BACK A FEW SECONDS LATER.
SIMPLE? THIS SPELL IS ***IMPOSSIBLE,*** BRIAN.
LOOK, IT REQUIRES ***PRECISE*** COORDINATION OF ***QUATERNARY*** CIRCUMSTANCES.
PAT? HOW BAD IS THAT?
THERE ARE ***SIXTY-FOUR*** QUATERNARY CIRCUMSTANCES.
FORGET IT, BRIAN. IT WOULD TAKE ***DAYS*** TO PREPARE A SPELL LIKE THIS.
AND IF WE GET EVEN ***ONE*** OF THE CIRCUMSTANCES WRONG, WE ***DIE*** AND THEN WE ***DON'T*** COME BACK.
EVER.
IT WOULDN'T TAKE DAYS TO PREPARE, ANDY. IT WOULD TAKE ABOUT FIVE MINUTES.
AND WE COULD DO IT PERFECTLY.

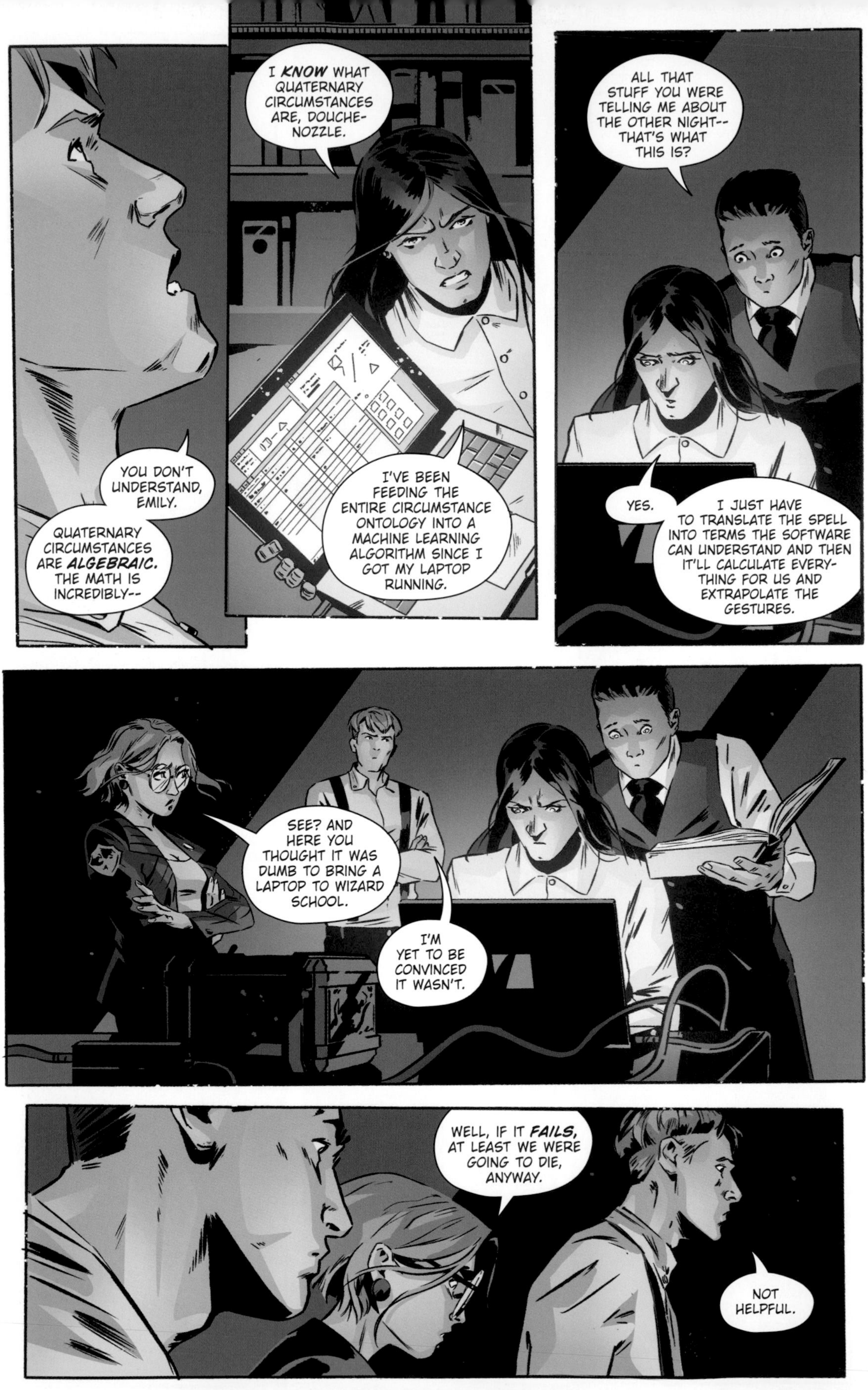

I KNOW WHAT QUATERNARY CIRCUMSTANCES ARE, DOUCHE-NOZZLE.
YOU DON'T UNDERSTAND, EMILY.
QUATERNARY CIRCUMSTANCES ARE ALGEBRAIC. THE MATH IS INCREDIBLY--
I'VE BEEN FEEDING THE ENTIRE CIRCUMSTANCE ONTOLOGY INTO A MACHINE LEARNING ALGORITHM SINCE I GOT MY LAPTOP RUNNING.
ALL THAT STUFF YOU WERE TELLING ME ABOUT THE OTHER NIGHT-- THAT'S WHAT THIS IS?
YES.
I JUST HAVE TO TRANSLATE THE SPELL INTO TERMS THE SOFTWARE CAN UNDERSTAND AND THEN IT'LL CALCULATE EVERY-THING FOR US AND EXTRAPOLATE THE GESTURES.
SEE? AND HERE YOU THOUGHT IT WAS DUMB TO BRING A LAPTOP TO WIZARD SCHOOL.
I'M YET TO BE CONVINCED IT WASN'T.
WELL, IF IT FAILS, AT LEAST WE WERE GOING TO DIE, ANYWAY.
NOT HELPFUL.

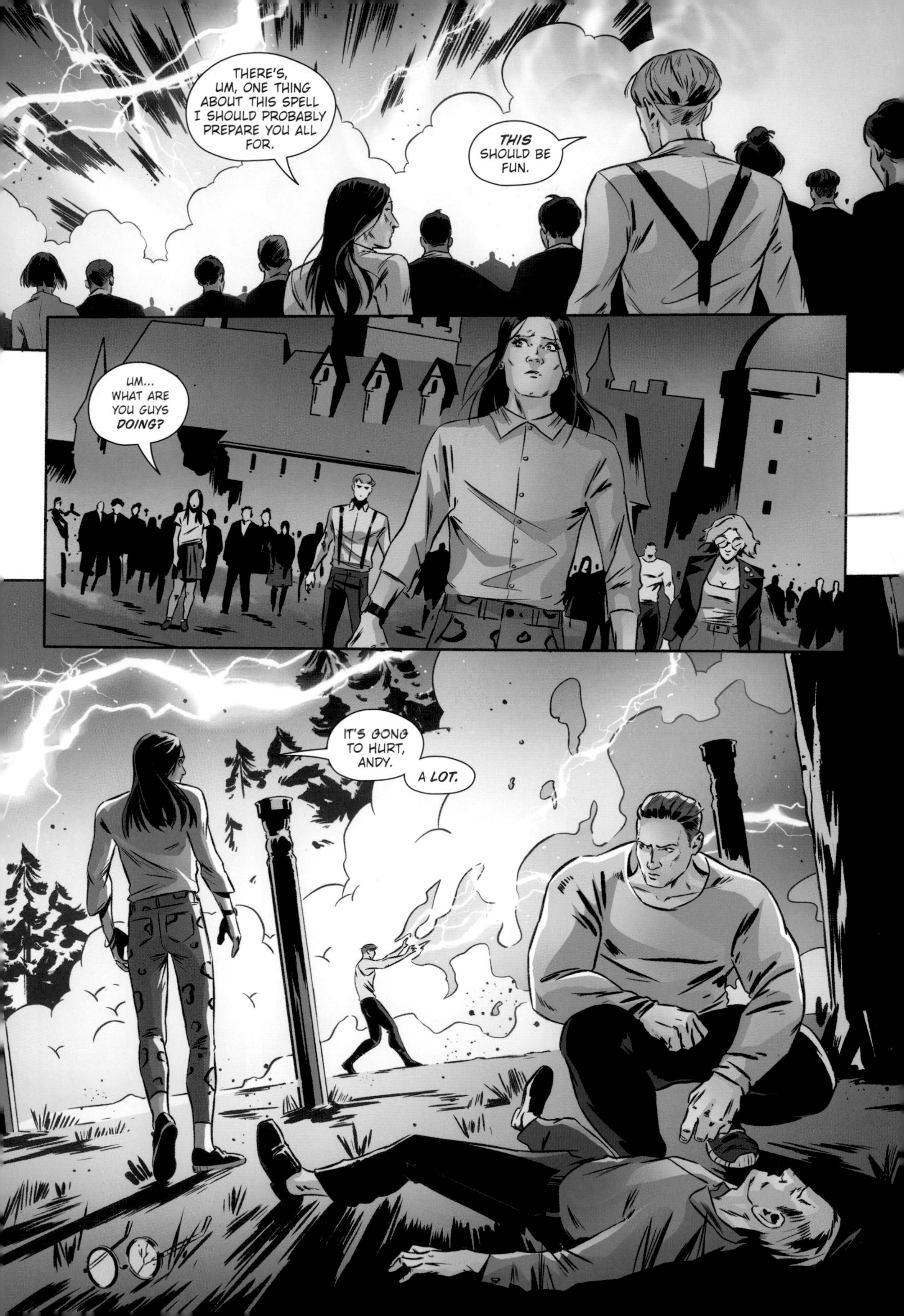

THERE'S, UM, ONE THING ABOUT THIS SPELL I SHOULD PROBABLY PREPARE YOU ALL FOR.
THIS SHOULD BE FUN.
UM... WHAT ARE YOU GUYS DOING?
IT'S GONG TO HURT, ANDY.
A LOT.

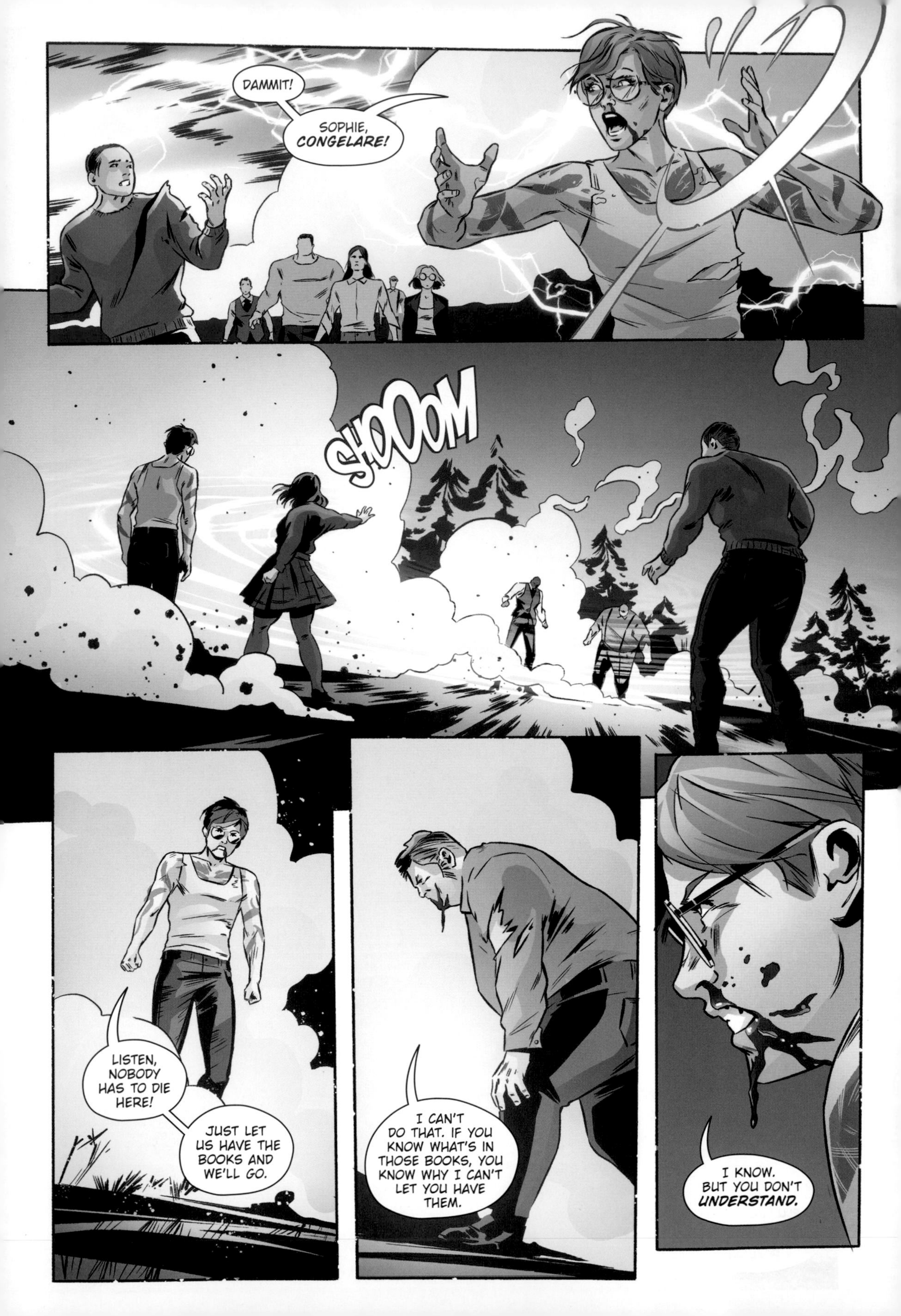
DAMMIT!
SOPHIE, *CONGELARE!*
SHOOOM
LISTEN, NOBODY HAS TO DIE HERE!
JUST LET US HAVE THE BOOKS AND WE'LL GO.
I CAN'T DO THAT. IF YOU KNOW WHAT'S IN THOSE BOOKS, YOU KNOW WHY I CAN'T LET YOU HAVE THEM.
I KNOW. BUT YOU DON'T *UNDERSTAND.*

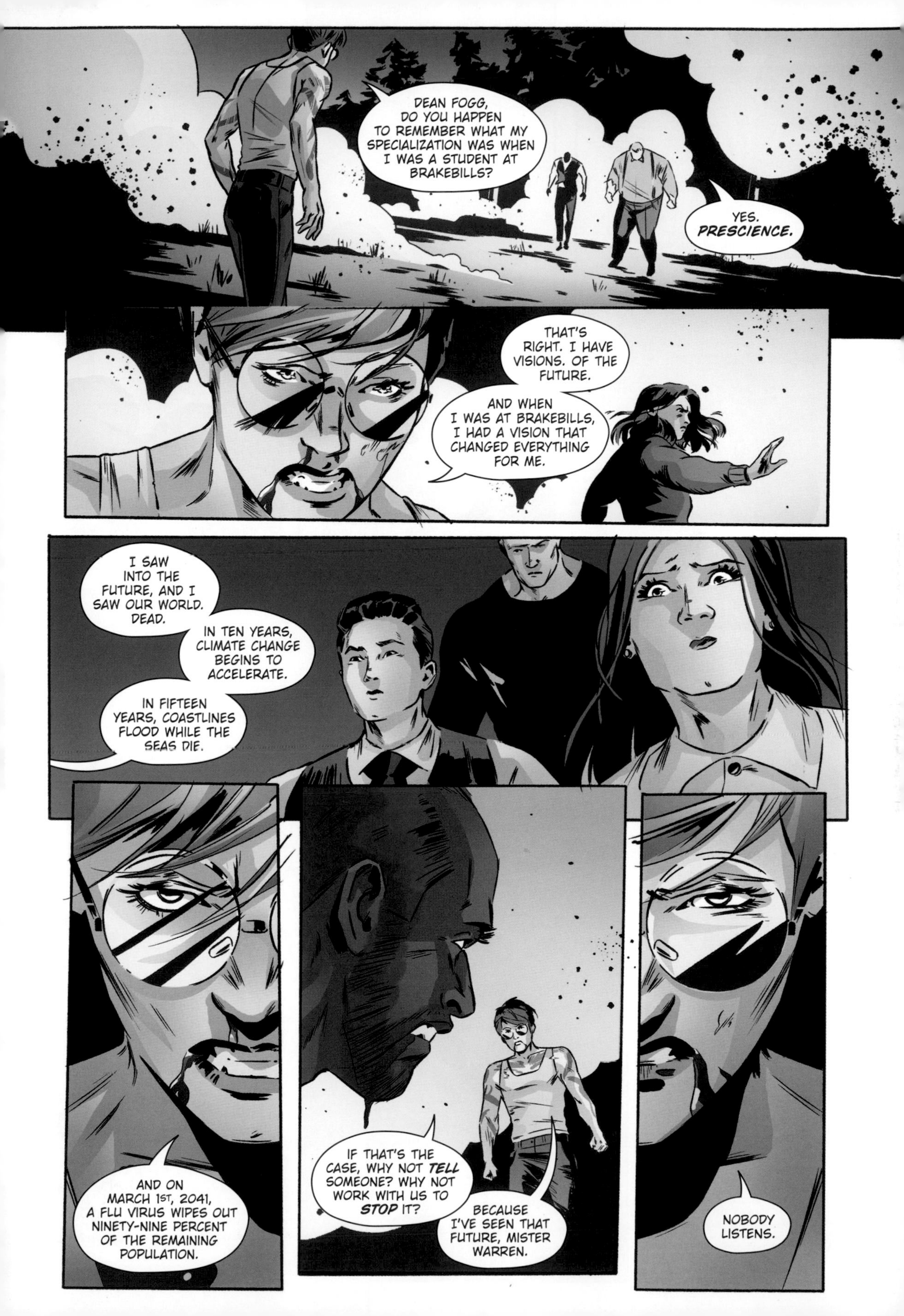
DEAN FOGG, DO YOU HAPPEN TO REMEMBER WHAT MY SPECIALIZATION WAS WHEN I WAS A STUDENT AT BRAKEBILLS?
YES. *PRESCIENCE.*
THAT'S RIGHT. I HAVE VISIONS. OF THE FUTURE.
AND WHEN I WAS AT BRAKEBILLS, I HAD A VISION THAT CHANGED EVERYTHING FOR ME.
I SAW INTO THE FUTURE, AND I SAW OUR WORLD. DEAD.
IN TEN YEARS, CLIMATE CHANGE BEGINS TO ACCELERATE.
IN FIFTEEN YEARS, COASTLINES FLOOD WHILE THE SEAS DIE.
AND ON MARCH 1ST, 2041, A FLU VIRUS WIPES OUT NINETY-NINE PERCENT OF THE REMAINING POPULATION.
IF THAT'S THE CASE, WHY NOT *TELL* SOMEONE? WHY NOT WORK WITH US TO *STOP* IT?
BECAUSE I'VE SEEN THAT FUTURE, MISTER WARREN.
NOBODY LISTENS.

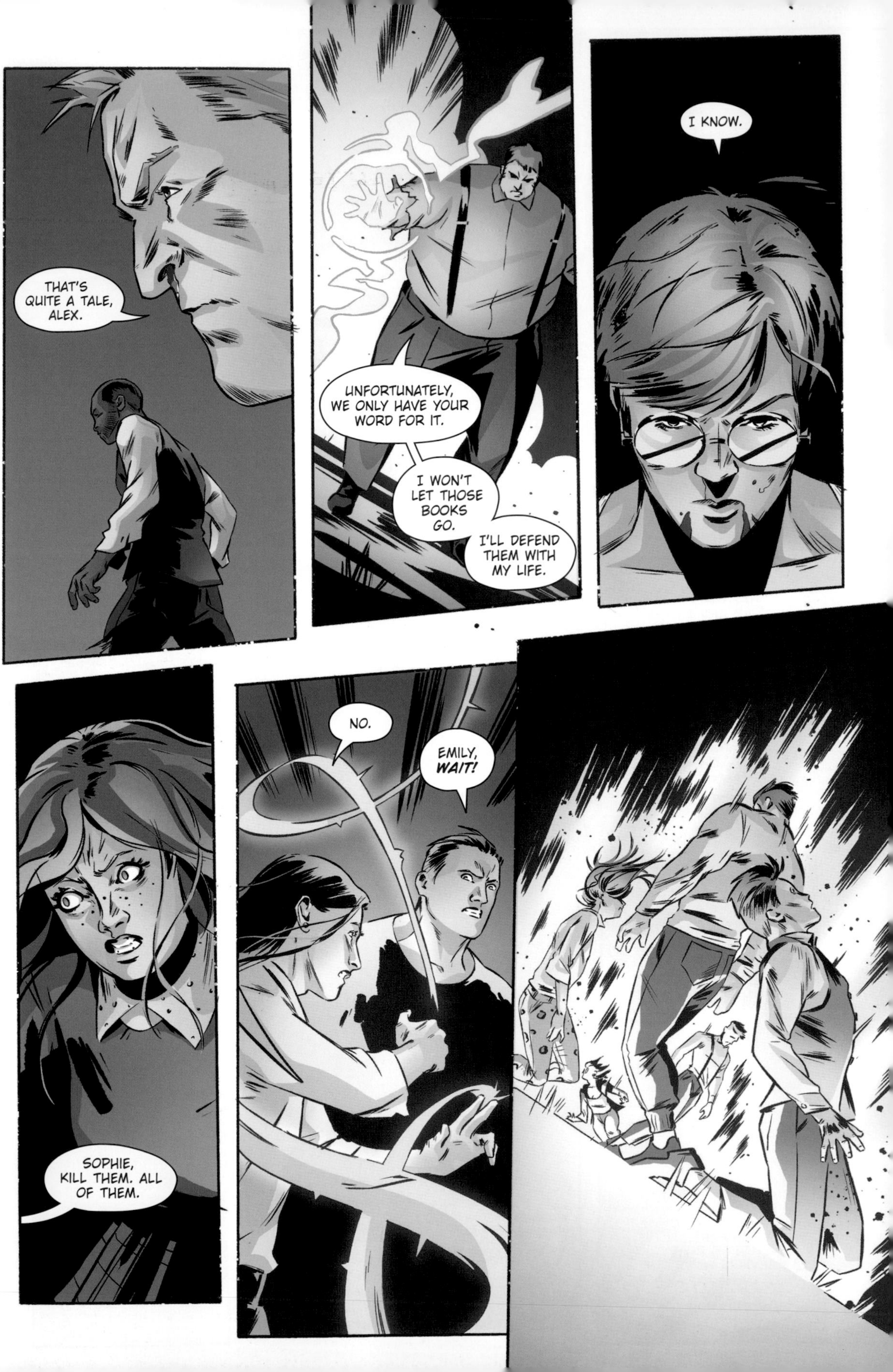
THAT'S QUITE A TALE, ALEX.
UNFORTUNATELY, WE ONLY HAVE YOUR WORD FOR IT.
I WON'T LET THOSE BOOKS GO.
I'LL DEFEND THEM WITH MY LIFE.
I KNOW.
SOPHIE, KILL THEM. ALL OF THEM.
NO.
EMILY, WAIT!

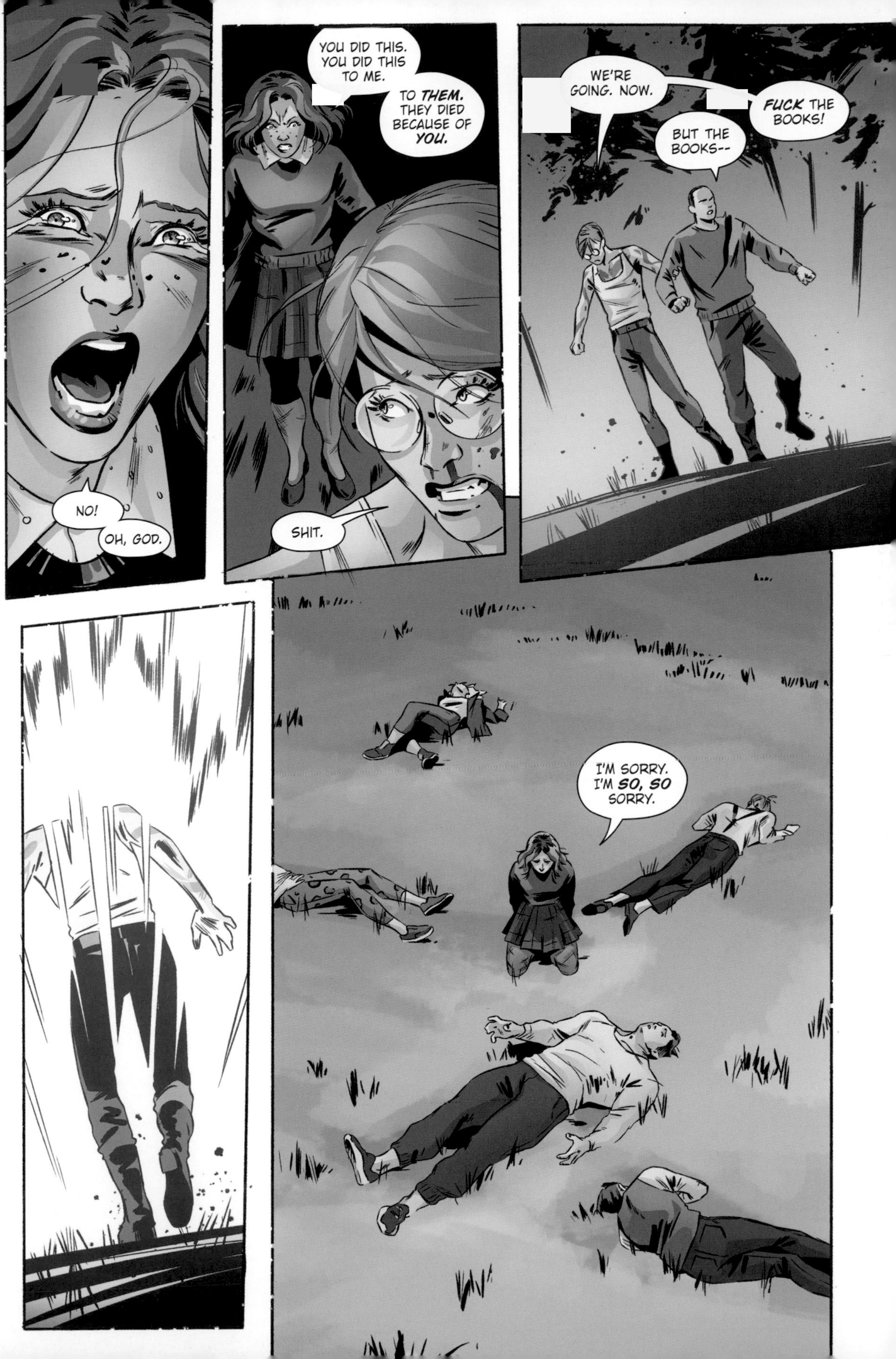

NO!
OH, GOD.
YOU DID THIS. YOU DID THIS TO ME.
TO **THEM.** THEY DIED BECAUSE OF ***YOU.***
SHIT.
WE'RE GOING. NOW.
BUT THE BOOKS--
FUCK THE BOOKS!
I'M SORRY. I'M ***SO, SO*** SORRY.

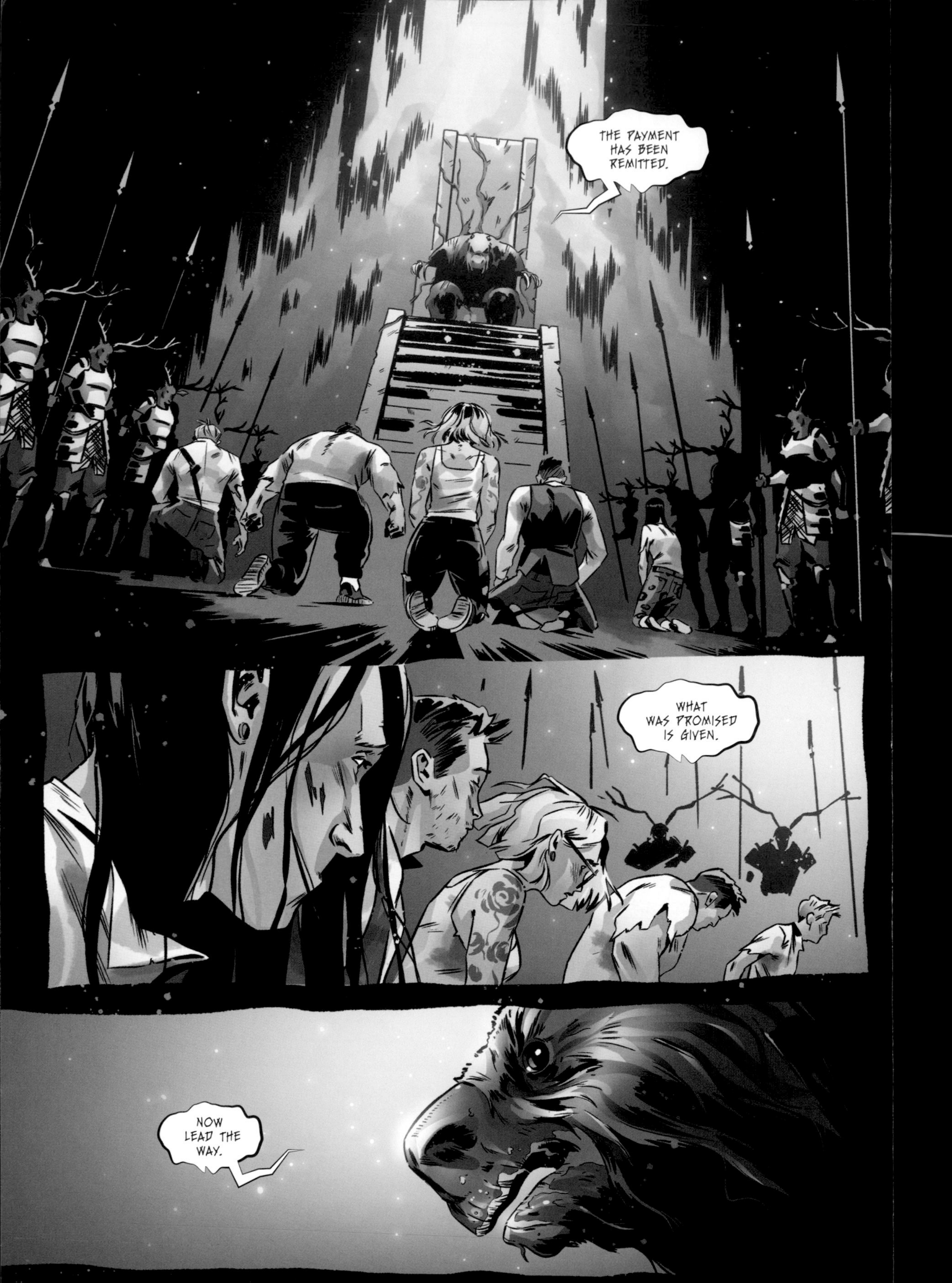
THE PAYMENT HAS BEEN REMITTED.
WHAT WAS PROMISED IS GIVEN.
NOW LEAD THE WAY.

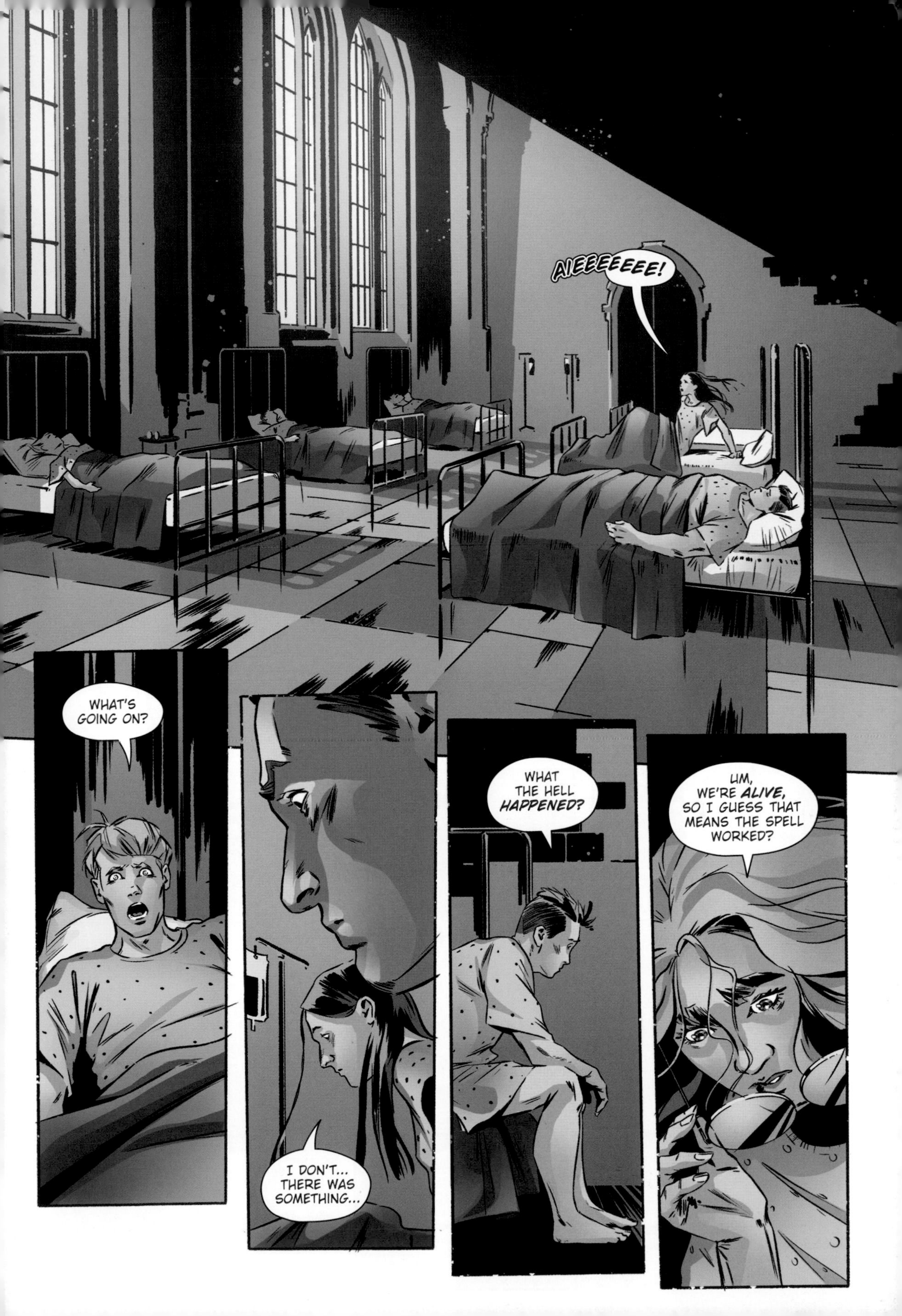
AIEEEEEEE!
WHAT'S GOING ON?
I DON'T... THERE WAS SOMETHING...
WHAT THE HELL HAPPENED?
UM, WE'RE ALIVE, SO I GUESS THAT MEANS THE SPELL WORKED?

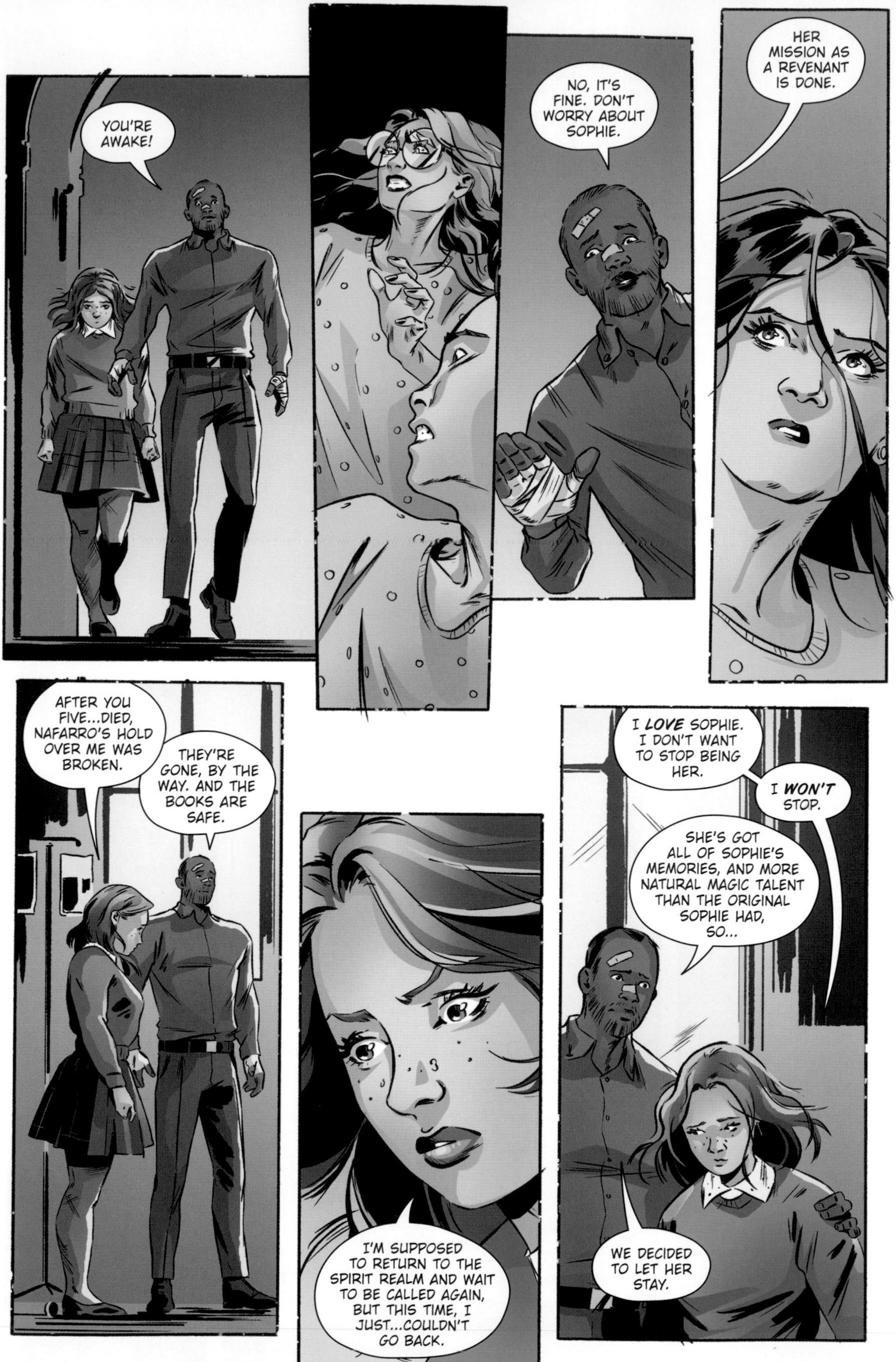

YOU'RE AWAKE!
NO, IT'S FINE. DON'T WORRY ABOUT SOPHIE.
HER MISSION AS A REVENANT IS DONE.
AFTER YOU FIVE...DIED, NAFARRO'S HOLD OVER ME WAS BROKEN.
THEY'RE GONE, BY THE WAY. AND THE BOOKS ARE SAFE.
I'M SUPPOSED TO RETURN TO THE SPIRIT REALM AND WAIT TO BE CALLED AGAIN, BUT THIS TIME, I JUST...COULDN'T GO BACK.
I **LOVE** SOPHIE. I DON'T WANT TO STOP BEING HER.
I **WON'T** STOP.
SHE'S GOT ALL OF SOPHIE'S MEMORIES, AND MORE NATURAL MAGIC TALENT THAN THE ORIGINAL SOPHIE HAD, SO...
WE DECIDED TO LET HER STAY.

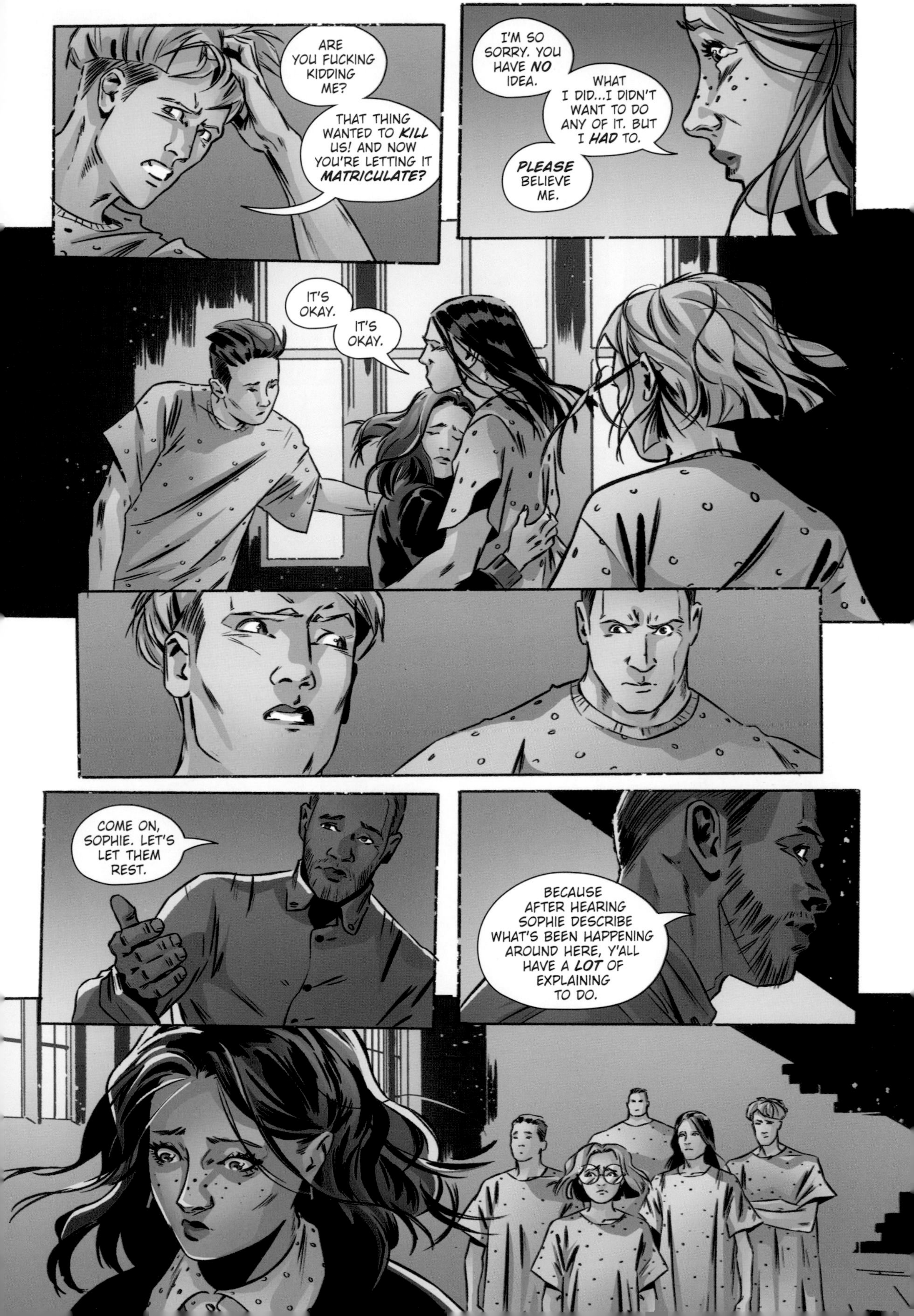
ARE YOU FUCKING KIDDING ME?
THAT THING WANTED TO **KILL** US! AND NOW YOU'RE LETTING IT **MATRICULATE?**
I'M SO SORRY. YOU HAVE **NO** IDEA.
WHAT I DID...I DIDN'T WANT TO DO ANY OF IT. BUT I **HAD** TO.
PLEASE BELIEVE ME.
IT'S OKAY.
IT'S OKAY.
COME ON, SOPHIE. LET'S LET THEM REST.
BECAUSE AFTER HEARING SOPHIE DESCRIBE WHAT'S BEEN HAPPENING AROUND HERE, Y'ALL HAVE A **LOT** OF EXPLAINING TO DO.

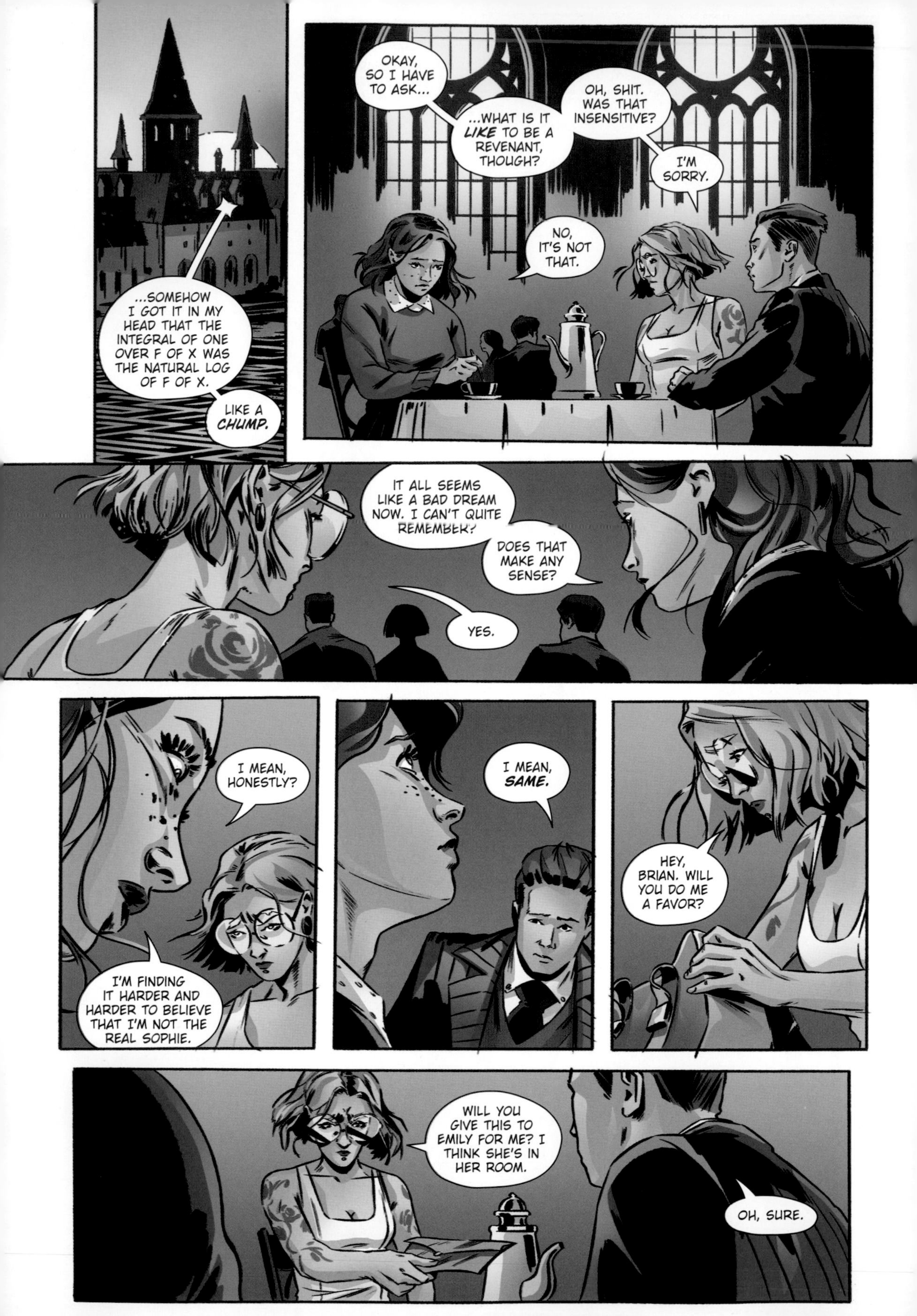
...SOMEHOW I GOT IT IN MY HEAD THAT THE INTEGRAL OF ONE OVER F OF X WAS THE NATURAL LOG OF F OF X.
LIKE A *CHUMP.*
OKAY, SO I HAVE TO ASK...
...WHAT IS IT *LIKE* TO BE A REVENANT, THOUGH?
OH, SHIT. WAS THAT INSENSITIVE?
I'M SORRY.
NO, IT'S NOT THAT.
IT ALL SEEMS LIKE A BAD DREAM NOW. I CAN'T QUITE REMEMBER?
DOES THAT MAKE ANY SENSE?
YES.
I MEAN, HONESTLY?
I'M FINDING IT HARDER AND HARDER TO BELIEVE THAT I'M NOT THE REAL SOPHIE.
I MEAN, *SAME.*
HEY, BRIAN. WILL YOU DO ME A FAVOR?
WILL YOU GIVE THIS TO EMILY FOR ME? I THINK SHE'S IN HER ROOM.
OH, SURE.

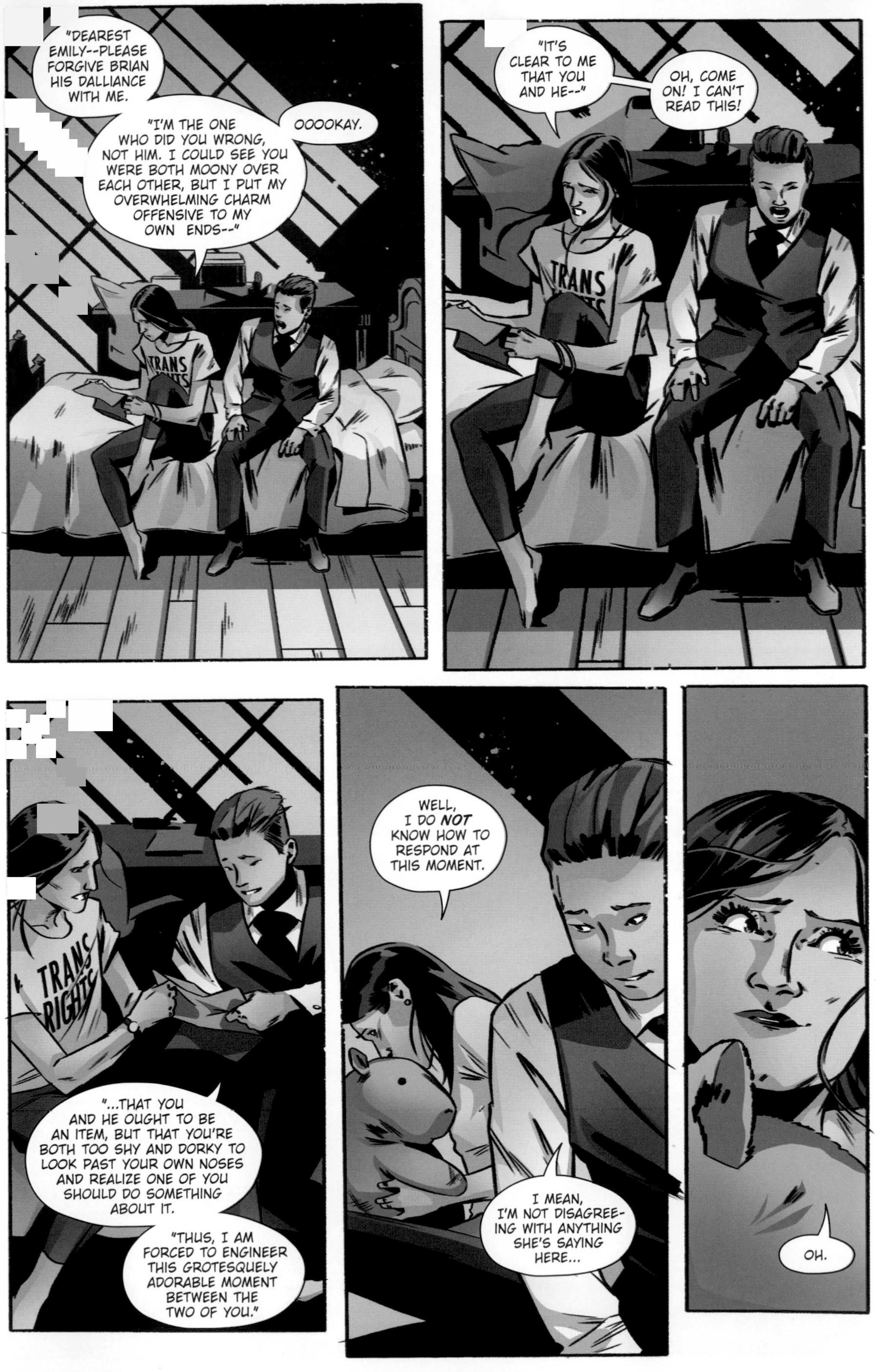
"DEAREST EMILY--PLEASE FORGIVE BRIAN HIS DALLIANCE WITH ME.
"I'M THE ONE WHO DID YOU WRONG, NOT HIM. I COULD SEE YOU WERE BOTH MOONY OVER EACH OTHER, BUT I PUT MY OVERWHELMING CHARM OFFENSIVE TO MY OWN ENDS--"
OOOOKAY.
"IT'S CLEAR TO ME THAT YOU AND HE--"
OH, COME ON! I CAN'T READ THIS!
"...THAT YOU AND HE OUGHT TO BE AN ITEM, BUT THAT YOU'RE BOTH TOO SHY AND DORKY TO LOOK PAST YOUR OWN NOSES AND REALIZE ONE OF YOU SHOULD DO SOMETHING ABOUT IT.
"THUS, I AM FORCED TO ENGINEER THIS GROTESQUELY ADORABLE MOMENT BETWEEN THE TWO OF YOU."
WELL, I DO ***NOT*** KNOW HOW TO RESPOND AT THIS MOMENT.
I MEAN, I'M NOT DISAGREE-ING WITH ANYTHING SHE'S SAYING HERE...
OH.

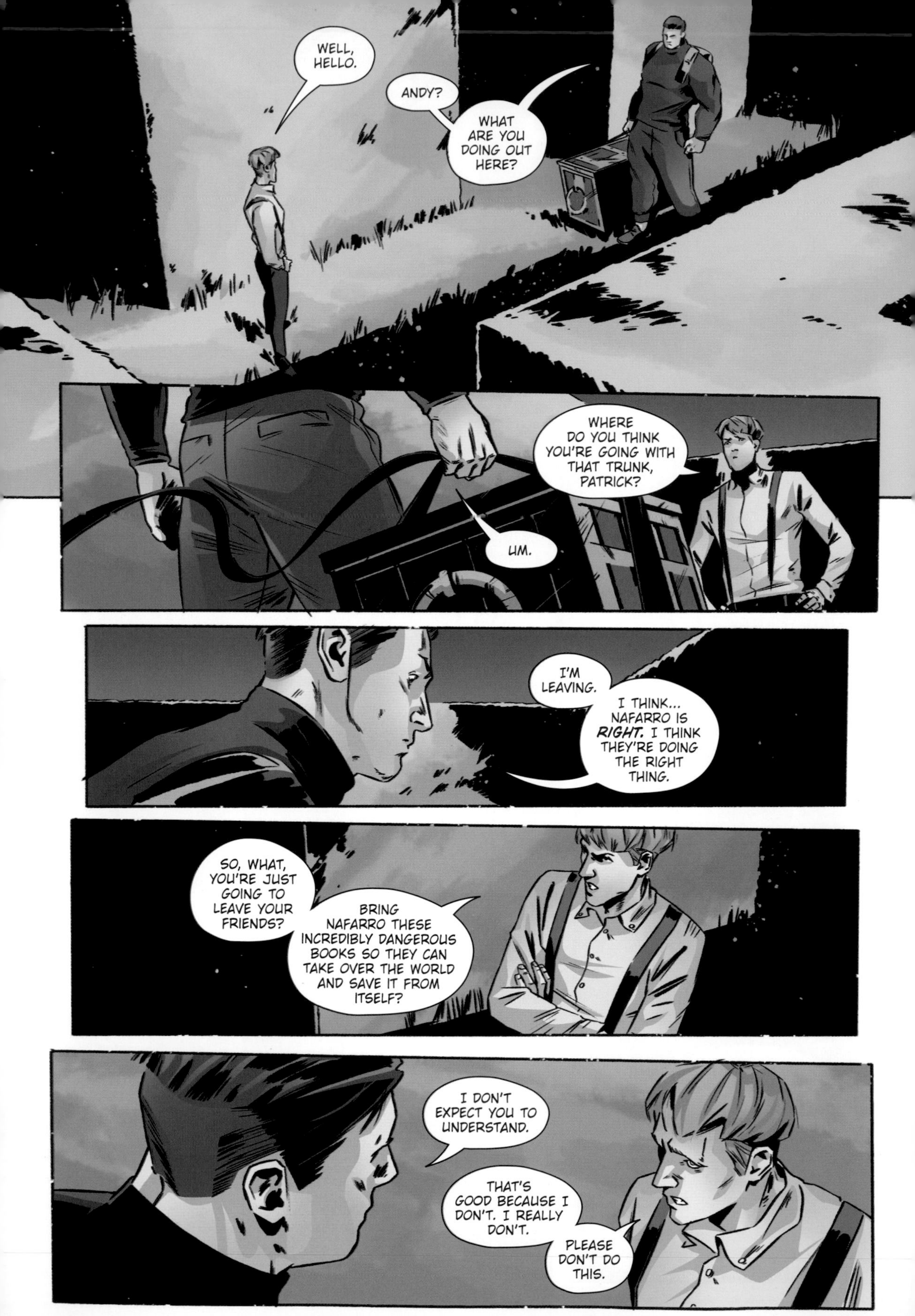
WELL, HELLO.
ANDY?
WHAT ARE YOU DOING OUT HERE?
WHERE DO YOU THINK YOU'RE GOING WITH THAT TRUNK, PATRICK?
UM.
I'M LEAVING.
I THINK... NAFARRO IS ***RIGHT.*** I THINK THEY'RE DOING THE RIGHT THING.
SO, WHAT, YOU'RE JUST GOING TO LEAVE YOUR FRIENDS?
BRING NAFARRO THESE INCREDIBLY DANGEROUS BOOKS SO THEY CAN TAKE OVER THE WORLD AND SAVE IT FROM ITSELF?
I DON'T EXPECT YOU TO UNDERSTAND.
THAT'S GOOD BECAUSE I DON'T. I REALLY DON'T.
PLEASE DON'T DO THIS.

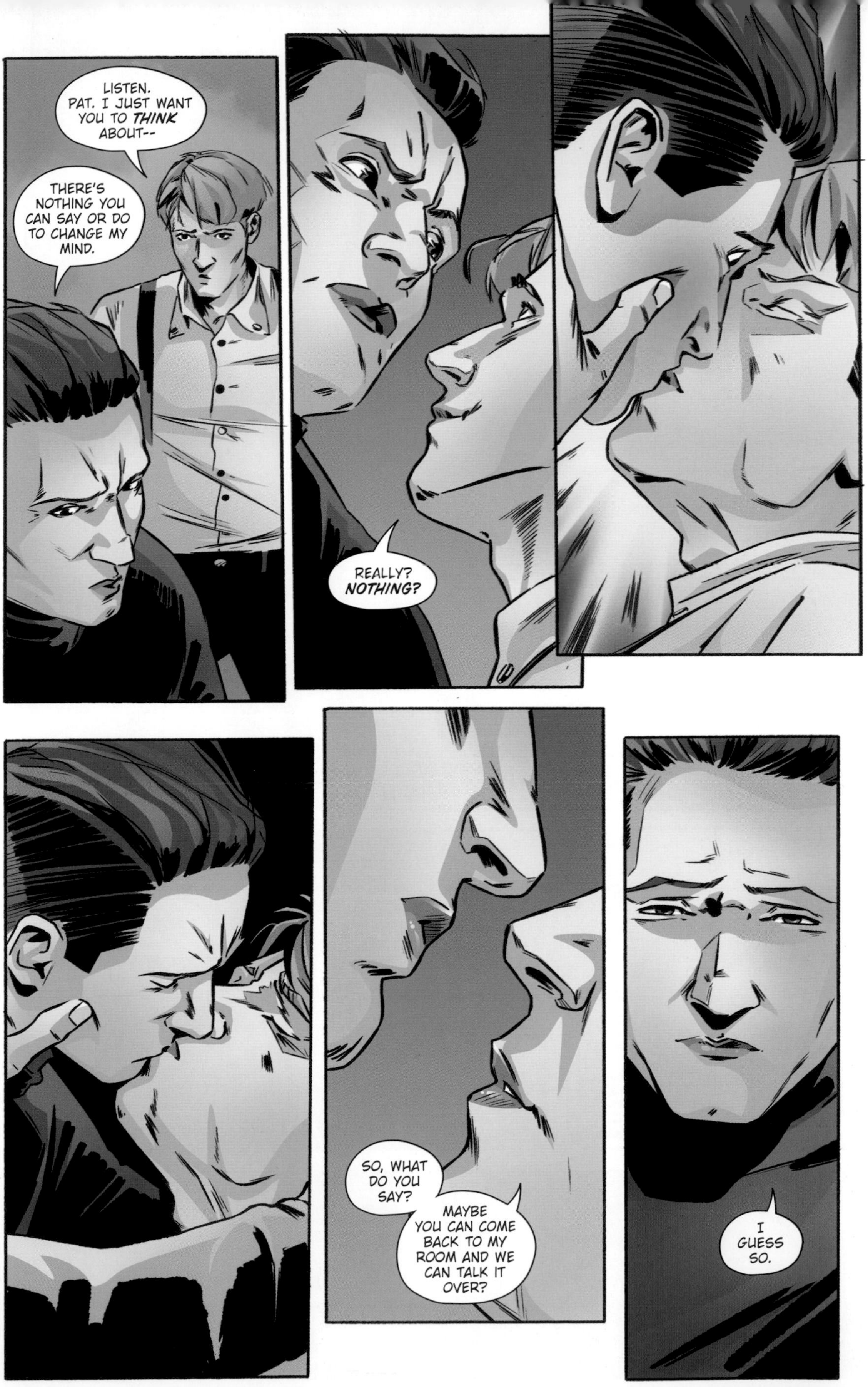
LISTEN. PAT. I JUST WANT YOU TO *THINK* ABOUT--
THERE'S NOTHING YOU CAN SAY OR DO TO CHANGE MY MIND.
REALLY? *NOTHING?*
SO, WHAT DO YOU SAY?
MAYBE YOU CAN COME BACK TO MY ROOM AND WE CAN TALK IT OVER?
I GUESS SO.

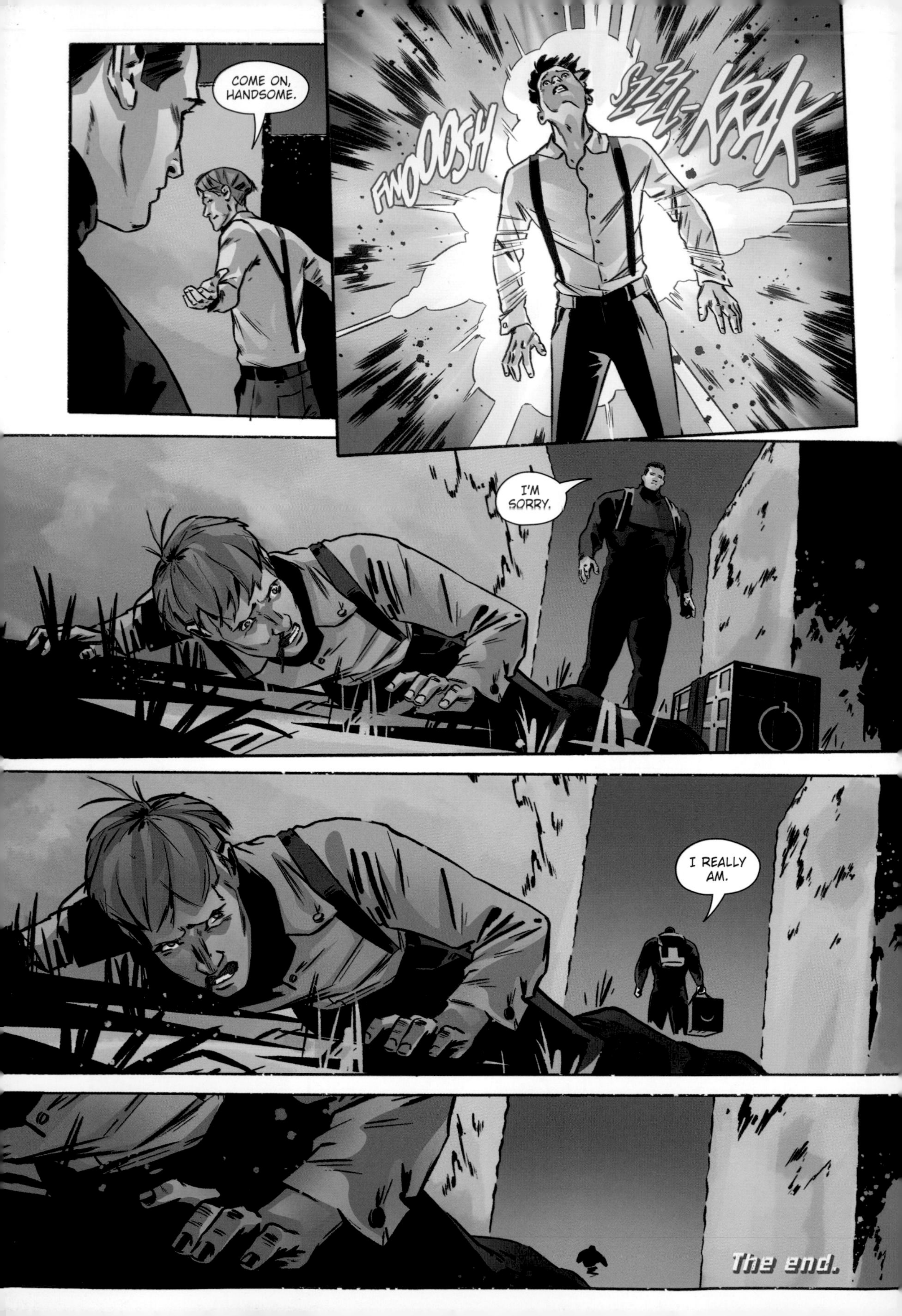
COME ON, HANDSOME.
FWOOOSH
SIZZL-KRAK
I'M SORRY.
I REALLY AM.
The end.

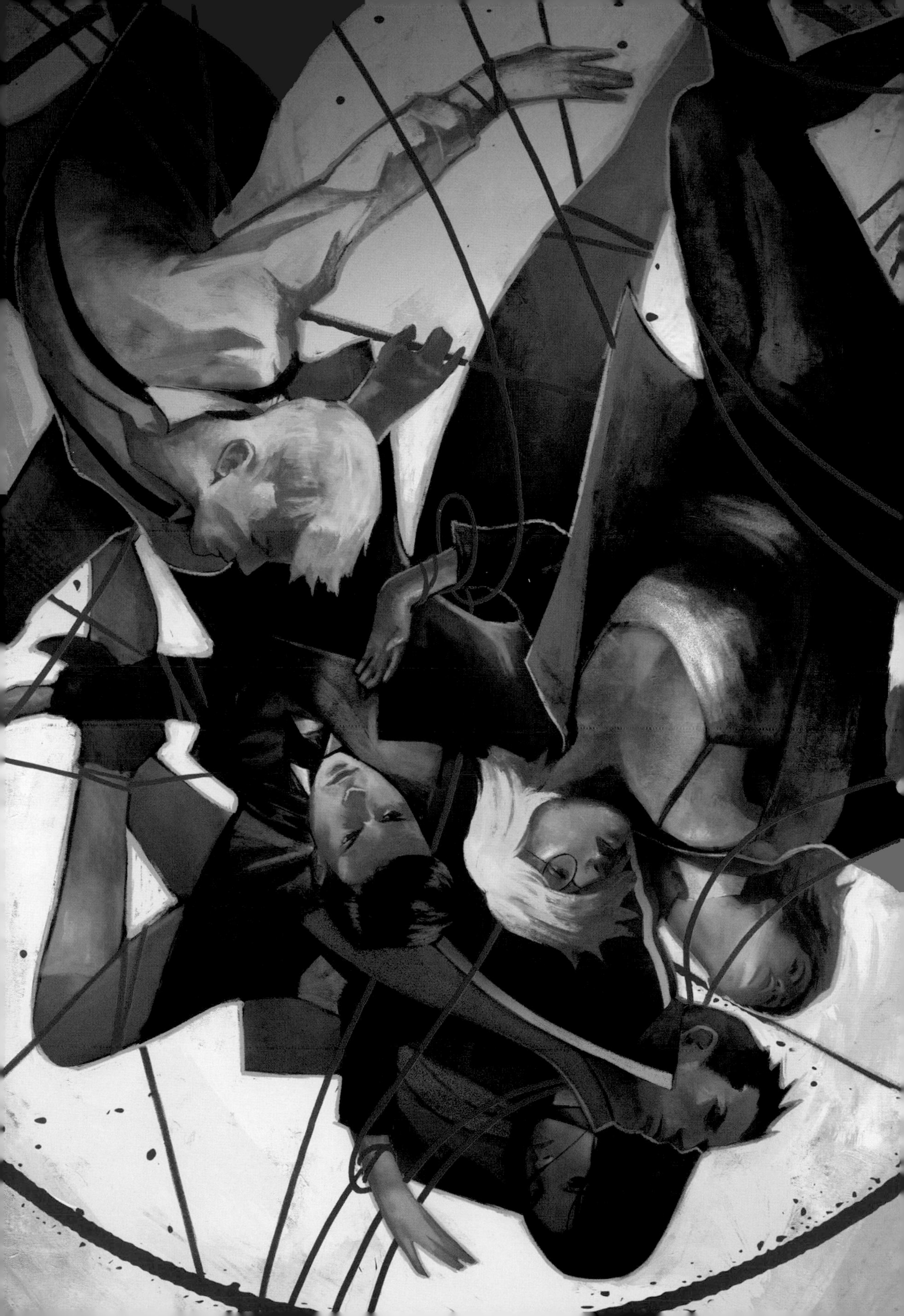

THE FOLLOWING GALLERY FEATURES
PREORDER COVERS #1-5 BY
ALEXA SHARPE

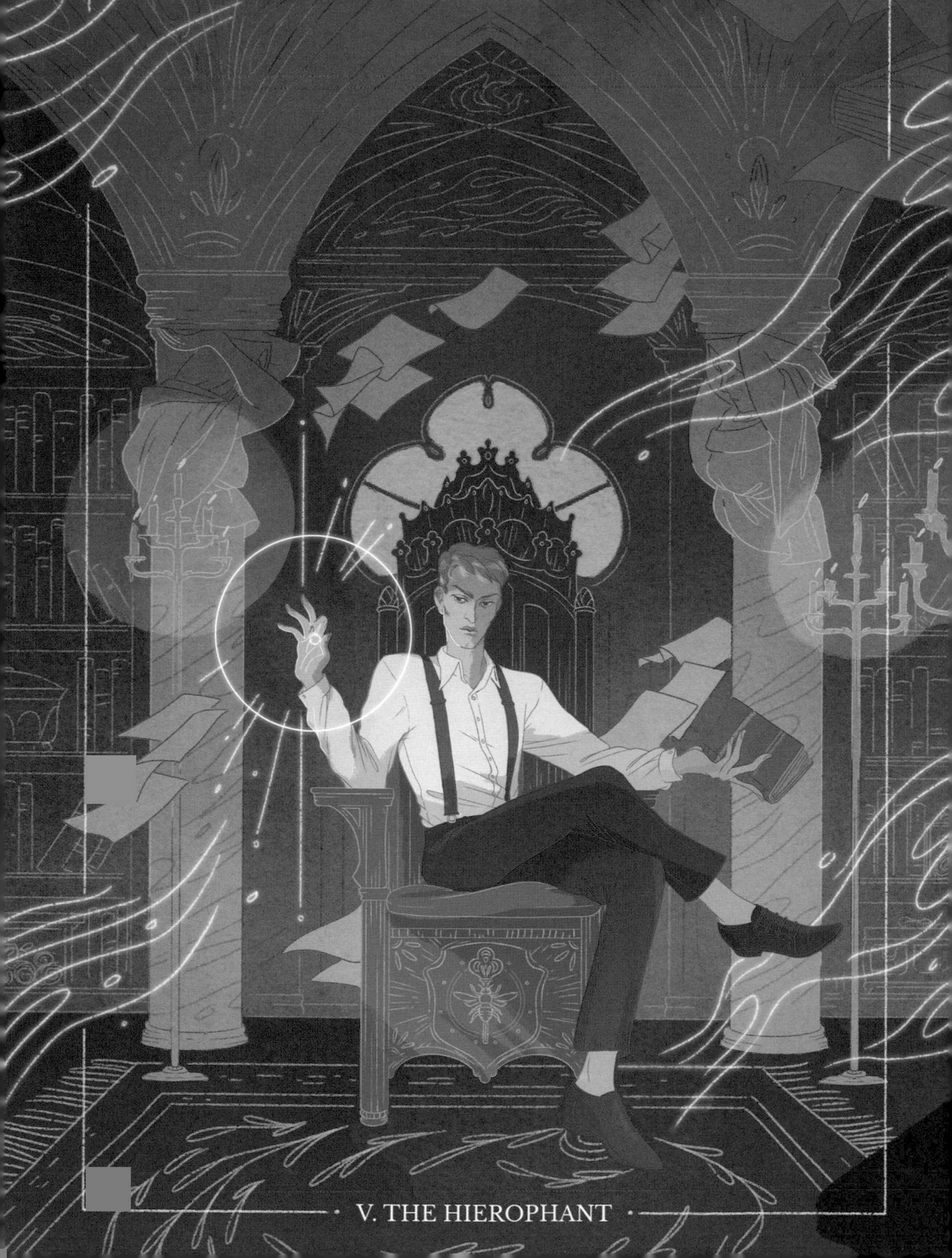

V. THE HIEROPHANT

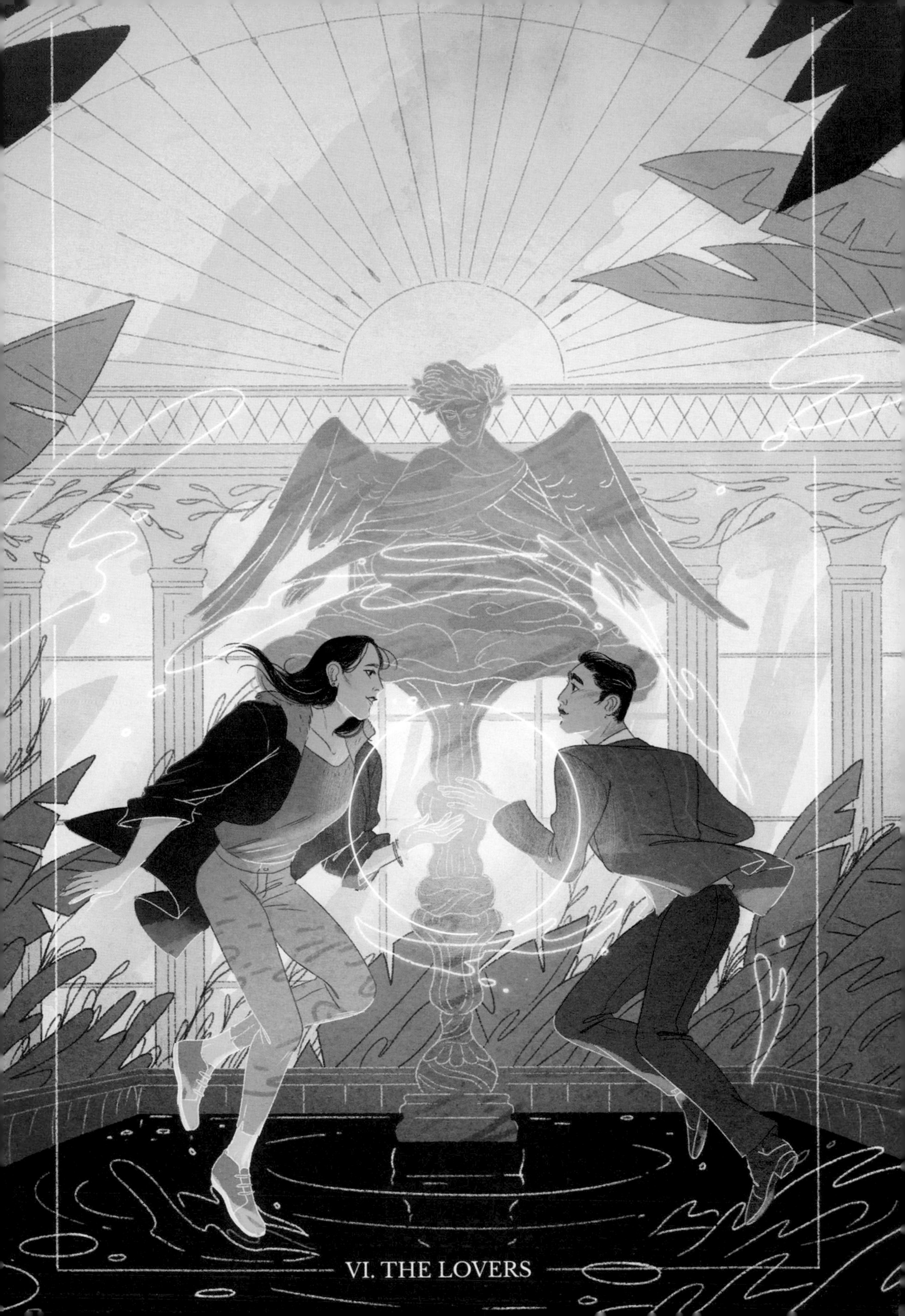

VI. THE LOVERS

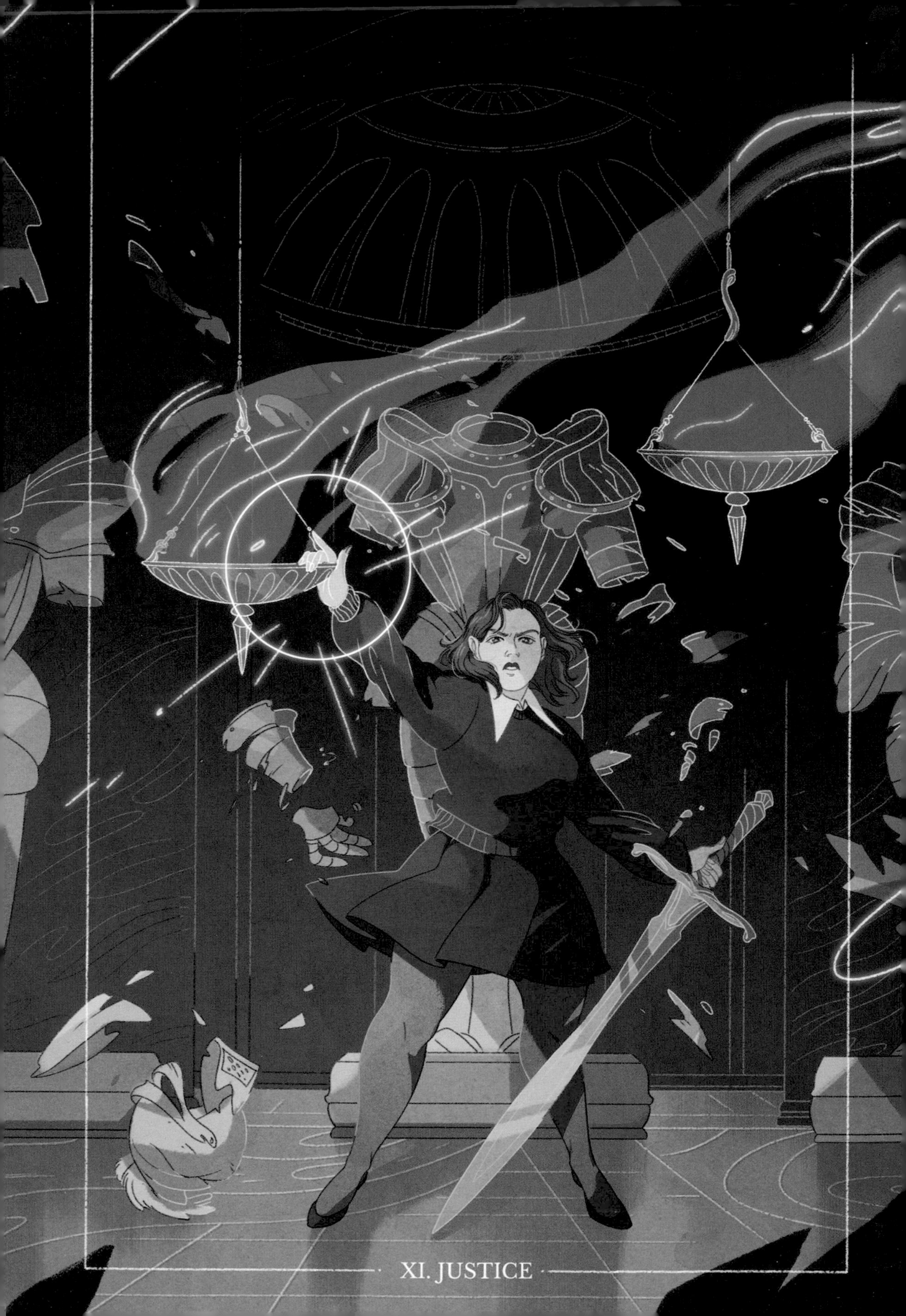
XI. JUSTICE

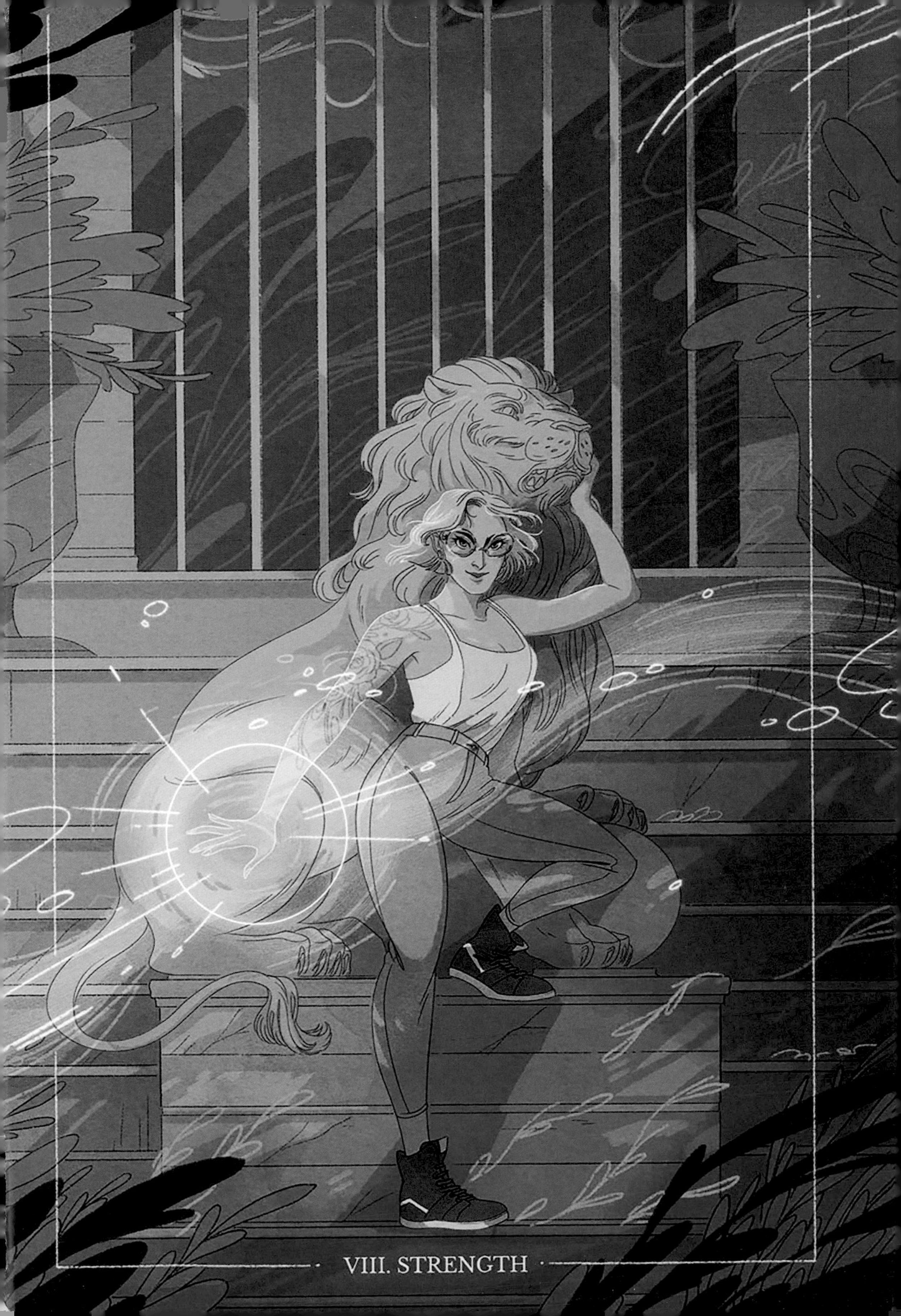

VIII. STRENGTH

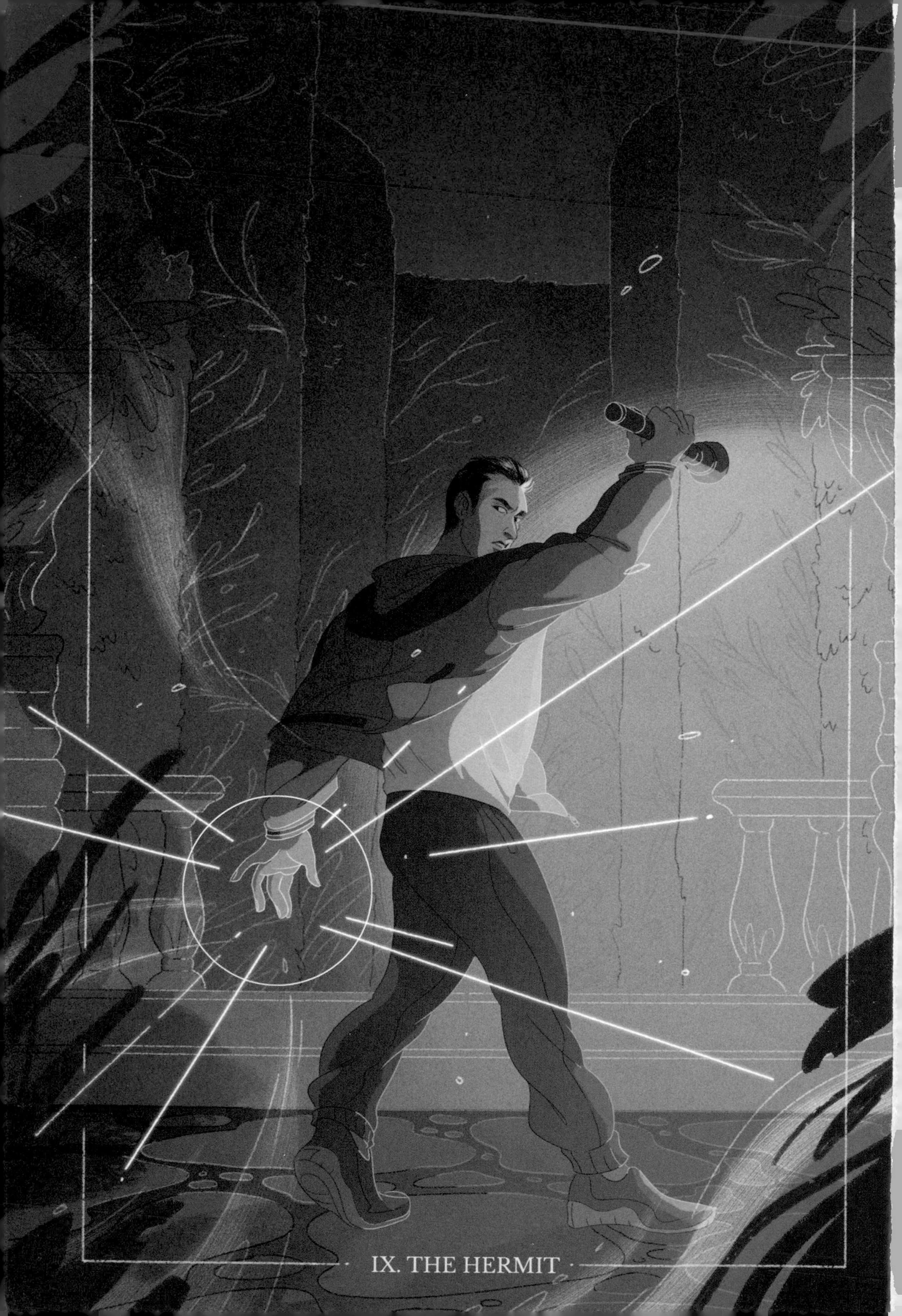
IX. THE HERMIT